Second Edition

Information Systems Methodologies

A FRAMEWORK FOR UNDERSTANDING

D1366844

Second Edition

Information Systems Methodologies

A FRAMEWORK FOR UNDERSTANDING

T. William Olle
T. William Olle Associates Ltd, UK

Jacques Hagelstein
Philips Research Laboratory, Belgium

Ian G. Macdonald
James Martin Associates Ltd, UK

Colette Rolland
University of Paris I, France

Henk G. Sol
Delft University of Technology, The Netherlands

Frans J.M. Van Assche
James Martin Associates BVBA, Belgium

Alexander A. Verrijn-Stuart
University of Leiden, The Netherlands

Addison-Wesley Publishing Company
Wokingham, England · Reading, Massachusetts · Menlo Park, California
New York · Don Mills, Ontario · Amsterdam · Bonn · Sydney
Singapore · Tokyo · Madrid · San Juan · Milan · Paris

The programs and design specifications presented in this book have been included for their instructional value. They have been prepared with care and diligence but are not guaranteed for any particular purpose. The publisher does not offer any warranties or representations, nor does it accept any liabilities with respect to the programs or design specifications.

Many of the designations used by manufacturers and sellers to distinguish their products are claimed as trademarks. Addison-Wesley has made every attempt to supply trademark information about manufacturers and their products mentioned in this book.

Cover designed by Hybert Design and Type, Maidenhead and printed by The Riverside Printing Co. (Reading) Ltd.
Typeset by Colset Private Limited, Singapore.
Printed in Great Britain by Mackays of Chatham plc, Chatham, Kent.

First edition published 1988. Reprinted 1989.
Second edition printed 1991.

British Library Cataloguing in Publication Data
Information systems methodologies: a framework for understanding
  1. Information retrieval
  I. Olle, T. William
  025.04

  ISBN 0-201-54443-1

Library of Congress Cataloging in Publication Data
Information systems methodologies : a framework for understanding / T.
  William Olle . . . [et. al.]. — 2nd ed.
    p. cm.
  Includes bibliographical references and index.
  ISBN 0-201-54443-1
  1. System design. 2. Information storage and retrieval systems.
  I. Olle, T. William.
  QA76.9.S88I533 1991
  004.2'1—dc20   90-26052
                                        CIP

Preface to the first edition

How to use this book

With the advent of large commercial information systems and major research projects working towards new systems for the future, it is crucial that students, professional analysts and systems designers should gain an understanding of the principles and practices involved. This book is written as a tutorial text on information systems methodologies, but with a perspective free of any particular methodology. A comparative approach is taken, covering the many different ways of analysing and designing a system for a specific purpose.

The book will appeal to three groups of reader:

- students and teachers
- practitioners and computing professionals
- researchers

The manner in which the book should be used by each group is described below.

Students and teachers

For students and teachers the book is a tutorial text on information systems methodologies. Some background knowledge is assumed: prior to using this text, a student will need to have assimilated at least one information systems methodology which covers some significant part of the information systems life cycle.

The book provides an understanding rather than a prescription of alternative ways of tackling information systems planning, analysis and design. It aims to present a framework for these stages in the information systems life cycle, against which most methodologies can be more clearly understood relative to each other. This understanding is felt to be vital to any graduate who may be called upon in practice to use any one of the multitude of methodologies in use today.

The subject matter covered in this text might be taught in a department of information systems, although in some institutions of tertiary education it is handled under computer science, software engineering or under business studies or business administration. The level of the material is such that it is appropriate for third year students.

The exercises at the end of selected chapters are intended to challenge students' understanding of the concepts introduced. Most of the exercises can be tackled by small groups of three or four students working together, as is the practice in some educational establishments.

When teaching this material, it is important to emphasize that the book defines a framework into which many existing methodologies can be fitted. It does not propose a new information systems methodology or even a synthesis of existing methodologies.

Practitioners and computing professionals

For the practitioner, this text is intended to put the problem of a methodological approach to information systems into a perspective independent of any specific methodology. It is unlikely that any practitioner who completed formal training prior to 1980 will have had any exposure during that training to information systems analysis and design methodologies, although he or she may have been taught certain techniques which, in this text, are associated with construction design.

The acceptance of a methodological approach by professionals is likely to receive considerable impetus in the coming years from the ever increasing availability of computerized tools, such as 'analyst's workbenches' and 'design aids'. These tools take much of the routine work out of performing an analysis and creating a design. However, the need for the basic skills required will remain and should be given more emphasis.

An experienced practitioner with exposure to at least one methodology will be able to make use of this text for individual study without having to have it presented by a teacher. The experienced practitioner will find the checklist of components in the final chapter particularly useful for comparing and evaluating alternatives being proposed by colleagues or by external consultants.

Researchers

For the researcher, the text is intended as a springboard, rather than as a piece of research work in its own right. The final chapter identifies a number of open issues on which research is clearly needed. This book does not fully take into account capabilities offered by some methodologies having a research status at the time of writing. It is more influenced by methodologies which have been successfully 'commercialized' and are in use in professional environments.

The researcher may be motivated to expand or modify the framework for planning, analysis and design to include methodologies of a research character. The research topics suggested in the final chapter will hopefully be helpful in indicating directions for follow-on work.

Evolution of information systems methodologies

The International Federation for Information Processing (IFIP) has several technical committees. Of these, TC8, founded in 1975, has the title Information Systems. TC8 has four working groups, each addressing a different aspect of information systems. In May 1982, Working Group 8.1, entitled 'Design and Evaluation of Information Systems', sponsored a very successful working conference, *Information Systems Design Methodologies: A Comparative Review*, chaired by T. William Olle (Olle *et al.*, 1982). The acronym CRIS (Comparative Review of Information Systems Design Methodologies) was first coined to identify this conference and subsequently adopted to refer to the overall activity.

It was this first conference which led to the work presented in this book. The conference gave a very useful insight into the state-of-the-art of information systems design and identified many issues requiring further research and analysis.

Some of the CRIS methodologies discussed at the conference were commercially marketed. Others came from a research environment. Some had been researched over many years and were in the process of being marketed. The 1982 conference was identified as Stage 1 of the overall activity.

The second part of the IFIP WG8.1 CRIS exercise involved an analysis of the features of the CRIS 1 methodologies. A second conference was held in July 1983 at which papers were presented on this theme. It was clear from the discussions and the proceedings of this conference (Olle *et al.*, 1983) that the comparative study of several methodologies by people previously engrossed in one design methodology led to an appreciation of the similarities and the differences. The third conference in the CRIS series was held in May 1986 with the theme 'Improving the Practice' (Olle *et al.*, 1986). The fourth in the series, held in September 1988, addressed the topic of 'Computerized Assistance During the Information Systems Life Cycle' (Olle *et al.*, 1988).

Despite these discussions, the juxtaposition of so many methodologies at these working conferences and in the published proceedings left one bewildered. Are there really so many different ways to analyse and design an information system? In what ways are they similar? Should we be using one methodology for one kind of information system and a different methodology for another? If so, which should we use for which kind of system?

These and other questions face those responsible for training the analysts and systems designers of the future and, more urgently, those concerned with the practicalities of information systems working today. It is with these problems in mind that this book has been prepared.

The aim of the book is to present the techniques used in information systems methodologies in a way that shows how the various techniques interact with each other and how such techniques may be integrated. It must be stated immediately that this book does not aim to propose a new all-embracing methodology, because any attempt to use all techniques in one design process would lead to considerable overlap and all the associated consistency problems.

Furthermore, it is not an aim of this book to endorse or promote any existing methodology. For this reason, all references to existing methodologies are grouped together in Appendix A. However, this book owes a great deal to the insight and understanding of the many who, over the years, have developed various information systems methodologies covering some part of planning, analysis and design.

Acknowledgements

This book has been prepared by the seven authors during a series of ten meetings held between 1985 and 1987. The Task Group also acknowledges the contributions of Mats Lundeberg, George Verheijen and Amilcar Sernadas who were early members of the group.

The parent committee of the Task Group, IFIP Working Group 8.1 (Design and Evaluation of Information Systems), reviewed and critiqued the work during its meeting in May 1987 and agreed to endorse the work as suitable for publication. As a result of this meeting, numerous improvements and clarifications have been made. The Task Group considers itself fortunate to have had such support, interest and constructive comment from a body representing such a wide international breadth and depth of technical expertise. Nevertheless, the work – even after modification – represents the collective view of the Task Group.

References

Olle, T. W., Sol, H. G. and Verrijn-Stuart, A. A. (eds). 1982. *Information Systems Design Methodologies: A Comparative Review*. Amsterdam: North-Holland.

Olle, T. W., Sol, H. G. and Tully, C. J. (eds). 1983. *Information Systems Design Methodologies: A Feature Analysis*. Amsterdam: North-Holland.

Olle, T. W., Sol, H. G. and Verrijn-Stuart, A. A. (eds). 1986. *Information Systems Design Methodologies: Improving the Practice*. Amsterdam: North-Holland.

Olle, T. W., Verrijn-Stuart, A. A. and Bhabuta, L. (eds). 1988. *Computerized Assistance During the Information Systems Life Cycle*. Amsterdam: North-Holland.

Preface to the second edition

The second edition incorporates a number of changes from the first edition. Most significantly, a new chapter is added on the subject of computer aided systems engineering (CASE) systems. This chapter relates the concepts in CASE to those established in the earlier chapters for information systems methodologies.

Chapter 2 on the subject of scenarios has been substantially rewritten and considerably amplified. The authors feel that this is an important topic, and hopefully the new Chapter 2 does it justice.

The explanation of the behaviour perspective in Chapter 3 has been extended and improved. It is the least familiar for most readers, and the new treatment should result in a more widespread recognition of the importance of analysing the temporal aspects of a business area and designing similar aspects of each computerized system. The concept of 'methodology dependent components' (formerly 'framework prescribed components') has been explained more fully and more clearly at the end of Chapter 3.

The first edition did not make it sufficiently clear that the three chapters itemizing components represent an analytic model rather than a prescriptive one. A component was included if it had been perceived by one or more authors as being supported in one or more methodologies. The structure diagrams in Chapters 4, 5 and 7 are not intended to be regarded as a piece of design work. To emphasize this, the title of each of these chapters has been changed to include the phase 'component analysis'. In all three of these chapters, there has been a cleaning up of the examples and of the text relating to the examples of components.

The chapter entitled 'Evolution of an installed information system' in fact corresponded to a life cycle stage identified in Chapter 3 of the first edition as 'extension and maintenance'. The name of the life cycle stage has now been changed to emphasize the fact that the system evolution is an inherent part of the information systems life cycle. The chapter has been extended to present the renovation of information systems through restructuring, reverse engineering and re-engineering.

The chapter on representation and documentation has been repositioned after the chapters on information systems planning and on evolution of an installed information system. The new chapter on representation has been substantially revised. In particular, the section showing examples of the representations has been extended.

The fact that the framework has three levels has been noted by many readers. The top level contains a definition of types, the instances of which are found in the second level. The second level contains a definition of types, the instances of which are found in the third level. These three levels are identified in the chapter containing the concluding remarks. The new chapter on CASE has been inserted as Chapter 10.

In addition to the above, there are numerous places in the text where extra text has been inserted to clarify a point. Despite the careful proof-reading by the authors themselves and by Addison-Wesley, several printing errors had crept into the first edition. They have now been removed.

In conclusion, the authors wish to acknowledge the support received from their colleagues in IFIP Working Group 8.1 for organizing a workshop on the first edition at Sesimbra in Portugal. The comments received at the workshop motivated the authors to prepare this second edition. Many of the comments made at the workshop have led to changes which it is hoped will improve the clarity of the second edition.

Contents

1

Key concepts used in the framework

1.1 Introduction

The term **information systems methodology** is used extensively in this text in the sense of 'a methodical approach to information systems planning, analysis, design, construction and evolution'. It is recognized that the term **methodology** should be used to mean 'a study of method'. However, the common practice over the past decade has been to use 'methodology' in place of 'method' and this text adopts the line of least resistance by following the current practice.

There are still many questions to be answered on the topic of information systems methodologies, the more significant of which include:

1.   Are there really so many substantially different ways to design a computerized information system?
2.   If not, how are these ways similar? If so, how are they different?
3.   Should we be using one methodology for one kind of information system and a different methodology for another?
4.   If so, which methodology should we use for which kind of system?

Apart from these questions, each of which is rather difficult to answer, further questions emerge. Is each methodology striving towards the same target by different routes? Is each methodology striving towards a different target? It is this issue of the route and the target which is the focus for discussion in this chapter.

An information systems methodology is used by one or more persons to produce a specification. Hence, the specification is the target referred to in the previous paragraph. This design specification (or target) will be referred to in this text as a **design product**. It is what a designer can hand to a system constructor after he or she has completed the design.

The route travelled in reaching the target will be referred to here as the **design process**. The design process is performed by the designer in order to arrive at the design product.

This separation into design product and design process is at the heart of what constitutes an information systems methodology. The aim of this chapter is to lay the foundation for a more detailed discussion of each in ensuing chapters.

1.2   Analysis, design and specification

Most information systems methodologies use the term 'analysis' to refer to an activity which precedes that of 'design', as depicted in Figure 1.1. An information system is always designed for use in a given environment. Before the design commences, it is logical enough to 'analyse' the environment in some way. However, it is not always clear when analysis finishes and design commences.

In general, one would use the term **analysis** to describe the process of looking at something that already exists. The term **design** is better used to refer to the process of prescribing the form of something that is not already in existence.

Designing an information system is very often a process of redesign. There is usually some kind of information system in use in the environment – possibly manual, possibly computerized. If it is a good system (in some

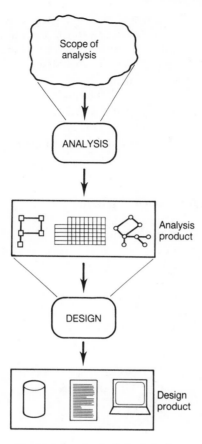

Figure 1.1   Analysis and design.

sense), then the emphasis will be on analysing what it does and computerizing or recomputerizing it more effectively. The analysis work can probably be done fairly quickly and the emphasis for the major part of the project will be on design. If the system is judged to be a poor or ill-designed system, or if there is no extant system of any kind, then there should be greater emphasis on analysis, followed by design when this is completed.

In a typical situation, some parts of the existing information system are well defined and others less so – or possibly not at all. This means that a typical project will contain a mix of analysis and design such that any sharp distinction between analysis and design becomes hard to establish. It is important to note that analysis should never be regarded as an end in itself, but rather a way of establishing a basis for the design work.

The term **specification** is used in this text in a generic sense and with no special meaning. A specification should result from any step in the design process. The design product, as introduced in the preceding section, is essentially a specification. Many would use the term 'design specification' instead of 'design product', but this term also introduces some ambiguity between 'the resultant design' and the activity of producing it.

The term **system development** is not used in this text, although it is widely used in practice and many methodologies claim to be 'development methodologies'. The reason for avoiding the term in the present context is because it tends to embrace part of the ground covered in this text plus part of what will be referred to here as **construction**. This issue will be discussed in more detail in Chapter 3.

1.3 Information systems planning

The term **information systems planning** is used in this book to refer to the strategic planning of computerized information systems. The planning is strategic in the sense that it identifies which information systems are needed, rather than planning in detail for any specific system. Information systems planning is a cornerstone for some information systems methodologies and it is clearly of vital importance. The emphasis here is on the fact that several systems will be needed in most sizable enterprises.

The term **enterprise** is used in this book to refer to any kind of company, government department, academic institution or other kind of organization, in which an information system of some kind might be used. Each enterprise belongs in some kind of environment and has at its disposal certain **resources**, as shown graphically in Figure 1.2. The term **environment** is used here in the generic sense and not in any sense specific to the use of hardware or software.

The question addressed as part of information systems planning is not only how to design and build *one* system, but rather which systems are needed in an enterprise, how such systems should interact, and how the right kind of phasing can be achieved from the existing situation to the future required set of systems. This kind of information systems planning calls for a very different kind of analysis from that needed as a precursor to the design of one information system. The boundaries for the information system are usually well defined.

Information systems planning calls for an analysis of business activities, but not in the same detail as if a specific system is being designed to support all or part of an activity. There is also a need to study the existing information systems and the benefits they provide. An information systems plan should indicate the new systems required and the sequence in which they should be implemented.

While recognizing the importance of information systems planning to the success of an individual design activity, this book will, for pedagogical reasons, present the analysis and design aspects of information systems

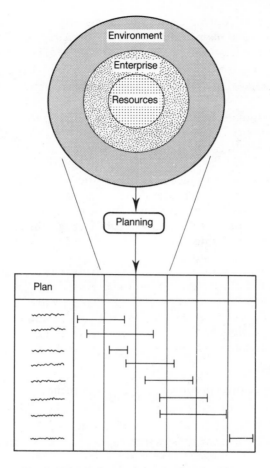

Figure 1.2   Information systems planning.

methodologies prior to information systems planning. It should be easier for the reader to come to terms with what is called for in designing one information system before tackling the far broader problems of planning as they relate to all the systems for an enterprise.

Each stage of a methodology typically has a given scope. The area covered in information systems planning may be quite extensive and it is common for the area covered by the ensuing analysis to be a subarea of that covered in the analysis. Furthermore, the area covered by a design stage may be a subarea of that covered in the preceding analysis stage.

The design work associated with one information system should result in one design product and there are several alternative design processes that may be used to prepare this design product. Similarly, with information systems planning, the outcome of the activity is a plan, here referred to as an **information systems plan**, which may be prepared in different ways. Discussion of these ways will be covered in more detail in Chapter 7.

1.4   Objectives of information systems design

It is important to understand the target clearly before concentrating on the routes that may be travelled to reach the target. The design product has its analogy in other kinds of human endeavour, such as architecture and engineering.

An architect will produce a set of specifications (which he or she will call a design) for a house, an extension to a house, a shopping centre or a cathedral. These specifications will consist of diagrams and narrative descriptions. The architect will, almost certainly, go through a number of iterations before finalizing the specifications. The product of the last iteration is aimed at the builder.

The houseowner, the shopkeeper and the bishop (as appropriate users for the kind of building referred to in the previous paragraph) may understand parts of these specifications – but many parts will be too technical. In certain cases, this may force the architect to produce simpler specifications, which they can understand and either accept or reject for further work. Normally, the architect will produce these plans on the way to the final design.

Moving from the building construction industry to the field of information systems design, we find a tendency here to confuse the specifications needed for review and acceptance by the shopkeeper and the bishop, with those needed by the builder. Does the bishop need to know where the drains will be laid? Does the prospective tenant of a shop in a shopping centre need to express an opinion on the type of insulating material used in the roof void?

The design product resulting from information systems design should be produced with the aim that it can be used by a builder and, in this sense, it must be acceptable to a builder. In some commercial situations, there may be a formal process of builder acceptance. In other situations, the builder's evaluation will manifest itself in the price estimate for building a system or, indeed, in whether the builder chooses to bid at all.

The design product should be a complete specification – complete in the sense that it should not leave any loose ends or open issues that will leave the builder uncertain as to how to proceed. Some builders with a more creative attitude towards their work may prefer the design product to leave them room for manoeuvre in their building work.

The prospective user of the system should not be forgotten. His or her opinion must be sought on many issues during analysis and design. In many cases, it will be necessary to provide the user with specifications, which will be referred to in this text as **user acceptor specifications**.

The intention is that a user acceptor can review and understand these specifications and, hopefully, accept them. If, by chance, a user is competent to read and react to the builder.'s specifications so much the better, but this should not be expected of him.

1.5 Human roles in information systems design

After the discussion in the previous section, it is possible to identify a number of human roles, each of which can be important during some stage of an information systems methodology. Some of these roles are depicted in Figure 1.3. The complete list of roles identified in this book is as follows:

1. executive responsible,
2. development coordinator,
3. business analyst,
4. designer,
5. user acceptor,
6. user,
7. constructor acceptor,
8. constructor, and
9. resource manager.

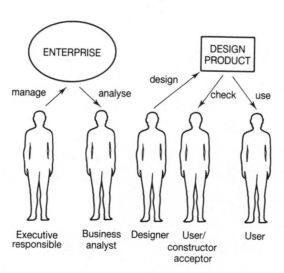

Figure 1.3 Some human roles in information system design.

The widely used term **developer** is covered by the roles 'designer' and 'constructor'. The somewhat ambiguous term **implementor** is also covered by the constructor role although, in some environments, an 'implementor' is a person who installs a copy of a previously designed and constructed system. Another widely used term in this context is **project manager**. This is broken down in the above list and covered by 'resource manager' and 'development coordinator'. These nine roles will now be discussed in turn.

1.5.1   Executive responsible

This is the person responsible to the management board for the successful progress and completion of the overall information systems project.

1.5.2   Development coordinator

In a large information systems project, where most of the human roles are played by different persons or groups, there should be a development coordinator to tie together the parts of the overall project on a day-to-day basis and to report to the executive responsible. In some environments, the development coordinator may have to coordinate the work on more than one project.

1.5.3   Business analyst

A business analyst is a person who analyses the business in order to develop a basis from which the design work can be done. There are various ways of performing such an analysis.

1.5.4   Designer

A person filling the role of designer is responsible for preparing what is referred to in this text as the design product. In some cases, the role of designer may be combined with that of business analyst.

1.5.5   User acceptor

A user acceptor is a representative of the users or of the executive responsible (or both), who approves the user acceptor specifications before construction starts.

1.5.6   User

A user is someone who will use the information system once it is available. There are typically many users, in some cases thousands. In such cases, it is important to distinguish between different types of user. More knowledge-able users need to be consulted by the designer during the design process.

1.5.7 Constructor acceptor

The role of constructor acceptor requires the builder specifications to be reviewed from the builder's point of view, to check that they meet whatever standards of acceptability are appropriate.

1.5.8 Constructor

A constructor is someone who builds the information system according to the specification given in the design product. Conventionally, a constructor may be an application programmer, but, with the gradual move towards higher level languages and more automated tools for building systems, the emphasis on programming as a required skill for a constructor is decreasing.

1.5.9 Resource manager

A resource manager is responsible for ensuring that the requisite resources are available for the design process to advance smoothly. This role may be combined with that of the executive responsible for the project. Alternatively, it might be combined with that of the development coordinator.

1.6 Components of a deliverable

A **deliverable** usually consists of several parts. For the sake of further discussion, a part of a design product is referred to in this text as a **component**. It is important to distinguish between a component of a design product and a component of the framework for understanding information systems methodologies as presented in this text.

One of the aims of this text is to identify typical components. A widely used component will be found in many products, where a product may be a design product or an **analysis product** or some other kind of product. This implies that the component is created as a deliverable in many different information systems methodologies.

Components are interrelated, in the sense that a component often cannot be created until some other component has been created. One could possibly evaluate a product based on the cohesion of its components.

One of the more subjective aspects of the concept of a component is deciding whether it should be regarded as part of the design product that is handed by the designer to the builder, or whether it is part of the analysis product which is for review by a user acceptor – or possibly both. In both these cases, the component can be regarded as a deliverable, but the question is: 'Who is the potential recipient of the deliverable?'

It is useful to note that some components can be created for the purpose of communicating with the user of the system or for building up some mutual understanding of the required functionality of the system. Such components are not necessarily part of the design product. However, no attempt has been made in this text to classify components in terms of their role in this respect. Such judgement would inevitably be subjective and controversial.

The term **product** can now be defined. A product for an information system is an output from a step or stage in a design process. For example, an analysis product is a set of components which can be given to a designer to serve as the basis for system design. A design product is a set of components which can be given to a builder so that the information system can be constructed according to the design.

The term **component** can also be defined. A component of the framework described in this text is a basic element of planning, analysis or design, which may be created as a result of a step in a design process. A step may result in more than one component, although, as will be discussed later, some steps do not result in any components.

Typically, a component is fairly elementary, such as a list of entity types, a list of business activities or a cross-reference between entity types and business activities.

Use of a design process calls for a business analyst to evaluate systematically the needs of the users and the constraints imposed by the executive responsible or resource manager, which influence the users' way of working. On the basis of this analysis, a designer can produce a prescriptive design, thereby completing the design process.

The whole design process, namely the results of the work of the analyst and the designer, can be seen as a project which needs to be managed using an appropriate project management technique. Further discussion of this issue, however, is outside the scope of this text. User needs and management constraints must always be balanced against resources available. The output of a design process must always be a design product.

One of the main arguments in this text is that there are many different design processes which may be used to arrive at the same design product. Using the analogy of the earlier section, one could assert that there are many different routes to the same target.

It is clear that, at present, the target reached is often dependent on the route travelled, but there is no apparent reason why this should necessarily be the case. The route travelled may well depend on the skill and experience of the designer, insofar as an experienced designer who has travelled many routes before may be able to pick a shorter or quicker route. If this route were chosen by a less experienced designer, he or she might never attain his or her target.

One of the many problems associated with the design process (which, as indicated, subsumes any analytic work necessary) is the starting point. Some people feel very strongly that an important part of an information systems design methodology is actually justifying the need for the system and evaluating the change that it will cause when introduced into the organization. Such justification will often include an analysis of existing work assignments, for example. Such activities are considered here to be part of information systems planning.

The starting point of a design process will be influenced strongly by whether an information systems planning activity has been performed. If so, this will necessarily have included an analysis of the business activities which can be further explored in the design process. If not, then the business activity analysis will usually need to be done from scratch.

1.7   Steps in a design process

There is a need to regard each design process as a number of steps. However, it is not useful to regard a step as something peculiar to a design process, but rather as something that can be used in one or more design processes. A **step** in a design process is defined as a piece of work that furthers a design process, which may result in zero, one or more components, depending on the type of step.

Steps are related to components, such that several of the steps will each cause zero, one or more components to be created. Not every step needs to create a component. This introduces the question of whether steps can be categorized in some way. It has been found convenient to regard each step as belonging to one of the following five step categories:

1.   abstraction,
2.   checking,
3.   form conversion,
4.   review with acceptor, or
5.   decision.

A more detailed description of each of these five step categories will be presented in Chapter 3.

1.8   Techniques used in information systems methodologies

The term **technique** is used in this text to refer to a part of an information systems methodology which may employ a well-defined set of concepts and a way of handling them in a step of the work. Some examples of techniques are:

- entity relationship modelling,
- functional decomposition,
- data flow analysis, and
- transition nets.

This list is not intended to be exhaustive and there is no significance implied in the sequence used.

Some of these techniques are analytic, in the sense that they examine and systematically describe the existing situation in the enterprise for which the computerized information system is being designed.

Other techniques are more prescriptive, in the sense that they are used to specify the required situation, rather than the existing one. Some techniques could be used either descriptively or prescriptively.

1.9   Perspectives and their impact

An examination of traditional information systems methodologies shows that they have tended to have differing emphases. Methodologies based on specifying the supposed functions of an information system are regarded as having a **process oriented perspective**. Methodologies derived from database technology have always emphasized what is referred to here as a **data oriented perspective**.

There has been a further realization that the time dependent (or temporal) aspects of an information system have not been given proper consideration in methodologies emphasizing the data and process perspectives. A third perspective has therefore developed, which is referred to here as the **behaviour oriented perspective**.

The three different **perspectives** are thus:

1.   data oriented perspective,
2.   process oriented perspective, and
3.   behaviour oriented perspective.

A design process may use one perspective as its driving force. Early methodologies tended to concentrate on one of these three perspectives to the exclusion of the other two. It is felt that a design process which aims to be complete should take into account all three perspectives. Each component of any design product is preferably regarded as having one perspective, thus allowing for the possibility of cross-referencing components which relate a component with one perspective to a component with a different perspective (Figure 1.4). These three perspectives will be described in more detail in Chapter 3.

A list of business activities would have a process oriented perspective.

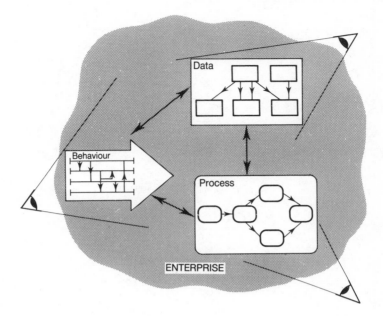

Figure 1.4 Perspectives.

A list of events would have a behaviour oriented perspective and a list of attributes would have a data oriented perspective. A cross-reference component, which indicates the attributes generated by a process, would have both data and process oriented perspectives.

1.10 Stages in information systems methodologies

There are many ways of breaking down what is usually referred to as the **information system life cycle**. The life cycle used in this book is described in more detail in Chapter 3. Most information systems methodologies are concerned with only a part of this life cycle, namely that leading to a design product, which can then be constructed for operational use. This book also limits consideration to that part of the information system life cycle leading up to the point at which a builder can start to construct a system.

For the purposes of presentation in this text, the following four stages in an information system life cycle are shown in Figure 1.5:

1.   information systems planning,
2.   business analysis,
3.   system design, and
4.   construction design.

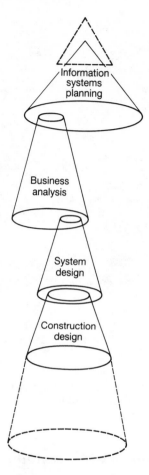

Figure 1.5   Stages considered in information systems methodology framework.

This list is given in a sequence which is felt to be natural for the work to be done. Existing information system methodologies do not necessarily conform to this breakdown and many of them do not cover all of these stages. Nevertheless, some breakdown is needed in this book in order to be able to present the material in a form understandable to the reader.

In theory, the above sequence of the stages should also be the preferred sequence for presentation in this text. For pedagogical reasons, a somewhat different presentation sequence has been chosen, with information systems planning placed after the other three. Each of the four stages will be described briefly here and in more detail in Chapter 3.

1.10.1 Information systems planning

As indicated in Section 1.3, information systems planning is a stage of activity in which one decides which systems, if any, need to be designed and built. An information systems planning stage will typically cover an area of the business which is more extensive than that covered in subsequent stages. The second and subsequent stages can be seen as focusing on an area of the business which may diminish for each stage.

The output from an information systems planning stage is a collection of components and hence a deliverable in the sense of Section 1.6. It may also be regarded as a product and referred to as a **planning product**.

From an expository point of view, the framework is made easily understandable by first presenting the stages associated with a more limited area of the business in Chapters 4, 5 and 6, and then treating information systems planning later in Chapter 7.

1.10.2 Business analysis

The stage of business analysis calls for examination and study of the existing state of affairs in a given business area of the enterprise. This study may be in terms of existing information systems (computerized or manual). It may call for an analysis of what is done in the enterprise and, furthermore, of what needs to be done given the support of more advanced information systems.

The output from a business analysis stage is also a deliverable in the sense of Section 1.6. It may also be regarded as a product and referred to as a **business analysis product**.

All business analysis activity is regarded as descriptive rather than prescriptive. The business analysis stage is considered in detail in Chapter 4.

1.10.3 System design

The system design stage consists of preparing a prescriptive statement about an information system – usually a computerized one. The scope of the application area covered in a system design stage may be more restricted than that of the associated business analysis stage on which it is based.

In many situations, it is useful to regard the output from a system design stage, namely the design product, as largely independent of the tools that will likely be used to construct the system. However, if it is known in advance which tools are to be used, it is quite likely that their capabilities and constraints may be factored in to the work of the system design stage. The system design stage is considered in detail in Chapter 5.

1.10.4   Construction design

The construction design stage introduces a major problem, to the extent that, in practice, it is highly dependent on the hardware and software tools chosen to do the job. This set of tools is referred to here as the **construction environment** and would typically include tools such as:

- database management system,
- data dictionary system,
- screen design aid,
- transaction processing system,
- programming language, and
- application generator.

The choice of a construction environment is ideally made after completion of the system design stage. This means that one chooses the tools to build the system after the system has been fully designed.

In practice, the designer is often aware of the environment to be used before the system design stage or even before the business analysis stage is initiated. This should enable an experienced designer to take shortcuts and hence reduce the overall time required.

The construction stage is not considered further in this text, although it is noted that many existing methodologies do address the problems of designing suites of programs. In addition, there are many computerized tools available which are having a significant effect on the way in which one can perform this stage.

1.10.5   Review of stages

To relate the concept of the above four stages in an information system life cycle to existing information systems methodologies, it is clear that existing methodologies emphasize different stages. Only very few seem to touch on the all-important first stage of information systems planning.

Some existing methodologies fail to identify a clear path leading to the construction of the information system. Others are essentially construction methodologies, which do not consider the early stages of planning and analysis. This latter kind of methodology can be categorized as **environment driven**.

Any breakdown into stages inevitably represents an element of subjectivity, but some breakdown is felt necessary in this report for the purpose of an organized presentation.

A design process, in the sense of this report, could cover two – or conceivably three – stages. Some existing methodologies can be seen to compact two stages into one. In each such methodology, it is impossible to distinguish a clear break between the completion of business analysis and the start of design specification.

1.11 Form of acceptor specifications

The output from the various stages identified in the previous section should include specifications which are comprehensible to the acceptors. These may be the user acceptors, namely the set of users who are required to review and submit positive approval of the design work. The lack of comment from users has all too frequently been interpreted as approval. In addition, the specifications may be reviewed by a constructor acceptor, who will apply very different judgements from the user acceptor.

The specifications may contain the following five elements:

1.   tabular data,
2.   formal specifications,
3.   informal narrative,
4.   graphic representations, and
5.   prototypes.

A given design product need not contain all five elements, but those that are used should be consistent with each other.

As in the case of the architect and the construction work, communication with the user acceptor must be seen very differently from communication with the constructor. Feedback from the user acceptor and from other users is important, especially during the analysis stage. Users should not be expected to react to specifications expressed in some highly mathematical form, however rigid and complete this may be.

The user acceptor must, in order to fulfil his or her role, be able to judge whether the information system to be built will meet his or her needs. The constructor acceptor will evaluate the design product to see whether it can be implemented and to ensure that it meets whatever standards of acceptability are appropriate.

Another role that makes use of the representation and documentation while performing its task is the analyst and designer role. Both of these produce specifications which need to be recorded. They use various representation techniques as a means of communicating with each other, as well as with the user and constructor. Such techniques also provide a means of managing the complexity during the design process.

The topic of representation and documentation will be considered in more detail in Chapter 9.

1.12   Evolution of an installed system

Design is always an iterative process. This implies a need to be able to revise
an interim or complete design product as easily as possible. If the information
system being designed is already built (based on the complete design product)
and installed, then the impact of design changes on the functioning information system will need to be assessed. Some data dictionary systems allow such
an **impact of change** analysis to be performed.

   The planned evolution of an installed system is a complex topic but
one that is unavoidable in any discussion of information systems methodologies. Evolving a design during the design process is a topic which is part
of the description of a design process.

   Performing a design revision after a system is built, installed and in
full use is a separate topic, which is covered in Chapter 8. An important concept in this connection is that of 'design for change' where a designer uses his
or her experience to attempt to predict the nature of future user requirements
with the aim of making them easier to incorporate as and when they arise.

1.13   Scenarios

There are several factors which collectively influence the way in which the
information system should be designed. Each factor has two or more alternative options. A **scenario** is a valid combination of such options, together with
a valid response.

   There are several acceptable scenarios in which an information system
could be designed. There are other scenarios, that is, combinations of factor
options, in which one would be better advised not to attempt to design an
information system at all.

   The implication is that there are, in fact, many ways of designing an
information system. The term already introduced for 'a way of defining an
information system' is the term 'design process'. Under certain circumstances one design process is best whereas under other circumstances, that is,
other scenarios, another design process is preferred.

   There are further circumstances in which, for a given information
system, every design process would be unsatisfactory. For example, any combination of options which combines a neophyte designer with a large and
complex system in an ill-defined environment, would clearly be an
unacceptable scenario.

   Typical factors which influence the scenario can be categorized as **contextual, technical** or as associated with one or more stages of an information
system life cycle. Examples of contextual factors are: scale of the information
system, well- or ill-defined business area, quality of analyst and designer skill
available. Technical factors to be considered are: type of system, con-

struction tools available, and so on. The factors relevant to a discussion of scenarios are discussed in more detail in Chapter 2.

1.14 Boundaries of a design process

In preparing this text, emphasis has been placed on the techniques used in the planning, analysis and design work associated with information systems.

Several associated problems have been consciously omitted, not because they are irrelevant, but rather to place a clear boundary round the problem area under consideration. Examples of omitted problems include:

- the design of a business environment,
- the management of a design team,
- implementation planning and cost estimating,
- estimating the cost of the design process, and
- the design of application programs.

Certain commercially available methodologies (including some of those referenced in Appendix A), which overlap to some extent with what are referred to here as information systems methodologies, do touch on some of these problems. For example, the discussion of design processes will identify the idea of checking steps, which are performed on the way to a design product. Management control should be based on such checking steps.

A major design activity that is not considered in this list is the design of the business environment in which an information system is ultimately required to function. It is noted that some people's use of the term 'information system' includes the business environment and that the information system described here is referred to as the 'technical system'. Design of the business environment, while of the utmost importance, is outside the scope of this book.

1.15 Use of diagramming techniques

This text uses various diagramming techniques to convey the concepts and ideas being put forward. For example, Figure 1.6 uses a data structure diagram to indicate the relationships among the key concepts introduced in this chapter and developed in subsequent chapters.

A similar diagramming technique will be used in Chapters 4 and 5 to indicate how the various components are interrelated.

Other diagramming techniques are used in Chapter 6 to indicate how the components produced in certain hypothetical design processes are represented.

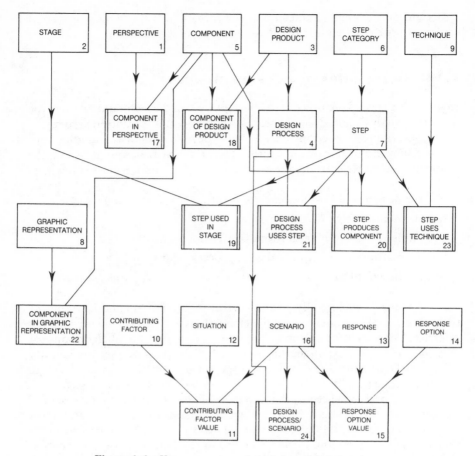

Figure 1.6   Key concepts and their interdependencies.

1.16   Summary of major concepts used in framework

The 16 key concepts discussed in this chapter are now presented in a tutorial sequence, together with details of the subsequent chapter in which the concept will be discussed more fully. Each key concept is shown as a rectangle in Figure 1.6.

Each interdependency of a key concept on another key concept is shown by an arrow. There are several cross-references between key concepts. These are regarded differently from interdependencies and are shown in Figure 1.6 as rectangles with double vertical lines. (The diagramming conventions are described more fully in Figure 3.8.)

1.   **PERSPECTIVE**   A PERSPECTIVE is a traditional way of categorizing

earlier information systems methodologies, the three alternatives being data, process and behaviour (see Chapter 3).

2. **STAGE**   A STAGE is regarded here as a convenient breakdown of the totality of the information systems life cycle activity described in this report. A breakdown is used for presentation purposes. Several STAGES are identified (see Chapter 3), but the emphasis in this report is on the following:

- information systems planning,
- business analysis, and
- system design.

3. **DESIGN PRODUCT**   A DESIGN PRODUCT for an information system is a set of specifications, such as those given to a builder, so that the system may be constructed. Each DESIGN PRODUCT consists of several COMPONENTS (see Chapter 3).

   Each DESIGN PRODUCT is generated by one DESIGN PROCESS, but some DESIGN PRODUCTS may be generatable by more than one different DESIGN PROCESS.

4. **DESIGN PROCESS**   A DESIGN PROCESS is a way of preparing a DESIGN PRODUCT. More than one DESIGN PROCESS may lead to the same DESIGN PRODUCT (see Chapter 6).

5. **COMPONENT**   A COMPONENT is the smallest part of the framework (see Chapters 4 and 5). The same COMPONENT could be used in several DESIGN PRODUCTS.

   Where possible, each COMPONENT in this text is described in tabular form. In a given DESIGN PRODUCT for an information system, there will be several instances of each COMPONENT. This means that the table representing the component will have several rows.

   Each COMPONENT is generated as a result of performing a STEP.

6. **STEP CATEGORY**   A STEP CATEGORY is a classification of a STEP into one of the following (see Chapter 3):

- abstraction,
- checking,
- form conversion,
- review, or
- decision.

7. **STEP**   A STEP is the smallest part of a DESIGN PROCESS and always belongs to one STEP CATEGORY (see Chapter 6). Each STEP may be part of more than one DESIGN PROCESS.

   Each abstraction STEP will generate one or more COMPONENTS. STEPS which are categorized as review or decision STEPS would not typically produce a COMPONENT. A checking STEP may or may not generate a COMPONENT, depending on the nature of the checking.

8.   **GRAPHIC REPRESENTATION** A GRAPHIC REPRESENTATION is a schematic convention for displaying one or more COMPONENTS (see Chapter 9).

If a DESIGN PRODUCT contains all the COMPONENTS needed in a GRAPHIC FORMALISM, then any DESIGN PROCESS used to prepare that DESIGN PRODUCT could use that GRAPHIC REPRESENTATION.

9.   **TECHNIQUE** A TECHNIQUE is employed in carrying out a STEP. It is a recognized part of a design methodology used in a STAGE to generate one or more COMPONENTS. A TECHNIQUE can support one or more STEPS and generates the COMPONENTS generated by those STEPS (see Chapter 6).

10. **CONTRIBUTING FACTOR** A CONTRIBUTING FACTOR is a factor which has two or more CONTRIBUTING FACTOR VALUES, and a combination of these values represents the given aspects of a SCENARIO. Each CONTRIBUTING FACTOR is independent of other factors (see Chapter 2).

11. **CONTRIBUTING FACTOR VALUE** A CONTRIBUTING FACTOR VALUE is a single value which a CONTRIBUTING FACTOR may have. It represents a feature of the business area or of the information system's environment which influences the identification of a SCENARIO and subsequently the choice of a DESIGN PROCESS.

12. **SITUATION** A SITUATION is what one observes in a business area as given. It comprises a set of CONTRIBUTING FACTOR VALUES.

13. **RESPONSE** A RESPONSE is a combination of values of RESPONSE OPTIONS.

14. **RESPONSE OPTION** A RESPONSE OPTION is a factor, the value of which may be chosen from a prescribed set of values.

15. **RESPONSE OPTION VALUE** A RESPONSE OPTION VALUE is one of two or more possible values of a RESPONSE OPTION.

16. **SCENARIO** A SCENARIO is a selected set of CONTRIBUTING FACTOR VALUES combined with a set of RESPONSE OPTION VALUES. A SCENARIO can also be defined as a SITUATION and an appropriate RESPONSE.

Each of the following cross-references is depicted in Figure 1.6 and relates two key concepts without either one necessarily constraining the other.

17. **COMPONENT IN PERSPECTIVE** Most COMPONENTS have only one PERSPECTIVE, that is, either data, process or behaviour. However, some COMPONENTS provide a cross-reference between a COMPONENT in one PERSPECTIVE and a COMPONENT in another PERSPECTIVE. It is consistent to regard such COMPONENTS as being in two PERSPECTIVES.

18. **COMPONENT OF DESIGN PRODUCT** Each DESIGN PRODUCT consists of one or more COMPONENTS and the same COMPONENT can be part of more than one DESIGN PRODUCT. The instances of a COMPONENT which is part of two or more DESIGN PRODUCTS will usually differ for the different DESIGN PRODUCTS.

19. **STEP USED IN STAGE** Each STEP may be used in one STAGE in one DESIGN PROCESS. A given STEP may, in fact, be used in different STAGES in different DESIGN PROCESSES, implying that the STEP is viewed differently by the DESIGN PROCESS from how it is viewed in this book. Each STAGE contains one or more STEPS.

    As mentioned earlier, the STAGES are introduced here merely to facilitate presentation of the material in this text. To understand a DESIGN PROCESS, it is more important to understand it in terms of the STEPS of which it consists.

20. **STEP PRODUCES COMPONENT** Each STEP produces zero, one or more COMPONENTS. Abstraction STEPS will always produce at least one COMPONENT. The same COMPONENT (implying different instances of the COMPONENT) can be produced in more than one STEP, although such STEPS must then belong to different DESIGN PROCESSES.

21. **DESIGN PROCESS USES STEP** Each DESIGN PROCESS uses two or more STEPS and a step can belong to one or more DESIGN PROCESSES.

22. **COMPONENT IN GRAPHIC REPRESENTATION** Each GRAPHIC FORMALISM can be used to present one or more COMPONENTS and some of the COMPONENTS can be presented in more than one GRAPHIC REPRESENTATION.

23. **STEP USES TECHNIQUE** Each TECHNIQUE supports either part of a STEP, one STEP, or more than one STEP. Since the TECHNIQUES are used in existing methodologies, the STEPS described in Chapter 6 are related, where possible, to existing known TECHNIQUES.

24. **DESIGN PROCESS VALID FOR SCENARIO** There is at least one DESIGN PROCESS valid for each SCENARIO, and a DESIGN PROCESS may be applicable to more than one SCENARIO as discussed in Chapter 2.

EXERCISES

A. Self-assessment

1.1 What is meant by the design process and how does it relate to the design product? What terms are used when referring to parts of these two? Which are the smallest and why would a further breakdown not make sense?

1.2   Three stages of the 'information system life cycle' used in this book are given primary attention:

- information systems analysis,
- business analysis, and
- system design.

Restate the significance of each of these. Explain why the way in which a methodology deals with these stages is a more important criterion for distinction than that regarding other stages.

1.3   In this book, a step is considered to fall into one of the following five categories:

- abstraction,
- checking,
- form conversion,
- review, or
- decision.

Discuss this choice and explain why it allows a complete description of the system design stage. Suggest another typing of design step categories.

1.4   In any information systems project, several parties will be involved in different human roles. How are these distinguished? Give an explanation of each. Suggest possible alternatives for categorizing human roles.

1.5   What is meant by a technique in the context of this book? Name some activities that would qualify as techniques for an information systems methodology.

B.   *Methodology related*

(for those familiar with one or more existing methodologies)

1.6   How does the terminology in this book compare with that employed by some existing methodology?

1.7   Is there a difference in the breakdown into stages?

1.8   If so, discuss whether such differences would make it difficult to achieve a systematic discussion of the features in order to understand the thrust of each methodology.

2

Scenarios for the use of information systems methodologies

2.1 Introduction

This book provides a framework within which information systems methodologies may be viewed. It also views information systems methodologies as a framework for the preparation of a design product.

A feature of a framework is that it supports a variety of different concepts, often combined in a number of different ways. Prior to using any information systems methodology, therefore, it is generally necessary to consider how, and within which context, it will be used.

This chapter addresses that context and examines typical features. It is positioned prior to the detailed description of stages and components to emphasize the fact that the framework to be described should always be used selectively and that it provides the rationale for these selections.

Each possible approach to the design of an information system depends on the characteristics of the business area in question. This dependency applies especially to the planning, analysis and design stages of the information systems life cycle. It is also desirable to build a certain amount of anticipation of future requirements into the design of the system (see Chapter 7).

In the light of this variety of concerns, any discussion of how methodologies might be applied and what relevant features they offer should be preceded by an analysis of possible options. In this book we shall do that by considering what sort of conditions are encountered (to be referred to as **situations**) and what elements contribute to these (called **contributing factors**). Given one's view of the situation, a decision is to be made about how to deal with it. Often, more than one **option** offers itself. The final **response** will then be that one option (or set of options) is selected. Such a choice will be named a **scenario**. The basic concepts in scenario selection are illustrated in Figure 2.1.

2.2   Situations and scenarios

A 'situation' is a very complex concept. It is established by many different factors. Of these, only those that could influence or would be influenced by the choice of a specific methodology (in the broadest sense of the word) are of interest here. The term 'situation' in the sense used in this book describes the result of an analysis. When combined with a certain chosen methodological

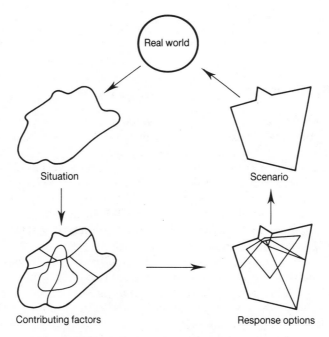

Figure 2.1   Basic concepts in scenario selection.

approach, that is to say, together with the prescribed response, it will be called the 'scenario'.

Two systems that require different approaches, even if the enterprise in question has adopted a standard methodology, would be the need for a 'crash' project, as opposed to one that may be fitted in smoothly, over a longer period of time. Likewise, if the application of a methodology allows the use of automated tools and if, indeed, one does decide to use them, then the factors to be evaluated might be quite different from the situation where such tools are ignored or the methodology does not provide any. These are examples of problems that might come up in specific cases. The factors involved might be termed 'time pressure' and 'tool automation'.

Some factors will always have to be considered, for instance:

- the 'business area' in general,
- information requirements,
- project type and size,
- skills available and obtainable, and
- tools available and obtainable.

Thus it is desirable to be able to select a design process which is appropriate for the specific circumstances. Many methodologies offer a variety of options, but require considerable study before a selection can be made. On the other hand, some are based on a single technique, thus sacrificing variety for unambiguous applicability.

This chapter examines some of the typical considerations that apply to various situations and alternatives. These are illustrated in terms of the components, steps and stages introduced in Chapter 1.

The considerations are presented in the form of 'relevant factor groups'. The reason for such grouping is that even the recognition of no more than two levels of assessment for individual factors (such as high and low, positive and negative, or similar) would lead to an unacceptably large number of scenarios. Three groups of factors are identified, namely:

1. Life cycle.
2. 'Contextual' factors concerning the enterprise and its information requirements.
3. 'Technical' factors concerning the design process alternatives.

Certain factors may be contextual in one situation and technical in another – 'designer skill', for example. On the one hand, this factor concerns the extent to which a certain level of technical design capability is provided; on the other, it is also a characteristic of the environment (or context) in which the project may be undertaken.

In general, one must consider a mix of factors. An example would be a relatively experienced organization wishing to add management information features to an existing transaction processing system, but with a limited number of experienced business analysts among its personnel and no applications development group in its data processing centre. In this case, the contextual factors are a particular need and a specific organizational experience. There are also explicit technical factors, such as a limited establishment of personnel trained for the new requirements, combined with otherwise reasonable technical facilities.

Other examples include the initial introduction of information system automation into a small enterprise (relatively small-scale extreme) and the changeover from a highly integrated conventional system to a fully fledged on line system, with advanced networks, enabling enterprise-wide *ad hoc* queries, messaging and decision support facilities (relatively large-scale extreme).

2.3   Significant factors

One way of describing the possible 'contingencies', namely the occurrence of situational factors of significance, would be to list all factors deemed important in a table and to assign an appropriate value to each. Although difficult to write down (each 'factor value' may consist of a short sentence and a particular combination may additionally require an entire paragraph), such a list would be very useful if each line could be coupled with a suitable corresponding strategy in a unique and stable way. Normally, both stability and uniqueness leave much to be desired. Additionally, the number of factors and different factor values might be prohibitive. By grouping the factors and accepting only classes of contingencies rather than individual cases, the presentation might become more manageable and hence more useful.

2.3.1   Aspects of a project approach

A project approach comprises a mix of choices for addressing each of the following activities:

- thinking,
- modelling,
- working, and
- controlling.

The way of *thinking* (sometimes called an enterprise's 'Weltanschauung') is of great importance. In an environment where the enterprise itself is viewed as the result of an explicit design process, the information system will be considered merely as one element in a larger engineered whole. On the other hand, the enterprise may be seen as an evolving, social phenomenon, within which each information system may be adapted according to perceived (changing) needs. The approach to information systems design will differ accordingly, and so will the options for applying methodologies.

Modelling means the extent to which business aspects are considered relevant (and hence are to be emphasized). It provides the abstractions that are used for expressing the 'real world' and the information streams for supporting and controlling them. The style and extent of the models chosen will influence the way in which a methodology might be used.

The way of *working* involves such things as the step sequence for the different actions to be undertaken, the use of of specialized tools and the selection of trained staff (own or hired). A methodology may fit in with a variety of approaches, but should be considered on that basis.

The *control* (or project management) of the work to be done may be subject to a variety of different styles. This will have its repercussions on the applicability and usage of the methodology chosen.

2.3.2   Selected combination of circumstances

The combination selected constitutes the strategy for the case in question. As said before, the term 'scenario' is used here as meaning 'the **combination** of a (perceived) **situation** and the (chosen) **response**'. All four aspects of the project approach may be relevant for a given situation. They would form the decision part of the scenario. As for the contextual and technical factors, a wide range may be viewed as potentially significant each time. However, just a small number of factors and factor values normally suffices to distinguish one situation from another.

An example of how to formulate a contingency-based approach would be the following. It is assumed that the contributing factors are:

1.   the scope of the problem to be solved,
2.   the extent to which existing systems are already structured,
3.   the size of the project,
4.   the experience of the users, and
5.   the quality of the design staff.

The factor values might all have a positive effect (implying little uncertainty or potential budget overrun) or, on the other hand, might all have negative effects and therefore suggest a high risk. These two extremes are combined in Figure 2.2 (where 'positive' is associated with a 'low' uncertainty and 'negative' with a 'high' uncertainty).

Factor	Uncertainty	
	Low	High
Problem	Well-defined	Ill-defined
Existing system structure	Well-structured	Poorly-structured
Project size	Small	Big
User experience	Extensive	Limited
Designer staff quality	High	Low

Figure 2.2   Example of a variety of factor values.

The strategies to be recommended for such a two-valued case, or for the more likely 'spectrum' of values, also typically depend on a life cycle (or time dimension) factor. They are business area dependent in that they differ for problems defined from the point of view of the enterprise. Typical examples of such problems are (1) a marketing information system needed to achieve better sales performance, and (2) a service improvement program for processing insurance claims.

The nature of the market information system referred to may well agree with the entries in the 'high' column of Figure 2.2 and possibly lead to the strategy 'data oriented perspective, iterative development, participative project team'. On the other hand, the insurance claims system would be closer to the 'low' column and probably require 'process oriented perspective, linear development, centralized project management'.

2.3.3   Role of the system life cycle

The **information system life cycle** may be broken down into a number of stages (see Section 1.10). Such a breakdown will be discussed in more detail in Section 3.2. Even if the sequencing of stage details may not always be fixed, it does suggest that there is a strict time scale applicable to all situations. However, most projects require iterations of various stages. Iteration may take different forms and thus impact differently on what one can do with a methodology. In this sense, the choice of sequencing and breakdown into stages leads to a separate factor category.

The life cycle aspects are connected with both the way of working and the way of controlling a project. That also applies to the way in which project teams are assembled. For instance, in the case of 'participative' design (users as active members of the design team), different forms of representation are used from in the case where an external consultant undertakes a turnkey project (for a fuller discussion, see Chapter 9).

Too many combinations exist for any completely general scheme of scenario representation to be proposed. However, it may be quite feasible in individual situations to precede planning or analysis with the systematic presentation of a number of relevant alternatives. This holds both for the overall information systems planning stage and for individual stages. This point will be addressed in Section 2.4.1.

As indicated, it is useful to reduce the number of options by grouping factors in a meaningful way. The emphasis is then on the contextual and technical factor groups and on the life cycle stages concerned. These form the three 'dimensions' of this task. The possible representation of scenarios on this basis is not considered further here, but the grouping of factors and their interaction are discussed in the following section.

2.4 Factor groupings

The point of departure is the three 'dimensions' represented by the life cycle, the contextual and the technical factors. The characteristics of the contextual and technical dimensions are illustrated by some specific examples.

2.4.1 Life cycle stages

This dimension is implicitly covered in Chapter 1 and in more detail in Chapter 3. Four stages (information systems planning, business analysis, system design and evolution) are discussed in later chapters. In addition, one may distinguish a certain number of steps to be performed in a design process (see Section 3.5). Each of the stages and steps has certain options associated with it. In fact, once chosen, the sequence of the steps might be considered a contributing factor in its own right. The same applies to one's emphasis on the stages.

As indicated in Section 2.3.3, there are more combinations of factors than are practical to be considered. For this reason, the range of subjects covered in this framework and the choice of terminology are difficult. The framework contains many typical time related 'scenario' elements, although these are not identified as such. It is certainly possible to set up a suitable time scale for such purposes on the basis presented here.

2.4.2 Contextual factors

Each enterprise (or at least those involved in designing the information systems for that enterprise) needs to develop its own view of the contextual factors. The following should usually be considered:

- the organizational structure and its environment,
- the nature of the information requirements, and
- the project type and size.

This grouping constitutes a general breakdown. As at the detailed level, these broader factor groups sometimes have typical technical factor aspects, in addition to their contextual origins. The nature of the requirements (typically dictated by the environment) also restricts the system one might build (on technical grounds).

It may be observed that no all-embracing guideline for selecting a scenario is proposed here. However, the consistency and completeness of one's view are enhanced by treating factors initially in broad outline rather than in detail. The above three category breakdown is one way of doing so.

The following seven examples illustrate the next lower level of detail to be considered in determining the approach to the ultimate scenario which is finally adopted.

1.   **Scale of information system**   Some systems are small; some are large. It is not clear to what extent the design processes used for these systems should be totally different. It is possible that some steps are irrelevant or an 'overkill' in a smaller situation.

The amount of data involved (for example, the size of the database) is not the only criterion of size. The number of different kinds of data, the transaction frequencies, the size of the user population and the number of information processes (usually synonymous with application programs) all contribute to the overall concept of scale.

2.   **Well- or ill-defined environment**   The relevant enterprise aspects and activities for which the information system is being designed may be 'well-defined'. This may be a result of the nature of the business or it may be because of some existing computerized system, use of which has caused the users to think in a more formalized way about their tasks.

In many business areas where computerization has never been seriously attempted, the situation may be classified as 'ill-defined'. The analyst will find an analysis of business activities quite difficult and it will be hard to reach a consensus on what is needed. The well-defined environment clearly contributes to an easier choice of scenario than the ill-defined one.

3.   **Quality of analyst and designer skill available**   Some designers have 15 years of varied design experience; others have one year of design experience repeated 15 times. Inevitably, some designers will have recently completed training. The experienced designer might well choose to omit certain precautionary analysis or design steps which would be highly recommended for the neophyte. The opportunity of hiring staff – if possible or desirable – must also be considered.

4.   **Quantity of analysts and designers available**   In some enterprises, there is a considerable shortage of technical skills. It can also be counterproductive to have too many people assigned to an analysis or

design project. The number of analysts and designers needed for optimum progression of the work is a difficult management problem which can influence the approach chosen. The extent to which extra staff may or may not be hired is also a contributing factor.

5. **Type of application** Different approaches apply to systems for transaction processing, management information reporting, decision support, and so on. These contextual factors also have a strong technical flavour and they are discussed from this angle in Section 2.4.3.

6. **Time pressures** A factor which all too often overrides others is that of pressure from the executive responsible, or from the prospective user community, for the system to be available by a certain deadline.

The availability of the system might be seen as vital to the conduct of the business. This kind of factor all too often leads the designer or the constructor to cut corners in an attempt to meet the deadline imposed.

7. **Economics** The options to be considered are also dependent on the capability of financing them and on the expected economics. For instance, there may not be funding for hiring more than a limited number of skilled staff, even if more might have been desirable. On the other hand, the anticipated productivity increase due to participation of experienced consulting personnel may far outweigh the loss of (other) productivity of one's own staff if the latter are inexperienced and now need further training before they can contribute satisfactorily to a project.

2.4.3 Technical factors

As with the contextual factors, one would expect each enterprise (or at least those involved in designing the enterprise's information systems) to develop its own view of the relevant technical factors.

A useful grouping for the technical factors might be the following:

1. Skills (of user, designer, builder staff).
2. Technical characteristics of the information system.
3. Tools (design/development, prototyping, libraries, languages).

The first two of these also have contextual aspects. In the case of the 'skills' factor, it is the availability of persons possessing them (both qualitatively and quantitatively). For the system, it is implied in the way the environment determines the requirements.

These points illustrate how each contributing factor interacts strongly with the others. Since the relevant ones vary from enterprise to enterprise and also carry different weights in different problem situations, one needs an overall view and a detailed one simultaneously, as applicable to the specific case. The broad grouping outline alone would make for a good starting point.

Four typical examples illustrate to what extent lower level detail may be of importance in the scenario selection:

1.   **Information system user and designer skills**   In an enterprise which begins using information systems for the first time (or starts using them company-wide instead of locally), there may be few staff members who have sufficient experience to be able to participate effectively in new projects. Where use of information systems has been commonplace for some time, one could consider setting up much more mixed user/designer teams.

   Similarly, newcomer enterprises normally do not have skilled designer and/or builder staff. Those that do have a longer tradition of using information systems may have decided long ago that they ought not to invest in specialized design staff, because that is not the prime scope of their activity. More often than not, there is a relatively limited number of persons immediately available with information system design and building skills. By contrast, some large enterprises do possess a pool of such staff. The scenario options vary accordingly.

2.   **Type of system**   There are many types of information system and, indeed, many taxonomies could be developed to categorize them. To set the scene for establishing relevant scenarios, the following categorization is used:

   - manual,
   - embedded system,
   - distributed system,
   - centralized system, and
   - federated system.

   An 'embedded system' is a system that forms part of a larger system, but is not generally perceived as a system in its own right.

   A 'distributed system', by definition, is designed to serve several geographic locations. The system may be wholly or partially distributed around these locations. Users may or may not be aware of whether the data in which they are interested is 'local' or held in another node of the system.

   A 'centralized system' is one which runs on one computer at one place and supports the work at either one geographic location or at several separate geographic locations. The information users may have access to the one system from their various locations.

   Finally, the term 'federated system' refers to the interaction of several nodes (each either centralized or distributed) that were not originally designed to function interactively, but are able to do so in some way, possibly based on a common use of industry standards.

Most systems currently under design are 'on line', with tasks invoked or initiated from a terminal. The need for an acceptable response time is a major design constraint.

One must question the relevance of many traditional design techniques to the distributed and federated systems being designed and built. On the other hand, the (formal or informal) procedures for using the resulting information do not differ fundamentally from the older traditions, so that the modern approach to designing the overall system may still have elements in common with that of the past.

This book does not explicitly consider the analysis and design issues involved with manual systems. It is interesting to note that many of the design techniques in use today were developed in the era of batch systems, when the computer merely served as a mechanized batch device.

3. **Construction tools available**   Tools currently available on the market vary from highly sophisticated, almost automatic, ones (see Chapter 10) to the more primitive conventional programming language facilities, such as those discussed further in Chapter 11.

     The aims of the more modern tools are to offer a reduction in the cost of constructing the system and to reduce the skill level required for the construction work. Although there is no way in which good construction tools can make up for bad design, the construction tools that the designer expects to use are an important factor in defining the scenario.

4. **Availability of 'prototyping' tools**   As discussed in Chapter 10, there are various kinds of prototyping tools available. The support provided by them is two-fold. If a business area is well defined, then it may be possible to accelerate the analysis stage by representing various options for using information in an easily understandable manner. This may be achieved by integrating the analysis and design stages, and presenting the user acceptor with a prototype of the final system on which to make an assessment. This approach is especially practicable where the use of a database management system is already established.

     On the other hand, if the area and its problems are ill defined, a prototyping tool may assist in eliciting relevant features of the business system. That is done by demonstrating the report formats using mock-up data.

     Thus, in the first situation assistance is given to the activity of output specification, in the second to that of defining required data elements. In other words, prototyping may perform an important role in the requirements analysis, and also support the design stage.

In addition to the support of analysis and design, it should also be possible to use prototyping tools in a construction design stage after the earlier stages have been completed. Such use would not be aimed at a user acceptor, but would have the objective of constructing the system as quickly and inexpensively as possible.

2.5   Cross-referencing the dimensions

To belong in two factor groups is a form of cross-reference (namely, between the two groups). The interrelationship between two different factors is another case. The explicit juxtaposition of entire factor groups is a combination of these two forms.

The usefulness of setting out one's options is evident. A well-phased selection can provide insight into what may be achieved and lead to early rejection of dead ends. It is important to consider to what extent such points are capable of expression in a methodology. The concept of a methodology is at variance with that of first considering a large number of options. As such, it is naturally prescriptive. The capability of applying it in a way dependent upon a range of (cross-referenced) factors, therefore, may not always be stated as an objective (let alone an explicit first task) of a methodology. However, one should be aware of the flexibility offered where it can be applied in this way.

A full enumeration of the factors relevant to the enterprise and its current information systems plans should be made from time to time. Ideally, this should be done in conjunction with the information systems planning stage. Another good time is in the early stages of a new project or prior to starting a major evolution stage (see Chapter 8).

2.6   Response options

Having highlighted the important aspects of a potential situation and having decided on the factor values to be attributed, the scheme must be completed with the choice of solutions to describe fully all scenarios of interest. In spite of the theoretical number involved, one would probably end up with only a dozen or so scenarios of interest. Of these, probably only three or four would be regarded as promising (or enjoy such evident preference), thus making the final selection relatively easy. The virtue of this approach is that one's *modus operandi* is determined beforehand, making it easier to be systematic in one's procedure.

The 'given' element in scenario selection consists of the contributing factors (and factor values) one recognizes. Part of that enumeration is expressed in appropriate cross-references between these, that is to say, by the dimensions discussed above. The response to be associated with that situational description states what methodological approach is taken. Specifically, one must decide what options exist and which are selected.

A number of methodological options may be open. The following three sections discuss some aspects that may be significant.

2.6.1 Step sequencing

In Chapter 6, examples are given of different sequences for various analysis and design steps. Some methodologies are very specific in the way such sequences are prescribed; others leave freedom of choice. In any event, planning any project for a new system or for the evolution of an existing system means that one decides on some schedule. Scenarios for such plans, therefore, may have to consider options for different sequences. This means that the time dimension of the information system life cycle is not continuous but consists of discrete portions, which may be combined in different ways.

Optimization of plans with discrete features is often difficult. Just as in the case of the factors, which were grouped to make them manageable, a sensible scenario for step sequencing would consider only a modest number of variations.

The classic example of two different step sequences is encountered in the contrast of so-called 'process oriented' and 'data oriented' methodologies. The former concentrates first on the business activities in enterprises and on the data processing tasks that support these; the data required is subsequently considered in that context. The latter first views the relevant entity types and relationships, leading up to the corresponding data model; their use in specific tasks is deferred until later in the life cycle.

The step sequencing aspect is an example of an area where there are different approaches to the specific 'way of working'.

2.6.2 Degree of formality

While communication in the design process demands unambiguous forms of expression (see Chapter 9), the nature of the messages exchanged – and consequently the degree of formality applicable – may vary from the unspecific verbal to the specific documentary. Most methodologies require a fair degree of precision. However, the formality implied may not be achieved in some of the exchanges leading up to the ultimate result. Hence, scenarios may have to be selected in which the style of the methodology proper is inter-mixed with some of the design steps, with informal intermediate products. Usually, this alternation between formal and informal is passed through unconsciously, but it might well be made explicit.

The same applies to the documentation accompanying the ultimate system. This book concentrates on the planning, analysis and design stages, but part of the activity in question is directed to that end product. Since usage of an information system involves people in their everyday tasks, informality of expression may be mixed with formality of operating the information system. Not all methodologies address the format of the finished system (with its computer based components and accompanying documentation). If the methodology available does not provide steps for dealing with usage procedures and documentation, the scenarios one formulates may have to state how those missing aspects are to be filled in. Irrespective of whether the methodologies considered address these points or not, the degree and mix of informality with formality deserves to be defined.

While this book is primarily concerned with the planning, analysis and design stages, the construction stage requires explicit unambiguity also. Some methodologies provide more specific guidance than others. The extent to which precision can and must be aimed for may vary. In any event, it should be considered worthwhile deciding beforehand what options offer themselves in this respect.

The degree of formality adopted constitutes an example of a specific 'way of thinking'.

2.6.3   Degree of flexibility

Regarding the selection of a design *process*, some methodologies offer one process and others more than one. Even if the required design product has been defined, that often leaves the choice still open. In considering the merits of methodologies, one should investigate what flexibility and which options are open.

2.7   Worked examples of scenarios

Three examples illustrate how scenarios may differ and to what extent these differences are relevant from the point of view of the methodologies available.

2.7.1   Example A: life cycle factor dominance

The situation assumed is that of a medium- to large-sized enterprise, within which a number of information systems are operational and where the need for improved performance is felt. Among possible ways of dealing with the problem, two are considered seriously: (1) individual reviews of the existing systems (leading to proposals for specific evolution), and (2) embarking on a new cycle of information planning. Relevant factors and options for the two cases are shown in the form of the scenarios in Figure 2.3.

Case 1 requires a methodology of limited range (or a limited selection of provisions out of a wider one), whereas case 2 must be provided with a full menu (or the capabilities of more than one methodology, for the different stages of the exercise). Both allow a degree of freedom. In the restricted approach (1), each individual system considered may be tackled as and when resources are available. In the full-scale planning approach (2), phasing would probably be applied whereby commitment of resources would be applied stage by stage. Any upgrading and/or new design project would be selectable at the most appropriate time.

Factor or response	Case 1	Case 2
Scope	Existing systems or selection	Existing and potential (new) systems
Risk	Reasonably well known (selection dependent)	Partially known (at best, for existing systems only)
Costs	Selection dependent upgrading costs	Planning plus subsequent work costs
Benefits	Improvement of selected systems	Overall (potential) plus selected improvements
Design process	Reverse engineering etc.	Information planning and all further stages

Figure 2.3 Two scenarios for a problem with life cycle options.

Whereas management's decision would mostly be based on an analysis of risk, costs and benefits, the enterprise's experience with methodological work might well be considered as well. For instance, if one has not been involved in information planning before, in choosing approach 2 it will be time consuming to bring user staff up to an effective level of participation. The most suitable scenario might then be one where external expertise is brought in. On the other hand, option 1 might even be chosen deliberately because of the training costs otherwise incurred.

From the example it is clear that at least four scenarios are conceivable, namely, case 1 or case 2 for either an experienced or an inexperienced enterprise (with further sub-scenarios depending on the nature of the experience or the lack thereof). That multiplicity is due especially to the potential scopes of the methodological consequences – covering a restricted part or a wide part of the life cycle.

2.7.2 Example B: contextual factor dominance

The situation assumed is that of a small enterprise, which is highly experienced in the application of specialized information systems, feeling the need to integrate some of their features. Obviously, many technical factors apply (such as technical knowhow invested in staff training, as well as in developing the systems themselves), but the overriding factor is the potentiality for linking the systems, with the intention of upgrading the informational capabilities of the enterprise as a whole.

Depending on the extent to which one wishes to invest in change, a sizable or a modest project may be appropriate. For instance, the approach may be one of stepwise extension, taking the existing systems as starting points (approach 1). Alternatively, an integral approach may be chosen, the linking network constituting the central concept (approach 2). In either approach, one must pass through some analytic stage, a design stage, a construction stage and an installation stage. These may be clearly separated, or possibly intermixed and or recursively applied. Methodologies may or may not lend themselves to assist here.

Some considerations connected with the organizational context are collected in Figure 2.4.

Factor	Approach 1	Approach 2
Scope	Linking together some existing systems	All-embracing network
Main issue	Value addded by linking specific systems	Enterprise-wide information aspects
Scale	Modest (choice)	Large (little choice)
Definition	Well defined (once selection made)	Ill defined (repercussions)
Economics	Well defined	Less defined
Methodology related	Requirements analysis and follow up	Requirements analysis and follow up

Figure 2.4   Two scenarios for a problem with contextual options.

Again, the economics play a dominant role. From the methodological point of view, the real issue is to what extent enhancement of information services is achieved. Although the same kind of requirements are to be considered – and the same stages are to be gone through – the scales and the degree of definition differ widely.

The perceived general need of the enterprise may lead to two main scenarios. The difference between them results from the choice of one contextual factor, namely the extent of linking the organization units. In choosing a methodology (or considering the suitability of an existing standard), the capability of supporting the consequent needs would have to weigh heavily.

2.7.3   Example C: technical factor dominance

The situation assumed is that of a large, centralized enterprise that contemplates reorganizing its information technology related activities. Contextual, namely reorganization related, factors apply as well, but the most obvious issue is that of reallocating the enterprise's technical capabilities. It may have become apparent, for instance, that having a data processing centre based section of analysts, designers and programmers no longer provides benefits commensurate with the cost involved. Alternatively, the experience of the user department staff may have grown over the years, so that they are in far less need of assistance than in the past, but now need information centre type support. Additionally, top management may feel that decentralization will make the departments operate more responsibly.

Some technical factors that might be considered when comparing the option of decentralization with that of retaining the current situation are listed in Figure 2.5.

Factor	No decentralization	Decentralization
Skills	Analysis, design construction central (technique oriented)	(Distant) information centre plus limited local skill (information oriented)
Systems	Coordination (technical aspects assured)	Coordination (explicit problem area)
Tools	Technique oriented	Support oriented
Economics	Well defined (technical, but not necessarily informational synergy)	Locally defined (departmental motivation, but not necessarily aimed at synergy)
Standards (general)	*De facto*	Problem area (information centre has no power)
Standards (methodology)	*De facto*	Variety possible (information centre is advisory)
Methodology related	Traditional (extensive skill)	Innovation possible (but limited skill)

Figure 2.5   Two scenarios for a problem with technical options.

Of the two main scenarios, the centralization alternative (leaving the organization as it was) probably has its well-known proponents, who argue that this is the only way to achieve effective coordination and standardization. Motivation through departmental autonomy is also a widely observed phenomenon. The main issue in this case, however, is to what extent the decentralization of skill influences information systems development and usage. In particular, the question must be asked whether decentralized application of methodologies (by motivated and information oriented staff) is preferable to centralized application (where the emphasis is bound to be technique oriented).

Since decisions to decentralize (or not) are usually made without much regard to information system aspects, this example highlights which skills have to be considered in externally enforced (by top management) circumstances. When centralization is maintained, or sometimes imposed where it did not exist before (for instance in the case of a merger between two companies), the scenario options centre around the transfer of knowhow and informational coordination.

On the other hand, when decentralization is aimed for (or exists), the possible scenarios may be concerned with the extent to which information centre services are to be preferred to external bureaux. In that case, informational coordination is an even greater problem, but obtaining methodology related knowhow might be much easier.

Where, in this example, the situation is caused by an organizational factor, the scenario options are specially related to technical factors, namely where to locate skills and how (technical) coordination and effective standardization are to be achieved in a set-up that by its nature is not geared for it. While enterprise-wide training in a (standard) methodology will serve to overcome some of the ensuing problems, this solution may not be cost effective. Also, too much emphasis on standardization for its own sake may inhibit innovation.

2.8 Summary

By exploring scenarios, one can focus on the most appropriate design process. Also, one may discover any limitations imposed by the information systems methodologies available, taking into account all options offered.

Meanwhile, the view taken in the chapters that follow is unconstrained by pragmatic scenario considerations. The reader should bear this in mind when using the book. From time to time it may be useful, therefore, to associate the problems and their treatment with some familiar scenarios, in order to bring some of the otherwise confusing detail to life.

EXERCISES

A. *Self-assessment*

2.1 Describe the importance of thinking in terms of a scenario when deciding on the applicability of an approach to information system design (and to the system life cycle in general).

2.2 What are scenario 'factors'? Why do the concepts of 'contextual' and 'technical' factors cover most points that might be relevant? Are there any factors that would be difficult to describe in this way?

2.3   Considering contexts and technical considerations as two dimensions, in what sense does 'time' form a third dimension as far as scenario options are concerned?

2.4   For a small project, such as the development of a reporting system extracting information from an existing database, consideration of a large number of factors may well be an 'overkill'. Discuss whether small systems should be designed using techniques that are different from those appropriate for large systems.

2.5   Discuss the extent to which analyst quality and quantity are technical and/or contextual factors.

2.6   Discuss the importance of formality and absence of ambiguity as ways of thinking when considering alternative scenarios.

B.   *Methodology related*

(for those familiar with one or more specific methodologies)

2.7   If a methodology involves a step resembling the consideration of the scenario, how is the step formulated? Are the relevant factors that may be considered categorizable as 'contextual' and 'technical', or would another terminology be more appropriate?

2.8   If there is no step resembling the consideration of the scenario, where could such a step be fitted into the methodology?

2.9   Discuss the following hypothesis. If it is not possible to introduce a choice of alternative approaches, a methodology is unnecessarily restrictive.

2.10   Discuss the examples given in Sections 2.7.1 to 2.7.3 in terms of an existing methodology.

2.11   Extend one of the examples of Sections 2.7.1 to 2.7.3 in terms of an existing methodology, so as fully to cover all points one might wish to include in a report to one's management.

3

Modelling — stages, perspectives and step categories

3.1 Modelling concepts

This chapter addresses three of the key modelling concepts introduced in Chapter 1 and amplifies the presentation of each. These concepts are the stages, the perspectives and the step categories.

3.1.1 Modelling in information systems methodologies

The concept of modelling is inherent in any information systems methodology. Some people find it useful to think of the information system as a model of a real world situation, although in the case of financial systems, for example, where there may be no physical aspects involved, the distinction between the real world system (sometimes called an object system) and the associated information system can become very blurred.

The term 'model', if taken in isolation, can be confusing. Typically, an information systems methodology should start with analytic modelling of a business area and continue with a prescriptive model for each information system which is to be constructed to support activities in that business area.

There is a tendency to confuse the descriptive and the prescriptive and, indeed, where the two are distinguished, the boundary between them can be a subject for intense debate.

Any analytic model can be seen to comprise a number of submodels. For example, it may contain a data model, an activity model, an organizational model and a behaviour model. A prescriptive model for design purposes can also consist of several submodels.

3.1.2 Integration of models

For both analysis and design, the constituent submodels may turn out to be fully or loosely integrated with each other depending on the methodology used. Clearly, there is merit in a full integration but whether this is achievable depends on the methodology used.

Whether full integration is achieved depends on the analyst or designer. A similar argument is valid when considering integration on a higher level, namely between analysis and design.

3.1.3 Framework as a model

This framework for information systems methodologies is itself a model. It is analytic in the sense that it is a result of analysing the capabilities of numerous extant methodologies (such as those listed in Appendix A). The framework does not attempt to be prescriptive because any such attempt would be premature in terms of the existing state of understanding on this subject. For presentation purposes, the framework has been broken down into a number of submodels and it is the aim of this chapter to discuss this breakdown prior to defining the framework in more detail.

3.2 Stages

As already indicated in Chapter 1, the three stages considered in detail in the framework for understanding are:

1. information systems planning,
2. business analysis, and
3. system design.

A more complete list of possible stages in an information systems life cycle is as follows:

1. strategic study,
2. **information systems planning,**

3.   **business analysis,**

4.   **system design,**

5.   construction design,

6.   construction and workbench test,

7.   installation,

8.   test of installed system,

9.   operation,

10.   evolution,

11.   phase out, and

12.   postmortem.

The stages considered in detail for the framework are hence the second, third and fourth, as highlighted in the above list. For each of these a detailed analysis is presented of the components which are found to be provided in existing methodologies. Two other stages considered in this text are construction design and evolution. Construction design is considered briefly in this chapter in order to establish the boundary between the system design and construction design. Evolution is considered in Chapter 8, although not in the form of a detailed component analysis. The breakdown into stages is the major presentation breakdown used in this book.

The stages suggested in the above list should not be confused with the concept of abstraction levels. There is no implication that the *amount* of detail increases from one stage to the next. Furthermore, there is no implication that one step is in any sense more concrete than its predecessor. Another inference which should be avoided is that, once one has completed one stage in the life cycle, it is not possible to return to that stage from a subsequent stage if circumstances so require.

There is considerable scope in the above breakdown for various kinds of feasibility study. The term 'feasibility study' on its own is felt to be too loose for use in this reference framework. However, the information systems planning stage has a strong element of an overall feasibility study and some of the other stages, such as business analysis and system design, should have a concluding step which investigates and evaluates alternative ways of performing the ensuing stage or stages.

Any breakdown of the systems life cycle into stages is arbitrary. The choice made in this book has been made for reasons of presentation expediency, in order to partition the material into chapters and sections such that it can be presented in a sequence which is logical for assimilation by readers.

Each of the stages considered in this book is now discussed in more detail. Each stage has a potential set of deliverables. These will include instances of the components identified in connection with the stage. Because this book does not prescribe a methodology, the deliverables are not defined in the detail that they should be for a specific methodology.

3.2.1   Information systems planning

This stage may begin with some analytic work, possibly carried out by someone external to the enterprise, to determine the broad nature of the information requirements in the enterprise, what business objectives have been identified, whether an information systems strategy exists (and, if so, what) and what objectives can be identified for further work.

The stage may include a feasibility study to determine the possible alternatives for proceeding further. It may be necessary to convince management of the merits of a selected approach.

The stage may also focus on the existing information systems, their scope, and whether they are due for phase out or are adaptable for future use. The stage can also focus on the need for new information systems and how they should be bounded.

The stage could typically include a broad brush analysis of data and of business activities. This analysis might be seen as proving the feasibility of the analysis techniques to be used.

3.2.2   Business analysis

The term 'business analysis' is used to refer to this stage in preference to the widely used term 'system analysis'. The reason for this choice is to emphasize that the business (or enterprise) is the subject of the analysis and not any kind of 'system' (extant or proposed).

The area of an enterprise covered by a business analysis stage is more constrained than for information systems planning. Whereas information systems planning could cover the whole enterprise, or a significant part of it in the case of a very large enterprise, business analysis should cover a subarea of that covered in the preceding information systems planning stage.

Business analysis includes an analysis of various aspects of the enterprise, depending on the methodology being used. It would usually include the business activities performed in the area of interest. It is important to note that a business activity is not synonymous with a computerized process. It is sometimes felt that an analysis of the processes to be performed by the computerized system is part of business analysis. Depending on the nature of the system and on the methodology adopted, an analysis of computerized processes can be useful, but this framework regards such work as appropriate to one of the later stages.

Another technique used in business analysis, sometimes as a starting point in the work, is to study the properties of the existing system irrespective of whether it is computerized or manual.

Another possible technique used in business analysis is, of course, data analysis. This could involve the preparation of a graphic representation, usually referred to generically as a data structure diagram.

The analysis of information flow in the organization and the associated analysis of material flow are both typical techniques here considered applicable to an analysis phase.

Any step in a business analysis stage might call for the preparation of narrative text for perusal by involved users.

3.2.3 System design

It is often difficult to determine exactly where business analysis ends and system design begins. Analysis involves describing what is extant and there to be analysed, while design is a more prescriptive or definitive activity.

In situations where there are only peripheral aspects of the problem to be analysed, possibly because the work calls for a straightforward reimplementation of the functionality of an existing system, the emphasis moves quite heavily towards an early need for creative system design. In cases where the extant manual or computerized system is known to be totally inadequate, then there will be an emphasis on in-depth business analysis prior to the system design.

A system design stage typically includes the preparation of components of different kinds. If the business analysis included the preparation of components with a behaviour perspective, then these may be a basis for the preparation of components with one of the other perspectives.

It is possible to prepare components of the system design stage in such a way that they are independent of the specific tools that will be used to construct the information system. In some environments, where flexibility to change tools is important, this tool independence is advantageous.

If the construction tools (such as the database management system (DBMS)) are known in advance, then the data oriented components can be prepared in such a way as to take the structuring capability into account. However, it should be noted that such an approach, while common in practice, would be contrary to recent thinking which emphasizes strongly the importance of design being independent of construction.

With the increasing emphasis on relational theory and the growing acceptance of the associated relational DBMS products, it has been felt advisable to refer to data oriented components resulting from the design stage in relational terms, namely in terms of tables, columns, rows and constraints.

Process design can be similarly performed in either a construction tool independent or dependent way. A process in this context is an item on a user menu which the user can invoke from a terminal.

The construction tool independent components of data design and process design can be referred to as a data model and a process model, respectively. The two should be cross-referenced to identify the data to be used by each process and also each process which uses a given part of the data.

3.2.4   Construction design

This stage involves designating how the system, as designed in the previous stage, is to be constructed. By definition, it involves a knowledge of the tools to be used to construct the system. If the system design stage has taken into account the construction tools to be used, then this stage may well be regarded as integrated into the previous stage.

The set of processes identified as part of system design will not necessarily equate on a one-for-one basis with the programming involved and it may be possible to construct the system cost-effectively, such that several processes as perceived in user terms can be handled by the same piece of programming.

Because there are so many different ways of constructing a computerized information system, and because construction technology is in a state of evolution at the time this text is being prepared, a detailed component analysis for the construction design stage has been omitted from this framework. It will be suggested in Chapter 11 as an appropriate research topic.

3.2.5   Relationship between stages

A simple view of the relationship between consecutive stages is shown in Figure 3.1. This is the traditional 'waterfall' model of the information systems life cycle.

The use of this simple model conceals the true complexity of what can actually happen in practice. Multiple small subprojects can exist at each stage, with complex timing dependencies and numerous interactions. The work each subproject is engaged on can be at any degree of completion, and several versions of the work may be current at any time.

Figure 3.2 shows an iterative model which is a more realistic view of the relationship between the life cycle stages. This model shows that there can be a loop back from any stage to any earlier stage. It should also be noted that in certain cases there may be several concurrent subprojects at, for example, the business analysis stage and that loop back may come from any subproject at any subsequent stage.

3.3   Stages and the three schema architecture

The three stages identified here as part of an information systems life cycle can be related to earlier work in the field of standardization. The 1975 ANSI/X3/SPARC report on database standardization suggested a three

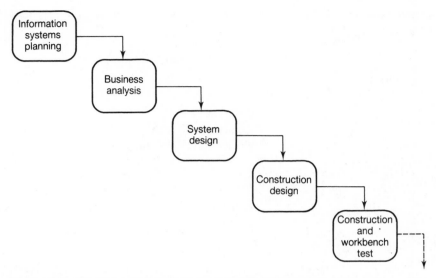

Figure 3.1   Traditional 'waterfall' model of the information systems life cycle.

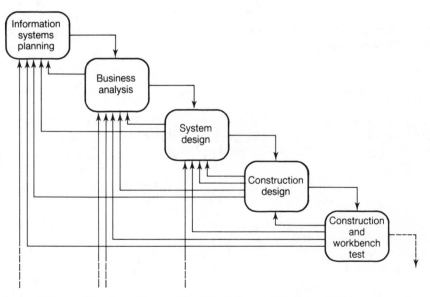

Figure 3.2   Iterative model of the information systems life cycle.

schema architecture as a cornerstone concept. The three schemas were identified as follows:

1. conceptual,
2. internal, and
3. external.

The conceptual schema could either be related to the data perspective components resulting from the business analysis stage or to those resulting from the system design stage. There has always been a divergence of views about the interpretation of the term 'conceptual schema'. In the sense that it is a representation of the 'real world', it should relate to the business analysis stage. In the sense that it is a construction tool independent (and hence storage independent) prescriptive definition of the data in a given system, it should relate to the system design stage.

The internal schema and external schema are felt to be concepts more appropriate to construction design than to system design. The term 'Universe of Discourse' used in the ANSI/X3/SPARC 1975 report and referred to extensively in the 1982 ISO report entitled *'Concepts and Terminology for the Conceptual Schema and the Information Base'* is not used in the present text. The more practitioner friendly term 'business area' is used instead, with the caveat that a business area may be located in any kind of enterprise and not only in commercial companies.

3.4   Perspectives

The inclusion of the concept of a perspective is intended to create a link with earlier information systems methodologies, some of which tended to emphasize one perspective to the exclusion of the other two. The three perspectives are:

1. data oriented,
2. process oriented, and
3. behaviour oriented.

Each of these will be discussed briefly in general terms in this chapter and then in more specific terms relating to the components involved in Chapters 4, 5, and 7.

3.4.1   Data oriented perspective

The advent of database technology in the mid-1960s was responsible for the data oriented perspective and the pendulum could be seen to swing from one extreme to the other. The radical data oriented perspective seemed, in some cases, to ignore the significance of processes to be performed on the data.

The data oriented perspective places emphasis on a complete and thorough analysis of the data and its relationships. There was an early emphasis on the provision of access paths to optimize performance of selected programs, but the slow emergence and acceptance of relational theory during the 1970s moved the consideration towards retrievability of all information, independently of storage representation, and subsequently towards the expressibility of the integrity constraints which the data must satisfy.

The data oriented perspective is seen to concentrate on different aspects as follows:

1. Business data.
2. Prescriptive, but construction and performance independent, data (sometimes called logical database design).
3. Prescriptive data, taking into account the construction tool to be used.
4. Stored representation of data, including indexes and access paths. This may be either the only option available with the construction tool, selected by the construction tool or, alternatively, selected by the construction designer.

These four aspects correspond to three stages in the information system life cycle – the first to business analysis, the second to system design, and the third and fourth to construction design.

3.4.2   Process oriented perspective

The earliest perspective to be recognized during the evolution of information systems methodologies was, without doubt, the process oriented perspective. In the early days of data processing, the computer was regarded as a convenient and quantifiably cost-effective tool for performing specific processes, such as generating a payroll or producing a set of invoices.

The need to analyse the process which the computer was required to perform was paramount and the programming languages available for constructing the application programs reflected this emphasis.

Many methodologies moved away from any emphasis on the computerizable process towards an analysis of the 'real world' activity as performed in the business, the understanding being that this activity could conveniently be computerized.

The process oriented perspective can be broken down conveniently into four distinct aspects, the first two relating to the business analysis and system design stages, respectively, and the remaining two aspects relating to the construction design stage:

1.   activity performed in business area,
2.   user perceivable task,
3.   computerizable process, and
4.   compilable unit of programming.

An activity is performed in a business area. Recognition of each activity is quite independent of the presence or absence of a computerized system. However, how it is performed may depend heavily on an information system.

A user perceivable task is a piece of work which is supported by a computerized information system. A list of tasks is typically to be found on a menu of such tasks, as presented to a user. The user understands these tasks and is able to select from the menu any of the tasks which he or she is authorized to initiate.

A computerizable process is an executable piece of software built by the builder, using whatever tools are appropriate. The computerizable process may support one or more user perceivable tasks, but the user does not have, and furthermore does not need, knowledge or understanding of the nature of the process. A typical computerizable process may consist of one or more compilable units of programming.

A compilable unit of programming is several lines of source code, prepared by a programmer using some programming language or other, which is prepared as part of the construction stage.

3.4.3 Behaviour oriented perspective

The most recent trends in information systems methodologies focus on the dynamic nature of the data and the need to analyse and understand events in the real world which impact data recorded in the information system. For convenience, this perspective is referred to here as the behaviour perspective.

The behaviour perspective suggests a dynamic view of the business area and of the information system. In both cases this view concentrates on the changes over time which may, and which are perceived to, take place. Both the business area and the information system are regarded as systems which are changing with time and which have a life span together with a life history of continuing changes.

During the business analysis stage, an analyst must place emphasis on the business events which take place in the business area. Each business event must be carefully distinguished from any business activity (see Section 3.4.2 on the process perspective). 'Receipt of a sales order' is an example of the former and 'sales order processing' is an example of the latter.

Similarly, during the system design stage, a designer should place emphasis on designating the system events which can take place and on the state transitions associated with each system event.

The behaviour perspective takes time into account during the work associated with the business analysis and system design stages. The business area is regarded within a time continuum rather than in terms of a snapshot.

Some business areas are 'event intensive' and careful analysis is required to determine which sequences of events are permissible and which are inadmissible.

Some business areas, such as those dealing with process control, indicate the importance of the behavioural perspective on the design of the system. Events happening in the real world can trigger a requirement for appropriate action in the computerized system.

The behaviour perspective can be broken down into four aspects as follows:

1. event occurring in a business area,
2. information system event,
3. triggering condition, and
4. invocation of transaction.

The first of these is addressed in the business analysis stage, the second and third in the system design stage, and the last in the construction design stage.

An event occurring in a business area is perceived as being pertinent to the business. An event happens at a given point in time and, once it has occurred, it does not undergo changes. Succedence and precedence relationships can exist between pairs of business events, and careful analysis is required to determine which sequences of events are permissible and which are inadmissible.

An information system event is an event which must be designated during system design as possibly taking place during the operation of the computerized system. A system event may be the result of an interaction between the computerized system and its users. It can be dependent on the time as given by a calendar clock or it may occur when a particular state of the computerized system has been achieved.

It may be necessary to specify a triggering condition to establish exactly the basis on which a system event may trigger a transition of the computerized information from one state to another. Precedence and succedence of system events determine the permitted ordering of all such state transitions.

Some existing information systems methodologies recognize the importance of the behavioural perspective and the problems it tackles. There is a preference for analysing business events as part of the business analysis stage and for prescribing the information system events which can happen while the information system is running as part of the design of the computerizable processes.

As indicated in Chapter 1, a typical design process would cover two or three perspectives. As will be illustrated in Chapters 4 and 5, a component can usually be classified as either data, process or behaviour, or, alternatively, as a cross-reference between a component in one perspective and a component in another.

3.4.4 Integration of perspectives

The fact that many methodologies emphasize one perspective or another is regarded as due to the technological developments which have taken place over two or three decades. Most of the techniques that are used in the various methodologies do have an orientation to a specific perspective. For example, data modelling has a clear data orientation and function decomposition has a process orientation.

It is emphasized in this framework that a comprehensive methodology should address components from all perspectives. It should achieve this by embodying several techniques. Furthermore, there should be relationships established between the components generated by a technique with one perspective and the components generated by a technique with another perspective.

A component which depends on (or interrelates) components from two different perspectives is here called a **cross-reference component**. Many of these will be illustrated in Chapters 4 and 5.

3.5 Step categories

Each design process consists of a number of steps, where the term 'step' is used in the sense described in this text. This can mean that the number of steps in a design process is possibly between four and ten. Each step in a design process can be categorized as being of one of the following five categories, each of which is depicted graphically in Figures 3.3 to 3.7:

1.   abstraction,
2.   checking,
3.   form conversion,
4.   review, and
5.   decision.

These five step categories will each be discussed in turn.

3.5.1 Abstraction steps

The majority of steps in any design process can be classed as abstraction steps. The act of abstraction is equally applicable in all three perspectives.

In the business analysis stage, there is a need to abstract accurately from a study of the business area under consideration, as shown schematically in Figure 3.3. When applied to data, abstracting often calls for experience and insight. Basically, it calls for the person involved to recognize that a set of objects have something in common and that the data pertaining to each of them can be handled in the same way.

For example, one might recognize that J. Smith, P. Brown and F. Jones are all 'customers' of the company for which the information needs are being analysed. This would lead the analyst to introduce what is usually referred to in many existing methodologies as an 'entity type' to represent the concept of a 'customer'. The three individuals referred to above plus others would then be regarded as 'entities' of the entity type 'customer'. The analyst has in this way **abstracted** from his or her observation of an area of interest.

In many cases, one has to address the question of 'abstraction level'. For example, should there be an entity type 'Customer' and an entity type 'Supplier'? If there is overlap between the populations of these two entity types, is it preferable to have only one entity type called 'Trading Partner'? Or is this kind of decision a design decision rather than an analysis decision?

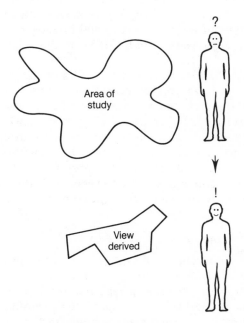

Figure 3.3 Abstraction.

Another example concerns the entity type 'Employee' and the entity type 'Manager'. Is the population of the latter wholly contained in the population of the former? If so, many existing methodologies would regard 'Manager' as a subtype of 'Employee'.

It is important not to confuse the action of performing an abstraction step with the concept of 'abstraction level'. In the first example in the previous paragraph, the entity type 'trading partner' is more abstract than 'customer' and 'supplier'; the concept of 'trading partner' subsumes the other concepts. Furthermore, the amount of work involved in carrying out the abstraction step is about the same whether one selects one abstract entity type or two less abstract entity types.

When applied to processes, abstracting can have similar pitfalls to those associated with finding the right abstraction level for the data oriented components. It may often be necessary for a conscious choice to be made between high abstraction level processes and low abstraction level processes.

Given that the results of the business analysis have to be reviewed by users, it could be better to choose a lower abstraction level which is easier for the users to comprehend (because this is the level on which they work), rather than go for abstract processes which may be more compact and more elegant. Another advantage of the separation of business analysis from system design is that it enables a lower abstraction level to be used during the business analysis stage and a higher one during the system design stage.

When applied to events, abstracting is an activity in which there is not a great deal of experience to call on. Some application areas are quite 'event intensive' which means that a fairly large number of different types of events can take place in the business environment. (This must not be confused with a situation where there is a large number of events of a relatively small number of event types.)

The problem facing the analyst – and also the designer – is how to group together events which may bear some similarity to each other. For example, should one treat 'guest check-in with confirmed reservation' at a hotel as a separate kind of event from 'guest check-in without reservation'? The alternative (as with data and processes) is to group the event types together into a more abstract event type (such as 'guest related event type') which is categorized accordingly. The low abstraction level events are essentially subtypes of the high abstraction events. This discussion will become clearer in Chapter 5 when examples of the components are presented.

3.5.2   Checking steps

One of the most important aspects of any piece of analysis or design is that the parts should be consistent with each other. In present terms, this means that components with the same perspective, or even with different perspectives, should be checked against each other to ensure consistency.

For example, the design process might include a 'business activity

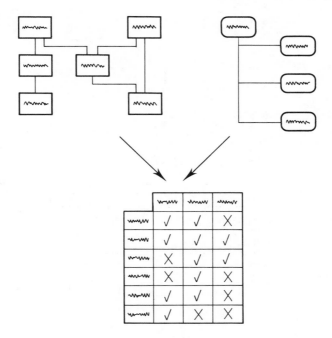

Figure 3.4   Checking.

analysis' and a 'data analysis'. These could possibly be performed by different groups. A simple consistency check would ensure that every entity type is used by at least one business activity and that every entity type is generated by one – or possibly more – business activities. This is shown schematically in Figure 3.4.

3.5.3   Form conversion steps

It is sometimes desirable, or even necessary, to convert the results of earlier steps from one form into another. This conversion may be from one computerized form to another, from printed form into computerized form or from one diagrammatic form to another, as shown in Figure 3.5.

The purpose of the conversion may be to produce the results in a form which is more easily acceptable to human users, or possibly to make the results acceptable as input to a piece of software which cannot accept the results of a step in its existing form.

3.5.4   Review steps

Chapter 1 has already stressed the importance of preparing specifications which can be understood and reviewed by users and by constructors. Where appropriate, the review activity may be formalized to the extent that approval

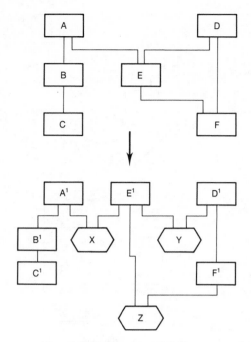

Figure 3.5   Form conversion.

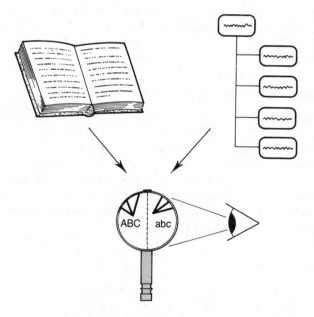

Figure 3.6   Review.

is needed by a user acceptor or a constructor acceptor as appropriate. Review steps are of particular relevance in the business analysis and system design stages. The concept of a review step is depicted in Figure 3.6.

It is not necessarily appropriate to have a review step after each abstraction or checking step. However, review steps need to be performed at carefully chosen points throughout any design process.

3.5.5 Decision steps

A decision step should be included after every review step and possibly even more frequently. The basic decision to be made is always whether to go forwards or whether to have another iteration over steps already performed. The concept of decision steps is illustrated in Figure 3.7.

3.6 Review of framework presentation

As indicated, the principal breakdown for the framework is that of stages. Chapter 4 presents the business analysis stage and Chapter 5 then presents the system design stage. Chapter 6 consists of examples of design processes, each defined in terms of a set of steps, with the components generated by each step identified in the same terms as in Chapters 4 and 5. Chapter 7 presents the information planning stage, and Chapter 9 discusses the different ways in which the results generated by steps can be represented and documented.

3.7 Diagramming technique

Chapters 4, 5, 6 and 7 use a diagramming technique for presenting and inter-relating the numerous components identified, variants of which are used in many information systems methodologies. The diagrams produced are referred to variously as data structure diagrams, entity relationship

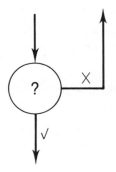

Figure 3.7 Decision.

diagrams, entity diagrams, object association diagrams, plus all of these with the word 'diagram' replaced by 'model'. The more neutral term preferred here is 'data structure diagram'.

Since there are even more variations in the style of these diagrams than there are terms used to refer to them, the style used here needs to be explained more thoroughly than in Figure 1.6, where the same diagramming technique was used to show the associations among the various concepts used in this framework.

In Chapters 4, 5, 6 and 7, each component is represented by a rectangle containing the name of the component. A line with an arrowhead drawn from one component to another component, from A to B as shown in Figure 3.8, indicates that there is a 'relationship' between A and B. The line may be continuous or broken. In some cases, the name of the relationship is included in the diagram.

The relationships indicated are widely used in many data analysis techniques found in information systems methodologies. As will be discussed

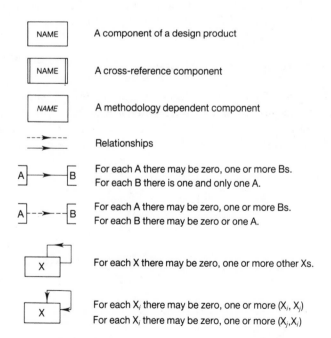

Figure 3.8   Diagramming conventions.

in Chapter 4, there are several possible kinds of relationship but, for simplicity of presentation, two kinds of relationship involving two components plus two kinds involving one component only are used in presenting the reference framework.

When a continuous line is indicated with an arrow head pointing from component A to component B, this means that each instance of component B is related to one and only one instance of component A. At the same time, for each instance of component A, there may be zero, one or more instances of component B.

When a broken line is indicated with an arrow head pointing from component A to component B, this means that each instance of component B is related to either zero or one instances of component A. At the same time, for each instance of component A, there may be zero, one or more instances of component B.

It may be, in both cases, that for an instance of A to exist without any associated instance of B represents a somewhat illogical situation. In precise design work, on the basis of which a system is to be constructed, such restrictions should be clearly identified.

The third kind of relationship used in depicting the framework is a recursive relationship. This means that there is a relationship among instances of one component.

The fourth kind of relationship is also recursive; to explain its meaning, avoiding confusion with the third kind of relationship, it is necessary to introduce a concept of directionality. The relationship means that for each instance of the component X, say X_i, there may be zero, one or more instances of associated components X_j (where $i \neq j$) in one direction. For each instance of component X, say X_i, there may be zero, one or more instances of associated components X_k (where $k \neq i$ and $k \neq j$).

It should also be noted that each component which is a cross-reference between two other components (of the same or different perspectives) is depicted using a rectangle with double vertical lines. In some data analysis diagramming techniques, such a component would be regarded as a relationship between the two components, rather than a component in its own right.

Chapters 4 and 5 are each broken down according to perspective and a data structure diagram is used for each perspective and for certain combinations of perspective.

3.8 Different kinds of component

This framework is defined in terms of components; there are two different kinds of components which will be referred to as **methodology dependent components** and **analyst and designer prescribable components**.

Each kind of component is a type, in the sense that several instances of that type will normally exist. The difference between the two kinds of component is based on who is responsible for prescribing the instances.

3.8.1   Methodology dependent components

Some of the components presented in the following chapters are components which are applicable to all methodologies, although instances of these components vary from one methodology to another. These components are called **methodology dependent components**.

Each methodology dependent component has a finite set of possible options, common examples of which are shown in the appropriate chapter. A person designing an information systems methodology would have the alternative of selecting some of the options illustrated in this text and would possibly identify others which are not shown.

The reason for introducing these methodology dependent components in this framework is to be able to combine two or more similar concepts into one component. The instances of components, other than methodology dependent components, have to be generated by the business analyst or system designer (as appropriate).

One example of a methodology dependent component is 'relationship class', which is used to categorize relationships as unary, binary or n-ary. A given information systems methodology may use any or all of these but, for the sake of illustration, it is assumed that only binary relationships are allowed. The user of the methodology then needs to understand what a binary relationship is, but he or she is not required to identify instances of the component 'relationship class'.

Other examples of methodology dependent components will be found early in Chapter 4 as part of the data perspective for the business analysis stage. For each methodology dependent component, a list of instances is presented as part of the worked example. In each case, the list is not intended to be exhaustive, although the instances presented are supported in existing methodologies.

Methodology dependent components are indicated in the data structure diagrams by the use of *italics*, as is shown in Figure 3.8.

3.8.2   Analyst and designer prescribable components

The majority of components are such that either an analyst, a designer or – in the case of information systems planner – a planner, would be responsible for specifying the instances of the component.

An example of this kind of component, which is found in many methodologies, would be 'relationship'. The methodology calls for the analyst to identify relationships. The component called 'relationship' is said to be generated by the methodology. This means that a user of the methodology will be responsible for identifying as many instances of this component as are relevant to the business area being analysed.

Analyst and designer prescribable components are indicated in the data structure diagrams using a plain rectangle, as indicated in Figure 3.8 for 'a component of a design product'.

This framework does not prescribe the prescribable components; it merely identifies many that could be prescribed. Such components become prescribable through their inclusion in a methodology by a methodology designer. It is then the intention of the methodology designer that an analyst or designer using the methodology should prescribe the instances of each such prescribable component during an appropriate life cycle stage.

3.8.3 Cross-reference components

A **cross-reference component** is a component which relates to two other components. Normally the two other components are analyst and designer prescribable components as described in the preceding section. The following possibilities exist with respect to the two other components on which a cross-reference component depends:

1. Both are in the same stage and have the same perspective.
2. Both are in the same stage but they have different perspectives.
3. Each is in a different stage, but both have the same perspective.

In all three cases, the cross-reference component is described only after both components to which it is related have been described.

It is possible for one of the two components to which a cross-reference component is related, to be a cross-reference component itself. It is even possible for both of them to be cross-reference components.

The name of a cross-reference component attempts to reflect the names of the two components to which it is related. However, all cross-reference components should be regarded as completely symmetrical and bidirectional, and the sequence of the other component names in the name of a cross-reference component should not be regarded as significant.

3.9 Role of component analysis

Each of Chapters 4, 5 and 7 presents the component analysis in four parts as follows:

1. list of components,
2. structure diagram,

3.   textual description of each component, and

4.   worked example.

Each chapter is divided into sections as discussed at the beginning of each chapter.

The list of components is established for a section. The sequence of the components is intended to be tutorial, and is such that forward references to components that have not yet been introduced are avoided.

Each structure diagram includes the components in the list plus any components already included in earlier lists to which a relationship must be explained. It is important to note that these structure diagrams do not attempt to capture the full and detailed semantics of the relationships between the components. The diagrams are used as a means of communicating the main features of an analytic model.

A textual description is given for each component in the list. These descriptions are in the sequence used in the list. Each component description attempts to mention the other components to which the subject component is related. To distinguish references to other components from nouns used in the text, all component names are printed in UPPER CASE.

Following on from all textual descriptions for a section, a worked example of each component is given. The worked examples are also in the tutorial sequence. Each worked example includes a table with several columns. In determining the columns to be included in each table, the relational principles of normalization have been applied. However, since the main thrust of the examples is to illustrate the component and not to present the principles of data design, the text supporting the table does not explicitly identify primary and foreign keys. The worked examples in each chapter are based on the same application area, namely an inventory control example.

EXERCISES

A.   *Self-assessment*

3.1   What is meant by the concept 'model'? Why is it necessary to represent the relevant aspects of a system to be designed in the form of a model?

3.2   What is meant by the three 'perspectives' (data oriented, process oriented and behaviour oriented)? Why are they perspectives for the same model?

3.3   Summarize the five step categories which are distinguished in connection with the design process. It could be said that 'abstraction' is a direct consequence of the need to model a business area (supported by an information system) and that 'decision' is part of the activity of managing the analysis and design project. Discuss suitable roles for the other three step categories.

3.4   In Figure 3.8, a rectangle represents a 'component' of the design and a box with double vertical lines indicates interdependency (a 'cross-reference'). In Figure 1.6 the same convention was introduced for the key concepts discussed in this book. The concept of a 'component' is only one of these. Explain why these forms of representation are consistent and justify the basis for this representation in a 'framework'.

3.5   What is the significance of a 'methodology dependent component'?

3.6   Two forms of relationship are shown in Figure 3.8 – one as a solid line with a single arrowhead and one as a broken line with a single arrowhead. The difference between these two relationships is that the former has one (and only one) component at the tail of the arrow whereas the latter may have zero or one. Why is this an important distinction?

B.   *Methodology related*

(for those familiar with one or more specific methodologies)

3.7   Describe a number of concepts in a methodology in terms of the corresponding concepts introduced in this chapter.

3.8   If applicable, explain how any of these concepts in the methodology fail to fit into the framework presented in this book and discuss why this situation should arise.

4

Component analysis for the business analysis stage

4.1 Introduction

This chapter presents a detailed description of many components which are created during a business analysis stage. In defining such components and how they interrelate, it is necessary to use some kind of presentation technique. As indicated in Chapter 1, the information systems analyst and designer (as opposed to the program designer) must also use various presentation techniques to communicate the results of the business analysis and the evolving design, first to the users involved and their representative acceptor, and then to the constructor (and possibly to a constructor acceptor).

In presenting the components of the business analysis stage in this chapter, the above systems analysts are seen as involved users with respect to these components. However, the components presented in this chapter are necessarily more abstract than would be the case with a more typical commercial application, such as order entry, payroll or cost accounting.

In order to arrive at the components presented in this chapter and the next, several methodologies have been taken into account. Some of these are listed in Appendix A. Each methodology produces various components at various stages and the terminology used varies considerably from one methodology to another. Certain components may be regarded as possible intermediate components, which are needed to record the understanding derived from the business analysis stage but which are not necessarily needed in the final design product to be used by the systems builders. However, it would be difficult to introduce a categorization of the components in these terms.

A business analysis component is something about which the analyst must present information for review by the user community. Examples of widely used components are:

1.   **Entity type**   An entity type is a class of object about which the information system under design must contain data.

2.   **Information task**   An information task is a type of task which can be initiated by the user of the information system under design. If the information system is wholly computerized, then each information task may be initiated from a computer terminal.

4.2   Choice of presentation sequence

The components of the design product are presented in this chapter in what is considered to be a tutorial presentation sequence in the business analysis stage. All three perspectives are felt to be relevant in this stage and they are treated in the following sequence:

1.   data oriented,
2.   process oriented, and
3.   behaviour oriented.

After the components in each of these three perspectives have been described, the components which cross-reference from one perspective to another are considered.

The presentation sequence used could conceivably be regarded as one of several acceptable sequences making up a part of a design process. There seems to be little value in presenting these components in an arbitrary sequence which has no relationship to any possible use. Other design processes would produce the same components in a different sequence, and yet other design processes would choose to omit certain components.

It should be noted that there is a certain interdependency among components. This means that the meaning of one component can depend on another component to the extent that any discussion of the first component is meaningless without reference to the second.

The important aspect of a presentation sequence is that it avoids forward references to components that have not yet been introduced and that it is hence more easily comprehensible.

The complete sequence of component presentation for the business analysis stage is as follows:

1. data oriented perspective,

2. process oriented perspective,

3. behaviour oriented perspective, and

4. cross-references between perspectives.

Each component is described in turn. For each component, a textual description is given. When this description makes reference to some other component, the name of that component is given in UPPER CASE.

At the end of each section, examples of each component are presented in the same sequence as in the section. These examples are based on an inventory control application.

4.3 Overview of each perspective in terms of components

The application area covered by a business analysis stage may be determined on the basis of a preceding information systems planning stage, if one was performed. Otherwise, the scope of the work may be defined organizationally or in terms of a set of business activities which the work must cover.

The overview for each perspective is intended to introduce the various components relevant to that perspective in a less formal and less structured way than in the remainder of the chapter. In order to distinguish formal components from other concepts, each reference to a component in the overviews and in the more structured definitions gives the name of the component in UPPER CASE. The components are not formally defined in the overviews and it would be advisable to read these overviews again after studying the formal descriptions.

It should be pointed out that the choice of component names in a framework of this kind is difficult. On the one hand, it is desirable to use terms which are familiar to some people rather than to exacerbate terminology pollution by introducing an artificial set of terms. On the other hand, any choice of terms already in use is bound to cause concern to those who prefer some other term to convey a given concept.

A further aspect of business analysis is the use of names. Different groups of people may regard what is essentially the same component as having two different names. One group may refer to an ENTITY TYPE 'Clients' and another to an ENTITY TYPE 'Customers'. There may be 100% overlap between Clients and Customers which means that there are two names for the same thing.

One group might refer to a BUSINESS ACTIVITY as Stock Control and another group of the same enterprise in a different country may refer to a BUSINESS ACTIVITY as Inventory Control. It is a typical task for a business analyst to recognize that these two names refer to what is essentially the same BUSINESS ACTIVITY.

4.3.1   Data perspective

There are various approaches to the data perspective of business analysis and the approach described here attempts to provide a framework in which many of these can be represented.

The usual starting point is for the ENTITY TYPES of interest to the environment to be identified. Each ENTITY TYPE will be involved in one or more RELATIONSHIPS with other ENTITY TYPES, where each RELATIONSHIP is usually of a given RELATIONSHIP CLASS and RELATIONSHIP TYPE. RELATIONSHIP CLASS is used here to categorize RELATIONSHIP TYPES as unary, binary or n-ary.

Binary RELATIONSHIP TYPES are the most widely used and they consist of a constraint such as that implied in a one to many relationship. Some approaches to data analysis use non-constraining RELATIONSHIPS (usually many to many RELATIONSHIPS).

The way in which ENTITY TYPES are regarded has an impact on the way in which the RELATIONSHIP TYPES that may relate them are handled. For example, one can choose to regard an Employee Number or a Date of Birth as ENTITY TYPES with a one to one RELATIONSHIP between them. Alternatively, one can choose to look for ENTITY TYPES on a 'higher level', such as Employees and Customers and leave consideration of the Employee Number until later.

Alternatively, a significant percentage (but not all) of the first group's clients may be customers of the other group but the second group may have many customers who are not clients of the first group. This may occur to the extent that less than half of the second group's customers are clients of the first group. This is sometimes referred to as the subtyping problem. The aim in the business analysis stage should not be to find a solution to this problem, but to ensure that it is recognized, both qualitatively and quantitatively, so that the ensuing system design stage can include an acceptable approach to the problem.

In this chapter, the list of components with a data perspective includes certain components which accommodate the analysis of both the multiple names problem and the analysis of overlapping subsets of entities of different ENTITY TYPES.

If the ENTITY TYPES recognized are of the 'higher level' kind, such as Employee, Supplier and Customer, then another part of the data perspective of the business analysis stage would normally involve identifying the ATTRIBUTES of each ENTITY TYPE.

There are different depths to which one can take this analysis of ATTRIBUTES. It is possible to do no more than just take stock of the ATTRIBUTES, without probing more deeply. It is also possible at this stage to try and identify the constraints which the values of the ATTRIBUTES are required to satisfy.

Some typical kinds of constraint on ATTRIBUTE values are:

- uniqueness,
- referential,
- intra-entity type, and
- dynamic.

These will be explained in more detail in the formalized descriptions.

Specifying constraints which the ATTRIBUTE values must satisfy is one of those activities which can be regarded as either part of business analysis or part of system design, or possibly of both. An analyst may recognize the relevance of a certain constraint during the business analysis stage and record it in an appropriate component. The designer may subsequently elect to specify a constraint that data values must satisfy as part of his or her definition of the data. The topic will be considered further in the discussion of system design.

4.3.2 Process perspective

From the process oriented perspective, the business analysis stage may contain an analysis of BUSINESS ACTIVITIES which are performed in the area of interest. Each BUSINESS ACTIVITY may be broken down into two or more lower level BUSINESS ACTIVITIES, possibly by a process of functional decomposition.

An analysis of the permitted sequences of BUSINESS ACTIVITIES may be performed in which the analyst identifies that a certain BUSINESS ACTIVITY cannot meaningfully be performed until one or more other BUSINESS ACTIVITIES have been performed.

The business analysis stage may also contain an analysis of the kinds of information and material used in (and produced by) the BUSINESS

ACTIVITIES. This kind of information is regarded as an INFORMATION/ MATERIAL SET. The set is a MATERIAL SET if it refers to physical goods or real estate, and an INFORMATION SET if it is a quantity of data. A set may also be composite, implying a combination of both. (A container of information is regarded as a MATERIAL SET only if it is necessary to monitor the physical movement of each such container.)

Another typical part of a business analysis stage covers which ORGANIZATION UNITS are responsible for which BUSINESS ACTIVITIES and, conversely, which BUSINESS ACTIVITIES fall in the area of responsibility of each ORGANIZATION UNIT.

The FLOW of INFORMATION/MATERIAL SETS can be analysed. A FLOW may be from an internal ORGANIZATION UNIT to an EXTERNAL UNIT (i.e. external to the environment being analysed) or from an EXTERNAL UNIT to an ORGANIZATION UNIT, or between two ORGANIZATION UNITS, depending on the FLOW TYPE. It is also possible to analyse the existence of FLOWS without bothering to identify what is flowing.

It is possible to analyse the involvement of ORGANIZATION UNITS in the FLOWS to and from EXTERNAL UNITS. If appropriate, FLOWS between any two ORGANIZATION UNITS may also be analysed. A FLOW may also be related to one or more BUSINESS ACTIVITIES in which the flow takes place.

4.3.3   Behaviour perspective

In addition to (or possibly instead of) the process oriented perspective, it is possible to use a behaviour oriented perspective in the business analysis stage. In some application areas, it is difficult to distinguish between BUSINESS ACTIVITIES and BUSINESS EVENTS, although the distinction is possibly subjective.

One analyst might regard 'order processing' as a BUSINESS ACTIVITY, thinking in general terms of the ongoing function of the group of people who handle sales orders. Another analyst, however, might regard 'order processing' as a BUSINESS EVENT, thinking in very specific terms of what happens when one sales order is received, thereby triggering a sequence of identifiable actions which, in turn, might be regarded as either BUSINESS EVENTS or BUSINESS ACTIVITIES.

If the analysis of BUSINESS ACTIVITIES is carried out in considerable detail, with each BUSINESS ACTIVITY decomposed in such a way that the results of the analysis are representable as a several level hierarchy, then on the lowest level it will be hard to distinguish activities from events and vice versa. Careful judgement is required to recognize situations where one form of analysis or the other (or both) is called for.

An application area can be 'event intensive' which means that there are several BUSINESS EVENTS that can occur and there are constraints on the sequences associated with BUSINESS EVENTS. Such constraints may be of different kinds. They may refer to events of the same type (a BUSINESS EVENT as perceived in a business analysis stage is, of necessity, an abstraction for a kind of event that can happen during the course of business). Constraints may be recognized on the occurrence of different BUSINESS EVENTS.

An application area may have only very few BUSINESS EVENTS, even though the potential number of occurrences of some of these BUSINESS EVENTS may be quite high.

Another analysis associated with the behavioural perspective is that of BUSINESS EVENT triggering, which typically involves different BUSINESS EVENTS. For example, the occurrence of one BUSINESS EVENT might initiate the occurrence of two other BUSINESS EVENTS.

The behavioural perspective of the business analysis stage calls for identifying the BUSINESS EVENTS which may or must occur in the business. Each BUSINESS EVENT will normally impact one or more BUSINESS ACTIVITIES in some way. BUSINESS EVENTS have their own EVENT PRECEDENCE/SUCCEDENCE which means that a BUSINESS EVENT of one kind cannot happen until some other BUSINESS EVENT has already happened.

4.3.4 Cross-references between perspectives

One possible checking step is to cross-reference the BUSINESS ACTIVITIES with ENTITY TYPES. Other possible checking steps are to cross-reference BUSINESS EVENTS with ENTITY TYPES and to cross-reference BUSINESS ACTIVITIES with BUSINESS EVENTS.

Any consistency that may be checked for in the resulting cross-reference tables is very much a matter of individual preference rather than consistency in a mathematical sense. For example, it is possible to insist that every ENTITY TYPE is created by at least one BUSINESS ACTIVITY and that it is referred to by at least one BUSINESS ACTIVITY. Each BUSINESS EVENT should be relatable to at least one ENTITY TYPE and to at least one BUSINESS ACTIVITY.

4.4 Abstraction level used for framework

In specifying this framework for information systems methodologies, one of the main problems encountered is that of choosing an appropriate abstraction level for the components making up the framework. This problem is identical to that faced by business analysts and system designers using any information systems methodology.

If the abstraction level of the components is low, there will be more components and more relationships between components, and the associated presentation will be more time consuming. If the abstraction level is high, there will be fewer components, fewer relationships and possibly a shorter presentation. However, the result would be harder to comprehend for the intended audience.

The abstraction level chosen is dictated largely by that of the majority of existing information systems methodologies which are known to be in practical use. It would be tempting to create a framework on a higher abstraction level which would be more powerful in the sense that it might be more 'all-embracing'.

The relationship between the ease with which a model can be understood and its abstraction level does not appear to be a simple one. As one attempts to be more all-embracing on a given abstraction level, the ease of understanding for the average reader will surely deteriorate.

As the abstraction level increases from the lowest possible level, the comprehensibility will initially increase because of the reduction in the number of concepts that the reader has to assimilate. As the abstraction level is raised further and further, the sheer abstractedness counterbalances the gains achievable by abstracting. The abstraction level of the components in this chapter is therefore based on that of existing methodologies and techniques. Further work on an ideal abstraction level is left as a research project.

4.5 Components of business analysis — data perspective

The components of the business analysis stage which belong to the data oriented perspective are identified as follows:

  1. ENTITY TYPE
  2. ENTITY TYPE NAME
  3. ENTITY TYPE USES NAME
 *4. RELATIONSHIP CLASS
 *5. RELATIONSHIP TYPE
  6. RELATIONSHIP
  7. ENTITY TYPE IN RELATIONSHIP
  8. ATTRIBUTE NAME
  9. ATTRIBUTE
 10. ATTRIBUTE GROUP
 11. ATTRIBUTE IN GROUP
 12. ATTRIBUTE OF RELATIONSHIP
*13. VALUE CONSTRAINT TYPE
 14. VALUE CONSTRAINT
*15. POPULATION OVERLAP TYPE
 16. POPULATION OVERLAP

Components with an asterisk are methodology dependent components.

Each of the components is presented in turn, in the same sequence as in the above list. Only those components included in the above list are mentioned in the description. The interrelationships between these components are depicted in Figure 4.1.

4.5.1 ENTITY TYPE

An ENTITY TYPE is a class of object perceived as being in the area of application about which the information system being designed will need to have information.

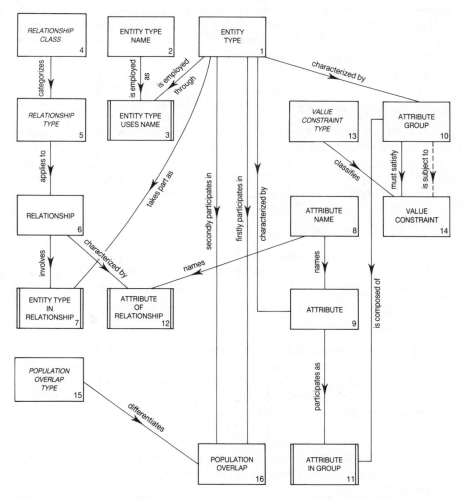

Figure 4.1 Business analysis stage – data perspective. The numbers in each rectangle correspond to the order of presentation in the text.

There are several ways of designating ENTITY TYPES. One is based on experience with previous, similar (but not identical) information systems. Another is by analysis of the INFORMATION SETS if such have previously been designated in connection with the BUSINESS ACTIVITIES in an earlier step in this stage.

In several design methodologies, there is no distinction made between ENTITY TYPES perceived (or perceived as needed) in the environment in which the information system will function, and the logical storage containers (such as files or tables) which will be discussed further in the system design stage.

In certain cases, the design oriented logical storage containers and the business oriented ENTITY TYPES could coincide. However, in many cases, numerous considerations will justify the separation between ENTITY TYPE and the logical storage containers which will be needed to record data about the ENTITY TYPES. The principal examples of such considerations are system performance and the limitations inherent in system construction tools (i.e. the DBMS) to be used.

4.5.2   ENTITY TYPE NAME

When ENTITY TYPES are being identified, it will often be apparent that there are some synonyms being used. In more complex situations, it is often helpful to carry out a systematic analysis of naming conventions, recognizing situations where two or more ENTITY TYPE NAMES are being applied to what is conceptually the same ENTITY TYPE.

4.5.3   ENTITY TYPE USES NAME

This component is a cross-reference between ENTITY TYPES and the ENTITY TYPE NAMES used to refer to them. It is also possible for the same ENTITY TYPE NAME to be used to refer to more than one ENTITY TYPE.

4.5.4   RELATIONSHIP CLASS

This component is methodology dependent. There are many different ways of categorizing the kinds of association which can be perceived between and among ENTITY TYPES. In order to categorize these ways, a two level scheme is used, the top level of which includes the RELATIONSHIP CLASSES. The following three classes are applicable:

U   unary relationship involving one ENTITY TYPE
B   binary relationships involving two ENTITY TYPES
N   n-ary relationships involving three or more ENTITY TYPES.

It should be noted that, in some cases, the term n-ary subsumes the definition of unary and binary as given above.

4.5.5 RELATIONSHIP TYPE

This component is methodology dependent. The number of RELATIONSHIP TYPES in each RELATIONSHIP CLASS varies from one design approach to another. A design process may make any selection.

For the binary RELATIONSHIP CLASS, ten alternatives are identified here for the purpose of illustration. Each RELATIONSHIP belongs to one of the limited number of RELATIONSHIP TYPES which are usually pre-designated for the design process.

Most RELATIONSHIP TYPES in widespread use involve two ENTITY TYPES. Different data analysis techniques use different RELATIONSHIP TYPES with a varying emphasis. Some permit several and make no value judgements on the relative merits of the different RELATIONSHIP TYPES. Another technique might use only one RELATIONSHIP TYPE in business analysis.

The following list is in an order of possible usefulness:

1. One to many, where many means zero, one or more.
2. Zero or one to many, where many means zero, one or more.
3. One to many, where many means one or more.
4. Zero or one to many, where many means one or more.
5. Zero or one to one.
6. Zero or one to zero or one.
7. Many (one or more) to many (one or more).
8. Many (zero, one or more) to many (one or more).
9. One to one.
10. Many (zero, one or more) to many (zero, one or more).

It should be noted that three of these are symmetric (namely numbers 6, 9 and 10) and the others are asymmetric. In the case of the asymmetric RELATIONSHIP TYPES, there is no need to list 'one to zero or one' (for example) as well as 'zero or one to one'. Some approaches to data analysis do not specify precise meanings of a prescribed set of permissible RELATIONSHIP TYPES. For example, it would be appropriate to add to the above list a fuzzy 'one to many' which would embrace types 1, 2 and 3 in the above list.

A one to many RELATIONSHIP of the first kind in the above list has been found to be the most useful in many methodologies encompassing some form of data analysis as a technique. In view of this, it is presented here in more detail. A similar presentation could be given for other RELATIONSHIP TYPES.

A RELATIONSHIP of the RELATIONSHIP TYPE 'one to many', where 'many' means 'zero, one or more', can be said to hold between two ENTITY TYPES, for convenience referred to here as A and B, if the following conditions both hold:

1.   Each entity belonging to ENTITY TYPE B is associated with 'one' entity belonging to ENTITY TYPE A.

2.   Each entity of ENTITY TYPE A is associated with 'zero, one or more' entities of ENTITY TYPE B.

Certain aspects of this RELATIONSHIP TYPE should be noted. Firstly, all RELATIONSHIPS of this RELATIONSHIP TYPE are asymmetric. Secondly, the first of the two conditions implies a constraint on entities of ENTITY TYPE B and is hence the more important of the two conditions. The second condition is simply an 'enabling' condition allowing any number of Bs to each A. The first condition gives rise to the use of the term 'dependency'. One can say B is dependent on A, or there is a dependency of B on A.

The second RELATIONSHIP TYPE in the above list, namely the 'zero or one to many', is very similar to the first, except that the first condition is relaxed slightly and reads:

1.   Each entity belonging to ENTITY TYPE B is associated with 'zero or one' entities belonging to ENTITY TYPE A.

The two first RELATIONSHIP TYPES are usually referred to (in relational database terminology) as 'dependencies' or 'functional dependencies' or (more recently) as 'referential constraints'. In the case of type 1, one could say 'B depends on A', in other words, there cannot be a B unless it is relatable to an A. In the case of type 2, there may be a B without it being relatable to an A. The dependency of B on A is hence only partial for type 2.

RELATIONSHIP TYPE 5, namely the 'zero or one to one', is frequently referred to as an 'is-a' relationship. The two conditions for this RELATIONSHIP TYPE are as follows:

1.   Each entity belonging to ENTITY TYPE B is an entity belonging to ENTITY TYPE A.

2.   Each entity of ENTITY TYPE A is associated with 'zero or one' entities belonging to ENTITY TYPE B.

One could also say that the population of As contains the population of Bs and that every B corresponds to an A.

A different RELATIONSHIP CLASS, namely the unary, has one RELATIONSHIP TYPE which is often called recursive. This is useful for associating entities of the same ENTITY TYPE, as opposed to associating entities of different ENTITY TYPES.

A widely promulgated RELATIONSHIP TYPE is 'many to many' (number 10). A many to many RELATIONSHIP between two ENTITY TYPES (where both uses of 'many' imply 'zero, one or more') is, by definition, completely 'enabling' in both directions. It serves little or no purpose in defining the constraints on the data which need to be identified in the business analysis stage. Some design processes will regard the identification of such RELATION-SHIP TYPES in the BUSINESS ANALYSIS stage as adequate and leave the more detailed work to the subsequent system design stage.

The n-ary RELATIONSHIP CLASS is used in some approaches to business analysis. A RELATIONSHIP may relate three or more ENTITY TYPES. Such RELATIONSHIPS are allowed in some methodologies and not in others. Where they are not allowed, the n-ary RELATIONSHIP would be treated as an ENTITY TYPE.

4.5.6   RELATIONSHIP

The designer of an information system will need to designate how the ENTITY TYPES are interrelated. Normally, each ENTITY TYPE is associated in some way with at least one other ENTITY TYPE. Occasionally, it is necessary to define a recursive relationship for an ENTITY TYPE.

Each RELATIONSHIP must be of a predefined RELATIONSHIP TYPE. For each RELATIONSHIP, it is also necessary to specify to which ENTITY TYPES or (for recursive relationships) to which ENTITY TYPE, the RELATIONSHIP 'belongs'.

It is also useful to analyse the cardinality of each RELATIONSHIP. This means that the analyst has to find out how many entities of each ENTITY TYPE will occur (often in a given unit of time), and then estimate the average number of entities of one ENTITY TYPE in the RELATIONSHIP that will exist for each entity of the other ENTITY TYPE. This quantity is sometimes referred to as the cardinality of the RELATIONSHIP, although the term cardinality is also used to convey the concept of RELATIONSHIP TYPE.

4.5.7   ENTITY TYPE IN RELATIONSHIP

Each ENTITY TYPE may be involved in one or more RELATIONSHIPS and each RELATIONSHIP consists of one or two ENTITY TYPES. (It is also possible to cater for situations where the n-ary RELATIONSHIP CLASS containing three or more ENTITY TYPES is allowed.)

Since the more frequently occurring RELATIONSHIP TYPES in the binary RELATIONSHIP CLASS are asymmetric, it is necessary for each such RELATIONSHIP to designate one ENTITY TYPE as the dependent on the other ENTITY TYPE.

It is also possible to designate various cardinalities of this component with respect to the RELATIONSHIP involved. For example, if there is a RELATIONSHIP between A and B, it is possible to analyse the minimum, average and maximum number of Bs for one A. In addition, it is possible to regard the minimum and maximum as constraining.

4.5.8   ATTRIBUTE NAME

As discussed earlier, there are many different ways of carrying out an analysis of data. Many ways call for a specification of the ATTRIBUTES of each ENTITY TYPE. Each ATTRIBUTE has an ATTRIBUTE NAME and it is common for one ATTRIBUTE NAME to be used for several ATTRIBUTES, provided the ATTRIBUTES belong to different ENTITY TYPES. For this reason, ATTRIBUTE NAMES are regarded as a separate component from ATTRIBUTES.

4.5.9   ATTRIBUTE

There is frequent confusion about the use of the term 'attribute' and some approaches to data analysis use the term as independent of ENTITY TYPE – implying the assertion that 'the same attribute can belong to more than one ENTITY TYPE'. This latter interpretation of the term 'attribute' is explicitly excluded here.

Some data analysis techniques require each ENTITY TYPE to have at least one ATTRIBUTE, where an ATTRIBUTE, by definition, belongs to only one ENTITY TYPE. An ATTRIBUTE must have an ATTRIBUTE NAME and, as indicated in the preceding section, it is a common requirement for ATTRIBUTES of an ENTITY TYPE to have ATTRIBUTE NAMES which are unique within the ENTITY TYPE.

In the case of data analysis techniques which analyse subtypes of an ENTITY TYPE, it is possible for an ATTRIBUTE of a subtype to be regarded as 'inherited' from the ENTITY TYPE to which the subtype belongs. This would take effect when there is a 'zero or one to one' RELATIONSHIP (also called an 'is-a' RELATIONSHIP) between the two ENTITY TYPES.

4.5.10   ATTRIBUTE GROUP

In order to be able to analyse the constraints that the values of ATTRIBUTES are required to satisfy, it is necessary to introduce the concept of an ATTRIBUTE GROUP. This is a set of one or more ATTRIBUTES belonging to the same ENTITY TYPE. (The case of an ATTRIBUTE GROUP comprising only one ATTRIBUTE is included only to simplify the definition of VALUE CONSTRAINTS.)

4.5.11   ATTRIBUTE IN GROUP

This cross-reference component identifies which ATTRIBUTES belong to a given ATTRIBUTE GROUP. It also allows an ATTRIBUTE to belong to two or more ATTRIBUTE GROUPS – a requirement that is seldom encountered.

4.5.12   ATTRIBUTE OF RELATIONSHIP

Some data analysis techniques allow RELATIONSHIPS, possibly only of certain RELATIONSHIP TYPES, to have ATTRIBUTES in the same way as ENTITY TYPES are commonly allowed to have ATTRIBUTES.

The component ATTRIBUTE OF RELATIONSHIP relates the component RELATIONSHIP with ATTRIBUTE NAME. This allows more than one RELATIONSHIP to have an ATTRIBUTE with the same ATTRIBUTE NAME.

4.5.13   VALUE CONSTRAINT TYPE

The values of the ATTRIBUTES can be subject to predefined VALUE CONSTRAINTS. Some approaches to data analysis regard the identification of such constraints as a major aim of the analysis.

The component VALUE CONSTRAINT TYPE is one that is introduced for definitional convenience. Two alternatives are identified here, although it may be possible to identify other alternatives and add to this short list. The three alternatives identified here are a part of relational theory. The terms used to identify these alternatives are:

> U   Uniqueness constraint
> R   Referential constraint
> C   Check constraint

A 'uniqueness constraint' is a constraint on the values of an ATTRIBUTE or ATTRIBUTE GROUP which simply asserts that the values must be different for all entities of the ENTITY TYPE.

A 'referential constraint' is a constraint on the values of an ATTRIBUTE or ATTRIBUTE GROUP for one ENTITY TYPE. These values must be equal to the values of some other ATTRIBUTE or ATTRIBUTE GROUP, usually of some other ENTITY TYPE. A referential constraint may be extended to place limits on the number of entities of one ENTITY TYPE for each entity of the other ENTITY TYPE. This kind of constraint is sometimes called a cardinality constraint.

A 'check constraint' is a potentially more complex condition expressed on the values of the ATTRIBUTES of one ENTITY TYPE but referring to the ATTRIBUTES of one or more other ENTITY TYPES. The condition must be satisfied at all times for the values involved to be collectively valid.

A check constraint is similar to a referential constraint in that both are imposed explicitly on the values of an ATTRIBUTE GROUP of an ENTITY TYPE and refer to the values of other ATTRIBUTES in the same or different ENTITY TYPES. However, they are different in that a referential constraint can refer to one other ENTITY TYPE only and can express only a simple equality condition, whereas a check constraint can refer to one or more other ENTITY TYPES and can express any kind of condition.

There may appear to be some overlap between this discussion of referential constraints and that for the component RELATIONSHIP TYPE. Whether the explicit identification of VALUE CONSTRAINTS as a separate component is called for depends on the way in which the RELATIONSHIPS are analysed.

4.5.14   VALUE CONSTRAINT

Each VALUE CONSTRAINT belongs to one of the VALUE CONSTRAINT TYPES prescribed for the approach to data analysis being used. For example, if the VALUE CONSTRAINT is a uniqueness constraint, it applies to one ATTRIBUTE GROUP and its meaning is as indicated in the previous section.

If it is a referential constraint, it applies to two ATTRIBUTE GROUPS. The two ATTRIBUTE GROUPS usually belong to two different ENTITY TYPES, but it is possible for them to belong to the same ENTITY TYPE.

A VALUE CONSTRAINT of any kind will often relate to an ATTRIBUTE GROUP consisting of only one ATTRIBUTE.

4.5.15   POPULATION OVERLAP TYPE

A POPULATION OVERLAP TYPE is used to identify the kind of overlap between the population of entities of one ENTITY TYPE and the population of entities of another ENTITY TYPE. There are three possible alternatives:

- D   Two completely disjoint populations
- P   Two partially overlapping populations
- C   One population completely contained in the other

It should be noted that these are assertions based on analysis of the respective populations. In many cases, the information derived from this kind of analysis can be invaluable in making the mapping from the business analysis component to the system design components.

The analysis of POPULATION OVERLAPS is often referred to in terms of 'subtypes'. An ENTITY TYPE may be referred to as a subtype of another ENTITY TYPE if there is a POPULATION OVERLAP of type C in the above list. This would mean that the population of the subtype is completely contained in the population of the other ENTITY TYPE. This situation is also regarded in terms of 'is-a' RELATIONSHIP TYPES as discussed in Section 4.5.5. The use of inherited ATTRIBUTES and CONSTRAINTS discussed in Section 4.5.9 is also relevant to this problem.

4.5.16   POPULATION OVERLAP

Each POPULATION OVERLAP relates to two ENTITY TYPES and defines how the populations of each intersect or overlap. It is quite possible for three or more ENTITY TYPES to have a communal overlap, in which case the situation has to be broken down into pairings, each of which is a POPULATION OVERLAP. For example, if it is necessary to investigate the overlap and intersection among three ENTITY TYPES, then it would be necessary to identify three POPULATION OVERLAPS – namely one for each pairing of the three ENTITY TYPES.

A POPULATION OVERLAP analysis may be qualitative, merely identifying the existence of an overlap. Additionally, the analysis may also be quantitative, including estimates of the degree of overlap in each case.

The component POPULATION OVERLAP is felt to provide a more flexible framework than the explicit introduction of a special component for subtypes, since it also allows for the analysis of partial overlaps and disjoint populations. Two or more ENTITY TYPES which are both subtypes of the same ENTITY TYPE may be disjoint from each other.

4.6 Examples of business analysis components from the data perspective

This section gives examples for 11 of the 15 components defined in the previous section. The four methodology dependent components are example independent, and a suggested list of alternatives has been given in each case in the preceding section. The four methodology dependent components are:

4.   RELATIONSHIP CLASS

5.   RELATIONSHIP TYPE

13.   VALUE CONSTRAINT TYPE

15.   POPULATION OVERLAP TYPE

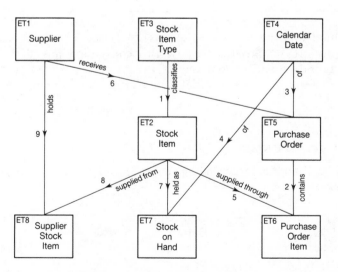

Figure 4.2 Inventory control example. The diagram is used to illustrate two components. ENTITY TYPES are shown as rectangles and RELATIONSHIPS as arrowed lines connecting two ENTITY TYPES. The ENTITY TYPE code introduced in Section 4.6.1 is included in each rectangle for ease of future reference.

For each of these, an indication is given of which alternatives are used in preparing the examples of the other 11 components. The following examples are based on an inventory control application used throughout this chapter for all perspectives. The sequence is the same as for the component description in the preceding section.

Figure 4.2 illustrates a data structure diagram of the same kind as was used to illustrate components. It shows eight ENTITY TYPES and nine RELATIONSHIPS.

4.6.1   ENTITY TYPE

The following table gives a list of the eight ENTITY TYPES. Each is given a code for future reference.

Entity Type Code	Description
ET1	Supplier
ET2	Stock Item
ET3	Stock Item Type
ET4	Calendar Date
ET5	Purchase Order
ET6	Purchase Order Item
ET7	Stock on Hand
ET8	Supplier Stock Item

It is common to write the names of ENTITY TYPES fully capitalized (for example, PURCHASE ORDER). Because this convention has already been introduced for the names of components, the examples of ENTITY TYPES and of other components will use initial capitals only (for example, Purchase Order).

4.6.2   ENTITY TYPE NAME

The following list of names could be generated by users to refer to the various ENTITY TYPES:

Stock Item	Consignment
Article	Delivery
Supplier	Issue
Purchase Order	Price
Stock Code	Supplier Number
Stock Item Name	

4.6.3   ENTITY TYPE USES NAME

Some of the eight ENTITY TYPES identified use one or more of the ENTITY TYPE NAMES listed for the preceding component. Some of the ENTITY TYPE NAMES may not be used by any of the ENTITY TYPES but need to be remembered as possible ATTRIBUTES of one (or even more) of the ENTITY TYPES.

The following cross-reference table indicates the association between ENTITY TYPES and ENTITY TYPE NAMES:

Entity Type Name	*Entity Type Code*							
	ET1	*ET2*	*ET3*	*ET4*	*ET5*	*ET6*	*ET7*	*ET8*
Stock Item		X						
Article		X						
Supplier	X							
Purchase Order					X			
Stock Code								
Stock Item Name								
Consignment								
Delivery								
Issue								
Price								
Supplier Number								

The fact that only four of the 11 ENTITY TYPE NAMES relate to any of the eight ENTITY TYPES indicates that seven of the ENTITY TYPE NAMES still need to be handled in some way.

4.6.4   RELATIONSHIP CLASS

The only RELATIONSHIP CLASS used in this example is 'binary', as described in Section 4.5.4.

4.6.5   RELATIONSHIP TYPE

The only RELATIONSHIP TYPE used in this example is the one to many, where many means 'zero, one or more'. This is discussed further in Section 4.5.5. It is convenient to identify this using the code M1.

4.6.6   RELATIONSHIP

Each RELATIONSHIP belongs to a RELATIONSHIP TYPE and is given a number and a name for possible future reference. The nine RELATIONSHIPS depicted in Figure 4.2 are listed in the following table:

Relationship Number	Relationship Type	Relationship Name
1	M1	classifies
2	M1	contains
3	M1	of
4	M1	of
5	M1	supplied through
6	M1	receives
7	M1	held as
8	M1	supplied from
9	M1	holds

The middle column in this table indicates that each RELATIONSHIP in the example is of the RELATIONSHIP TYPE 'one to many', where 'many' means 'zero, one or more'.

4.6.7   ENTITY TYPE IN RELATIONSHIP

Each RELATIONSHIP involves two ENTITY TYPES. However, the RELATIONSHIPS are asymmetric and it is therefore necessary to distinguish between the two ENTITY TYPES. This is done by identifying one as independent (I) and the other as dependent (D). All RELATIONSHIPS are given identifying numbers, which correspond to those in Figure 4.2.

Relationship Number	Entity Type Code	Dependency Code
1	ET3	I
1	ET2	D
2	ET5	I
2	ET6	D
3	ET4	I
3	ET5	D
4	ET4	I
4	ET7	D
5	ET2	I
5	ET6	D
6	ET1	I
6	ET5	D
7	ET2	I
7	ET7	D
8	ET2	I
8	ET8	D
9	ET1	I
9	ET8	D

4.6.8   ATTRIBUTE NAME

To start the list of ATTRIBUTE NAMES, the 11 ENTITY TYPE NAMES from Section 4.6.2 would be used. The list is then supplemented with other names – possibly provided by users. The following list gives some examples:

- Stock Code
- Stock Item Name
- Consignment
- Delivery
- Issue
- Price
- Supplier Number
- Supplier Name
- Stock Item Type Code
- Stock Item Type Description
- Date of Purchase
- Date of Delivery
- Purchase Order Number
- Purchase Order Item Number

4.6.9   ATTRIBUTE

Each ATTRIBUTE must be an ATTRIBUTE of an ENTITY TYPE. This means that each of the above ATTRIBUTE NAMES should be assignable to one of the eight

Attribute Name	Entity Type Code							
	ET1	ET2	ET3	ET4	ET5	ET6	ET7	ET8
Stock Code		X				X	X	X
Stock Item Name		X						
Consignment **								
Delivery **								
Issue **								
Price								X
Supplier Number	X				X		X	X
Supplier Name	X							
Stock Item Type Code		X	X					
Stock Item Type Description			X					
Date of Purchase				X	X			
Date of Delivery				X				
Purchase Order Number					X	X		
Purchase Order Item Number						X		

ENTITY TYPES already identified. It may transpire that some of these ATTRIBUTE NAMES cannot be assigned to an ENTITY TYPE. It may also appear that there are some synonyms among the list of ATTRIBUTE NAMES.

The cross-reference table on page 89 indicates the initial assignments.

The three ATTRIBUTE NAMES which are unassignable to an ENTITY TYPE are indicated with two asterisks.

4.6.10   ATTRIBUTE GROUP

The need for ATTRIBUTE GROUPS is based on the requirement to be able to specify the CONSTRAINTS which are to be imposed on the values of the ATTRIBUTES.

The first ATTRIBUTE GROUP consists of the following two ATTRIBUTES:

- Purchase Order Number
- Purchase Order Item Number

These two will be necessary to identify each occurrence of the ENTITY TYPE Purchase Order Item.

The second ATTRIBUTE GROUP consists of the following two ATTRIBUTES:

- Supplier Number
- Stock Code

These two ATTRIBUTES will be necessary to identify each entry in the cross-reference table Supplier Stock Item.

The third ATTRIBUTE GROUP consists of the following two ATTRIBUTES:

- Stock Code
- Date

These two ATTRIBUTES identify the level of a Stock Item on a given Date.

4.6.11   ATTRIBUTE IN GROUP

This example uses three ATTRIBUTE GROUPS, each of which contains two ATTRIBUTES. In a more comprehensive application, in which many ATTRIBUTE GROUPS would be needed, and in which it may be necessary for an ATTRIBUTE of an ENTITY TYPE to belong to more than one ATTRIBUTE GROUP of that ENTITY TYPE, a cross-reference table may be useful.

4.6.12   ATTRIBUTE OF RELATIONSHIP

The nine RELATIONSHIPS identified for this example belong to a RELATIONSHIP TYPE which does not usually have ATTRIBUTES. If the ENTITY TYPE called Supplier Stock Item had been identified as a many to many RELATIONSHIP between the ENTITY TYPE called Supplier and the ENTITY TYPE called Stock Item, then it would have the ATTRIBUTES here associated with the ENTITY TYPE Supplier Stock Item.

4.6.13   VALUE CONSTRAINT TYPE

The permitted VALUE CONSTRAINT TYPES are prescribed for each approach to data analysis. In this example, all three kinds of VALUE CONSTRAINT TYPE are used (see Section 4.5.12).

4.6.14   VALUE CONSTRAINT

In this example, one uniqueness VALUE CONSTRAINT is defined for each ENTITY TYPE. Each such VALUE CONSTRAINT is expressed either for a single ATTRIBUTE or for an ATTRIBUTE GROUP of that ENTITY TYPE. The uniqueness VALUE CONSTRAINTS for the eight ENTITY TYPES are as follows:

Entity Type Name	Attribute Name or Attribute Group Name
Supplier	Supplier Number
Stock Item	Stock Code
Stock Item Type	Stock Item Type Code
Calendar Date	Date
Purchase Order	Purchase Order Number
Purchase Order Item	Purchase Order Number
	Purchase Order Item Number
Stock on Hand	Stock Code
	Date
Supplier Stock Item	Supplier Number
	Stock Code

Each of the nine RELATIONSHIPS listed in Section 4.6.6 represents a referential VALUE CONSTRAINT. This is because the technique used in this example to identify RELATIONSHIPS considers only constraining RELATIONSHIPS.

Each of the nine referential VALUE CONSTRAINTS derivable from the nine RELATIONSHIPS then represents a VALUE CONSTRAINT on the values of one or more ATTRIBUTES in one of the ENTITY TYPES involved in the RELATIONSHIP. These ATTRIBUTES to which the VALUE CONSTRAINTS apply are always 'matchable' with the values of ATTRIBUTES in the other ENTITY TYPE in the RELATIONSHIP.

The following table indicates the ENTITY TYPE and the constrained ATTRIBUTES for each of the nine RELATIONSHIPS.

Relationship Number	Relationship Description	Entity Type Code	Attribute Name or Attribute Group Name
1	classifies	ET3	Stock Item Type Code
2	contains	ET6	Purchase Order Number
3	of	ET5	Date
4	of	ET7	Date
5	supplied through	ET6	Stock Code
6	receives	ET5	Supplier Number
7	held as	ET7	Stock Code
8	supplied from	ET8	Stock Code
9	holds	ET8	Supplier Number

A check VALUE CONSTRAINT is difficult to represent in tabular form since it can be of any complexity. The following example of a check constraint is expressed on the ATTRIBUTE Stock Code of the ENTITY TYPE Purchase Item.

> The Stock Code of a Purchase Item which is sent to the Supplier designated in the Purchase Order to which the Purchase Item belongs must be a Stock Code which is to be found in Supplier Stock Item for the Supplier.

> In simpler terms, there is a VALUE CONSTRAINT on ordering Stock Items from Suppliers which means that the Supplier must be known to handle any Stock Item ordered.

4.6.15   POPULATION OVERLAP TYPE

The inventory control example, as constituted, does not provide any meaningful example of POPULATION OVERLAPS. However, an example of a partial POPULATION OVERLAP is shown.

4.6.16   POPULATION OVERLAP

The ENTITY TYPES defined so far in this example do not call for any illuminating population analysis. In order to illustrate this technique, it is assumed that the ENTITY TYPE 'Customer' has been defined and that there is known to be some overlap between customers and suppliers. This could be tabulated as follows:

Population Overlap Type	First Entity Type	Number	Percentage also in second Entity Type	Second Entity Type	Number	Percentage also in first Entity Type
P	Supplier	300	10	Customer	3000	1

4.7 Components of business analysis — process perspective

The components of the business analysis stage which belong to the process oriented perspective are as follows:

1. BUSINESS ACTIVITY
2. BUSINESS ACTIVITY NAME
3. BUSINESS ACTIVITY USES NAME
4. ACTIVITY PRECEDENCE/SUCCEDENCE
*5. INFORMATION OR MATERIAL
6. INFORMATION/MATERIAL SET
7. SET NAME
8. INFORMATION/MATERIAL SET USES NAME
*9. INVOLVEMENT TYPE
10. ACTIVITY USES SET
11. ACTIVITY PRECONDITION
12. PRECONDITION ENABLES ACTIVITY
13. ORGANIZATION UNIT
14. ACTIVITY RESPONSIBILITY
15. EXTERNAL UNIT
*16. FLOW TYPE
17. FLOW
18. ACTIVITY INVOLVES FLOW
19. FLOW INVOLVES INFORMATION/MATERIAL SET
20. FLOW OF SET IN ACTIVITY
21. FLOW PRECONDITION
22. PRECONDITION ENABLES FLOW

The components preceded by an asterisk are methodology dependent.

Each of these is presented in turn. Only those components included in tha above list are mentioned in the description. The interrelationships between the components are depicted in Figure 4.3.

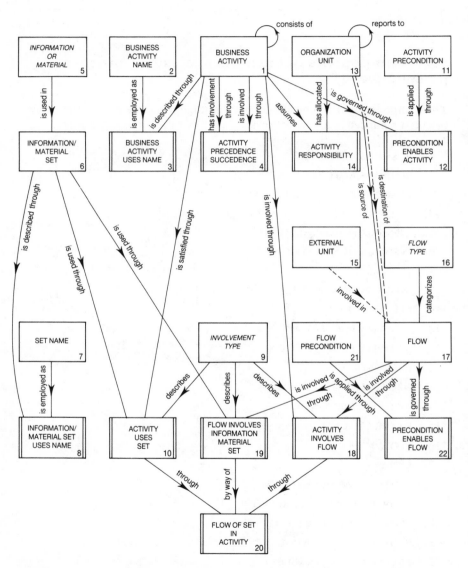

Figure 4.3   Business analysis stage - process perspective. The numbers in each rectangle correspond to the order of presentation in the text.

4.7.1 BUSINESS ACTIVITY

In the environment in which the information system is to be used, there are always several BUSINESS ACTIVITIES being performed. It should be one aim of the information system to support these BUSINESS ACTIVITIES, possibly by having them performed by a computer or possibly by providing the kind of information needed by people in order to perform the BUSINESS ACTIVITIES more effectively.

It would be adequate to list between 10 and 20 BUSINESS ACTIVITIES in a smaller scenario. In a larger one, it would be necessary to define BUSINESS ACTIVITIES on up to three or four levels, such that there is a small number of top level BUSINESS ACTIVITIES, each comprising more detailed lower level BUSINESS ACTIVITIES.

On a given level, there is some kind of sequencing to the BUSINESS ACTIVITIES. This may mean that a given BUSINESS ACTIVITY must be preceded by certain other BUSINESS ACTIVITIES. It may mean that a given BUSINESS ACTIVITY triggers other BUSINESS ACTIVITIES.

The possible decomposition of a BUSINESS ACTIVITY into further BUSINESS ACTIVITIES is designated in Figure 4.3 by a circular arrow in one corner of the rectangle representing BUSINESS ACTIVITY. This is called a recursive relationship. It is used to designate a relationship between entities of the same type, in this case between BUSINESS ACTIVITIES. Each BUSINESS ACTIVITY has zero or one other BUSINESS ACTIVITY of which it is a part. A BUSINESS ACTIVITY on the top level has no 'superior' BUSINESS ACTIVITY.

4.7.2 BUSINESS ACTIVITY NAME

In some environments, the same BUSINESS ACTIVITY may be identified by different names. This may be because of a multilingual environment or because of traditional uses in a single language environment. The separate identification of the BUSINESS ACTIVITY NAMES from the actual BUSINESS ACTIVITIES enables this kind of analysis to be carried out.

4.7.3 BUSINESS ACTIVITY USES NAME

This component is a cross-reference between BUSINESS ACTIVITY and BUSINESS ACTIVITY NAME indicating which names are used for which BUSINESS ACTIVITIES and vice versa.

4.7.4 ACTIVITY PRECEDENCE/SUCCEDENCE

This component designates the possible and/or necessary sequence in time in which the BUSINESS ACTIVITIES (on the same level in a multilevel situation) are to be performed. The resultant overall picture will typically represent an activity network.

The designer with experience in the application area may be able to designate the ACTIVITY PRECEDENCE/SUCCEDENCE associations among the BUSINESS ACTIVITIES without further analysis. More often than not, this information can only be derived after other components have been created. For example, it could be derived from the flows of information and/or material which are observed between BUSINESS ACTIVITIES.

It should be noted that an ACTIVITY PRECEDENCE/SUCCEDENCE should only be recorded for BUSINESS ACTIVITIES on the same level.

4.7.5   INFORMATION OR MATERIAL

This is a three-valued code which is used to designate an INFORMATION/MATERIAL SET as either a set of physical entities, a collection of information, or both. It is important in any analysis requiring both, to distinguish between the physical goods and information or data referring to the physical goods.

4.7.6   INFORMATION/MATERIAL SET

An INFORMATION/MATERIAL SET may be some kind of information which is either input to a BUSINESS ACTIVITY or generated by a BUSINESS ACTIVITY. Alternatively, an INFORMATION/MATERIAL SET is a collection of goods, parts, supplies or even real estate, which is of relevance to the organization. This component is also commonly referred to as a 'data store'.

In many cases, an INFORMATION/MATERIAL SET generated by a BUSINESS ACTIVITY is also needed as an input to one or more other BUSINESS ACTIVITIES. As was the case with BUSINESS ACTIVITIES, it may be useful in a complex environment to decompose INFORMATION/MATERIAL SETS, such that several lower level INFORMATION/MATERIAL SETS 'belong' in some sense to a higher level INFORMATION/MATERIAL SET.

An analysis of the INFORMATION/MATERIAL SETS associated with each BUSINESS ACTIVITY is often a useful design step towards determining ACTIVITY PRECEDENCE/SUCCEDENCE. Not all environments are concerned with material sets but, when they are, it is important to analyse their use by BUSINESS ACTIVITIES and also the FLOW.

4.7.7   SET NAME

In some environments, the same INFORMATION/MATERIAL SET may be identified by different names. This may be because of a multilingual environment or because of traditional uses in a single language environment. At the same time, the same SET NAME may be used to identify one or even more INFORMATION/MATERIAL SETS. The separate identification of the SET NAMES from the actual INFORMATION/MATERIAL SETS enables this kind of analysis to be carried out.

4.7.8 INFORMATION/MATERIAL SET USES NAME

This component is a cross-reference between INFORMATION/MATERIAL SET and SET NAME indicating which names are used for which INFORMATION/MATERIAL SETS and vice versa.

4.7.9 INVOLVEMENT TYPE

This is simply a code used to indicate how a data oriented component (such as an INFORMATION/MATERIAL SET) is involved in a process oriented component (such as a BUSINESS ACTIVITY). The data may be used by the process, in which case the process has to retrieve the data from wherever it is available, or else the process will cause the data to be created, modified or deleted.

This code is also used in other parts of this chapter and in the chapter on system design, where the breakdown may need to be more precise.

4.7.10 ACTIVITY USES SET

This component is a cross-reference between BUSINESS ACTIVITY and INFORMATION/MATERIAL SET. It indicates which INFORMATION/MATERIAL SETS are input to the BUSINESS ACTIVITY and which are generated by the BUSINESS ACTIVITY. Only a few BUSINESS ACTIVITIES will generate material sets. It should be noted that this cross-reference is independent of the FLOW of INFORMATION/MATERIAL SETS and of the involvement of ORGANIZATION UNITS and EXTERNAL UNITS.

4.7.11 ACTIVITY PRECONDITION

An ACTIVITY PRECONDITION is a condition which has to be satisfied in the business area for one (or more) BUSINESS ACTIVITY to be able to take place.

4.7.12 PRECONDITION ENABLES ACTIVITY

There may be several ACTIVITY PRECONDITIONS, all of which may need to hold before a BUSINESS ACTIVITY can take place. Alternatively, one ACTIVITY PRECONDITION may contribute to the initiation of several BUSINESS ACTIVITIES. This component is a cross-reference between the two components – BUSINESS ACTIVITY and ACTIVITY PRECONDITION.

4.7.13 ORGANIZATION UNIT

The term ORGANIZATION UNIT is used to refer to all kinds of department, section, group, bureau, directorate, centre, etc., that are typically found in any enterprise.

The relationships between ORGANIZATION UNITS in the same enterprise may be indicated. A relationship between two ORGANIZATION UNITS indicates that one of the ORGANIZATION UNITS reports to the other. There may be several ORGANIZATION UNITS reporting to any given ORGANIZATION UNIT. An ORGANIZATION UNIT at the top of an organization structure would not report to any other ORGANIZATION UNIT.

ORGANIZATION UNITS may be needed in the business analysis stage to record who is responsible for the various BUSINESS ACTIVITIES and also in flow analysis.

4.7.14   ACTIVITY RESPONSIBILITY

This component is a cross-reference between BUSINESS ACTIVITIES and ORGANIZATION UNITS indicating which ORGANIZATION UNITS are responsible for performing which BUSINESS ACTIVITIES and vice versa.

4.7.15   EXTERNAL UNIT

An EXTERNAL UNIT is a kind of organization which is external to the one under analysis. It is not normally a specific organization. These EXTERNAL UNITS are needed to analyse FLOWS of information and FLOWS of material between the business and the outside world.

4.7.16   FLOW TYPE

This component is introduced to allow the various kinds of FLOW to be categorized. It is not necessary to distinguish information FLOWS from material FLOWS because this will be determined by the kind of INFORMATION/MATERIAL SET. The main distinctions to be made between different FLOW TYPES are on the kind of source of a FLOW and on the kind of destination of a FLOW. Both source and destination can be ORGANIZATION UNITS, implying that the FLOW is external to the enterprise. Alternatively, either the source or the destination (but probabably not both) could be an EXTERNAL UNIT.

4.7.17   FLOW

A FLOW is a movement of either information (i.e. an information set) or of material (a material set) between EXTERNAL UNIT and ORGANIZATION UNIT, in one direction or the other, or else in internal flow between two ORGANIZATION UNITS. In some cases, the ORGANIZATION UNIT involved in a FLOW is not specified.

4.7.18   ACTIVITY INVOLVES FLOW

This cross-reference component allows for an analysis of each BUSINESS ACTIVITY of the FLOWS which are involved in it in some way.

4.7.19 FLOW INVOLVES INFORMATION MATERIAL SET

This component gives more detail about each FLOW, indicating which INFORMATION/MATERIAL SETS are involved in a FLOW and, conversely, in which FLOWS an INFORMATION/MATERIAL SET is involved.

4.7.20 FLOW OF SET IN ACTIVITY

This component cross-references FLOWS of INFORMATION/MATERIAL SETS with the BUSINESS ACTIVITIES which use the INFORMATION/MATERIAL SETS involved in the FLOW. The resulting cross-reference shows, for each FLOW, the BUSINESS ACTIVITIES in which it is involved and how. Conversely, it also shows, for each BUSINESS ACTIVITY, the FLOWS in which it is involved and how. The various options indicating the way in which a BUSINESS ACTIVITY is involved in a FLOW need to be defined as instances of the methodology dependent component INVOLVEMENT TYPE. An analysis which involved this cross-reference would also need to have produced the previous two.

4.7.21 FLOW PRECONDITION

A FLOW PRECONDITION is a condition which has to be satisfied in the business area for one or more FLOWS to be able to take place. It is not necessary for a FLOW to have a PRECONDITION in order for the FLOW to take place. For analysis purposes, a FLOW may be perceived as a continuous happening.

4.7.22 PRECONDITION ENABLES FLOW

There may be several FLOW PRECONDITIONS, all of which may need to hold before a FLOW can take place. Alternatively, one FLOW PRECONDITION may enable several FLOWS. This component is a cross-reference between the two components FLOW and FLOW PRECONDITION.

4.8 Examples of business analysis components from the process perspective

The following tables give examples of each of the 22 components defined in the previous section. The examples are based on the same inventory control application as used for the data perspective. The sequence is the same as for the component descriptions. The three methodology dependent components are included, to indicate which alternatives are used in this example.

4.8.1   BUSINESS ACTIVITY

Activity Number	*Description*
1	Inventory Control
1.1	Handling new stock
1.1.1	Categorization of new stock items
1.1.2	Registration of alternative supplier
1.2	Ordering stock required
1.2.1	Select supplier
1.2.2	Send purchase order
1.3	Monitoring stock levels

The numbering system used in the first column indicates the hierarchical decomposition of BUSINESS ACTIVITIES. For example, activity number 1.1 is decomposed into 1.1.1 and 1.1.2.

The above table contains only one name for expository purposes. Since a BUSINESS ACTIVITY can have one or more BUSINESS ACTIVITY NAMES (see next component), it is not strictly necessary to associate any one of these with the activity number unless the intention is to identify it as a preferred name.

4.8.2   BUSINESS ACTIVITY NAME

Name ID	*Business Activity Name*
1	Stock Management
2	Inventory Control
3	Inventory Management
4	Handling new stock
5	Categorization of new stock items
6	Registration of alternative supplier
7	Ordering stock required
8	Select supplier
9	Send purchase order
10	Monitoring stock levels

Each BUSINESS ACTIVITY NAME is assigned a Name ID to make it easier to show the references to this table from other tables.

4.8.3 BUSINESS ACTIVITY USES NAME

Activity Number	Name ID
1	1 (Stock Management)
1	2 (Inventory Control)
1	3 (Inventory Management)
1.1	4 (Handling new stock)
1.1.1	5 (Categorization of new stock items)
1.1.2	6 (Registration of alternative supplier)
1.2	7 (Ordering stock required)
1.2.1	8 (Select supplier)
1.2.2	9 (Send purchase order)
1.3	10 (Monitoring stock levels)

A BUSINESS ACTIVITY (as identified by an Activity Number in the first column of this table) may have one or more BUSINESS ACTIVITY NAMES. For example, the table shows that Activity Number 1 has three different names.

4.8.4 ACTIVITY PRECEDENCE/SUCCEDENCE

Preceding Activity	Succeeding Activity
1.1 (Handling new stock)	1.2 (Ordering stock required)
1.3 (Monitoring stock levels)	1.2 (Ordering stock required)

The codes used are the same as those given for BUSINESS ACTIVITY.

4.8.5 INFORMATION OR MATERIAL

Set Type Code	Description
I	Information Set
M	Material Set
C	Composite

This component is methodology dependent and would be the same for all examples.

4.8.6   INFORMATION/MATERIAL SET

Set Type Code	Set Number	Description
I	1	List of suppliers
I	2	List of items stocked
M	1	Stocks of goods
I	3	Reorder levels
I	4	Purchase orders
I	5	Price of goods items

The first column in this table shows how each INFORMATION/MATERIAL SET is classified. The second column contains a Set Number which, together with the Set Type Code, distinguishes each INFORMATION/MATERIAL SET. The last column contains a narrative description.

4.8.7   SET NAME

Name Number	Set Name
1	List of suppliers
2	List of items stocked
3	Stocks of goods
4	Reorder levels
5	Purchase orders
6	Price of goods items
7	Unit prices

This table lists the possible SET NAMES which may be used. Each SET NAME is assigned a Name Number which is used in other tables when referring to this one.

4.8.8   INFORMATION/MATERIAL SET USES NAME

Set Type Code	Set Number	Name Number
I	1 (List of suppliers)	1 (List of suppliers)
I	2 (List of items stocked)	2 (List of items stocked)
M	1 (Stock of goods)	3 (Stock of goods)
I	3 (Reorder levels)	4 (Reorder levels)
I	4 (Purchase orders)	5 (Purchase orders)
I	5 (Price of goods items)	6 (Price of goods items)
I	5 (Price of goods items)	7 (Unit prices)

This cross-reference shows that two names are used for the last INFORMA-TION/MATERIAL SET.

4.8.9 INVOLVEMENT TYPE

Involvement Type Code	Description
R	Data component input to process component
U	Data component output from process component

This component is methodology dependent. It would be the same for all examples using a given activity analysis technique. Other techniques might use a more extensive code breakdown, distinguishing the different kinds of involvement.

4.8.10 ACTIVITY USES SET

Activity Number	Involvement	Set Type Code	Set Number
1.1	U	M	1
1.1	U	I	2
1.2	U	I	4
1.2	R	I	5
1.2	R	I	1
1.3	R	I	3
1.3	R	I	2

For example, the fifth row in this table indicates that Business Activity 1.2 (Ordering stock required) retrieves (i.e. uses) Information Set I1 (List of suppliers). The third row indicates that this same activity will update Information Set I4 (Purchase orders).

4.8.11 ACTIVITY PRECONDITION

Precondition Number	Precondition Description
1	New stock item selected
2	Stock below reordering level
3	Supplier goes out of business
4	Space for stock expanded
5	Purchase order lost in post
6	New supplier makes competitive bid

The specification of the details of an ACTIVITY PRECONDITION is considered in Section 4.11.

4.8.12 PRECONDITION ENABLES ACTIVITY

Precondition Number	Activity Number
1	1.2.1 (Select supplier)
2	1.2.2 (Send purchase order)
3	1.2.1 (Select supplier)
4	(No activity identified)
5	1.2.2 (Send purchase order)
6	1.2.1 (Select supplier)

This table shows the cross-references between ACTIVITY PRECONDITIONS and BUSINESS ACTIVITIES. For the particular examples in this table, any one of the PRECONDITIONS is sufficient to trigger the BUSINESS ACTIVITY.

4.8.13 ORGANIZATION UNIT

Organization Unit Code	Organization Unit Name
P	Purchasing
W	Warehouse
G	Goods Receiving Unit
A	Accounting

This table lists the possible names and codes for each ORGANIZATION UNIT.

4.8.14 ACTIVITY RESPONSIBILITY

Organization Unit Code	Activity Number
G	1.1
P	1.2
W	1.3

This cross-reference component shows, for example, that the Purchasing department is responsible for BUSINESS ACTIVITY 1.2, namely 'Ordering stock required'.

4.8.15 EXTERNAL UNIT

External Unit Code	Description
S	Supplier
T	Transport Agency

This table lists the possible codes and descriptions for each EXTERNAL UNIT.

4.8.16 FLOW TYPE

Flow Type Code	Description
EI	External to internal
IE	Internal to external
II	Internal

As in the case of the components INFORMATION OR MATERIAL and INVOLVEMENT TYPE, this component is methodology dependent.

4.8.17 FLOW

Flow Type Code	Flow Number	Organization Unit Source	Organization Unit Recipient	External Unit
IE	1	P	—	S
EI	3	—	G	S
II	4	G	W	—
II	2	P	A	—

It should be noted that each FLOW involves at least one ORGANIZATION UNIT. This example does not allow for each FLOW to have a name, but this might be done with some techniques, for example by using the components FLOW INVOLVES INFORMATION/MATERIAL SET, INFORMATION/MATERIAL SET and SET NAME. In this way, the name of the FLOW would be the same as the name of the INFORMATION/MATERIAL SET.

4.8.18 ACTIVITY INVOLVES FLOW

Business Activity Number	Flow Number
1.2	1
1.1	1
1.2	2

The first example shows that FLOW 1 involves BUSINESS ACTIVITY 1.1 'Handling new stock' and BUSINESS ACTIVITY 1.2 'Ordering stock required'.

4.8.19 FLOW INVOLVES INFORMATION/MATERIAL SET

Set Type Code	Set Number	Flow Number
I	4	1
I	5	1
M	1	1
I	4	2

The first example shows that FLOW 1 is a flow of INFORMATION/MATERIAL SET 4, which is an information set representing 'Purchase orders'.

4.8.20 FLOW OF SET IN ACTIVITY

Flow Type Code	Flow Number	Activity Number	Set Type Code	Set Number
IE	1	1.2	I	4
IE	3	1.2	I	5
EI	4	1.1	M	1
II	1	1.1	M	1
II	2	1.2	I	4

The first example shows that FLOW 1 (from Purchasing to a Supplier) is an 'internal to external' flow of the information set representing 'Purchase orders' and is part of BUSINESS ACTIVITY 1.2, which is called 'Ordering stock required'.

4.8.21 FLOW PRECONDITION

Precondition Number	Precondition Description
1	New stock item selected
2	Stock below reordering level
3	Supplier goes out of business
4	Space for stock expanded
5	Purchase order lost in post
6	New supplier makes competitive bid
7	Invoice received from supplier

It should be noted that these examples of FLOW PRECONDITIONS are identical to those used to illustrate ACTIVITY PRECONDITIONS in Section 4.8.11. Some techniques may have these two components combined into one component. The specification of the details of FLOW PRECONDITION is considered in Section 4.11.

4.8.22   PRECONDITION ENABLES FLOW

Precondition Number	Flow Type Code	Flow Number
2	IE	1
7	II	2

The first example shows that the precondition for a flow of information from Purchasing to a Supplier is that the level of stock goes below the reordering level.

4.9   Components of business analysis — behaviour perspective

The components of the business analysis stage which belong to the behaviour oriented perspective are as follows:

1.   BUSINESS EVENT
2.   BUSINESS EVENT NAME
3.   BUSINESS EVENT USES NAME
4.   EVENT PRECEDENCE/SUCCEDENCE
*5.   BUSINESS EVENT ROLE
6.   BUSINESS EVENT CONDITION
7.   CONDITION FOR BUSINESS EVENT

The component indicated with an asterisk is methodology dependent. The relationships between the components are depicted in Figure 4.4.

4.9.1   BUSINESS EVENT

A BUSINESS EVENT is a type of event which is perceived in the application environment as being pertinent to the business. A BUSINESS EVENT must not be confused with a BUSINESS ACTIVITY, as identified from the process oriented perspective.

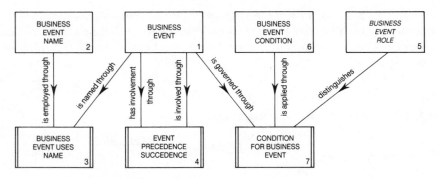

Figure 4.4   Business analysis stage – behaviour perspective.

A BUSINESS ACTIVITY consumes resources and lasts for a measurable period of time. A BUSINESS EVENT does neither of these. It happens at a given point in time, possibly identified to the nearest second, and does not in itself consume resources.

4.9.2   BUSINESS EVENT NAME

A BUSINESS EVENT NAME is a name used to identify a BUSINESS EVENT. Analysis may show that two BUSINESS EVENT NAMES are synonyms for the same BUSINESS EVENT.

4.9.3   BUSINESS EVENT USES NAME

This cross-reference component identifies the different possible BUSINESS EVENT NAMES used for the same BUSINESS EVENT. There may also be cases of one BUSINESS EVENT NAME covering two or more BUSINESS EVENTS.

4.9.4   EVENT PRECEDENCE/SUCCEDENCE

EVENT PRECEDENCE/SUCCEDENCE captures the permitted or required sequence of BUSINESS EVENTS. One BUSINESS EVENT may be a necessary precursor to the occurrence of an event related to the same or another BUSINESS EVENT.

An occurrence of a BUSINESS EVENT may not happen unless occurrences of one or more other BUSINESS EVENTS have already happened. When modelling BUSINESS EVENTS, it is usually necessary to identify (implicitly or explicitly) starting BUSINESS EVENTS and terminating BUSINESS EVENTS.

4.9.5   BUSINESS EVENT ROLE

This component is methodology dependent. It is used to distinguish between preconditions and postconditions in the component CONDITION FOR

BUSINESS EVENT. Some event modelling techniques use conditions in both roles (namely pre- and post-) and others use only preconditions. Expressing postconditions on BUSINESS EVENTS is not normally allowed in most methodologies.

4.9.6 BUSINESS EVENT CONDITION

A BUSINESS EVENT CONDITION is a condition which can be identified by an analyst as either necessary for the triggering of a BUSINESS EVENT or else required to indicate that an event has satisfactorily taken place.

There may be several BUSINESS EVENT CONDITIONS, all of which are preconditions, which must hold concurrently for a BUSINESS EVENT to take place. Alternatively, the logical combination of BUSINESS EVENT CONDITIONS may be more logically complex. A BUSINESS EVENT CONDITION may be defined in detail in terms of the ATTRIBUTES of ENTITY TYPES (see Section 4.12).

4.9.7 CONDITION FOR BUSINESS EVENT

This cross-reference component identifies the BUSINESS EVENT CONDITIONS applicable to a BUSINESS EVENT in the sequence in which they should be evaluated. It also indicates, for each BUSINESS EVENT CONDITION, the BUSINESS EVENTS to which it applies.

4.10 Examples of business analysis components from the behaviour perspective

The following tables give examples of each of the seven components described in the previous section. The examples are based on the same inventory control application as used for the data perspective and process perspective.

4.10.1 BUSINESS EVENT

Event Number	Description
1	Stock depletion
2	Stock below reordering level
3	Issue purchase order
4	Consignment received
5	Consignment added to stock

This table gives a list of the BUSINESS EVENTS which may happen in the business area. Each BUSINESS EVENT has an Event Number and a Description.

4.10.2   BUSINESS EVENT NAME

Name Number	Business Event Name
1	Stock depletion
2	Stock withdrawal
3	Stock below reordering level
4	Stock rupture
5	Issue purchase order
6	Prepare purchase order
7	Consignment received
8	Consignment added to stock

Each BUSINESS EVENT NAME is assigned a Name Number to make it easier to show the references to this table from other tables.

4.10.3   BUSINESS EVENT USES NAME

Event Number	Name Number
1 (Stock depletion)	1 (Stock depletion)
1 (Stock depletion)	2 (Stock withdrawal)
2 (Stock below reordering level)	3 (Stock below reordering level)
2 (Stock below reordering level)	4 (Stock rupture)
3 (Issue purchase order)	5 (Issue purchase order)
3 (Issue purchase order)	6 (Prepare purchase order)
4 (Consignment received)	7 (Consignment received)
5 (Consignment added to stock)	8 (Consignment added to stock)

This cross-reference table shows that a BUSINESS EVENT as identified by an Event Number can have one or more BUSINESS EVENT NAMES.

4.10.4   EVENT PRECEDENCE/SUCCEDENCE

Succeeding Event Number	Preceding Event Number
2 (Stock below reordering level)	1 (Stock depletion)
3 (Issue purchase order)	2 (Stock below reordering level)
4 (Consignment received)	3 (Issue purchase order)
5 (Consignment added to stock)	4 (Consignment received)

This table represents the network of interrelated BUSINESS EVENTS, showing which event has to happen before another event can happen.

4.10.5 BUSINESS EVENT ROLE

Event Role Code	Event Role Description
B (before)	Precondition
A (after)	Postcondition

This table shows the possible roles that a BUSINESS EVENT CONDITION can fill with respect to a BUSINESS EVENT.

4.10.6 BUSINESS EVENT CONDITION

Condition Number	Condition Description
1	Stock below reordering level
2	No phase out indication given

The second condition means that no indication has been made to phase out a Stock Item due to such factors as deterioration or obsolescence. Such a condition would inhibit the reordering of further stock, even after the reordering level had been reached.

4.10.7 CONDITION FOR BUSINESS EVENT

Event Number	Event Role Code	Row Number	Condition Number	True Row	False Row
3	B	1	1	2	F
3	B	2	2	T	F

This table indicates that BUSINESS EVENT CONDITIONS 1 and 2 both have to hold for BUSINESS EVENT 3 (Issue Purchase Order) to take place. BUSINESS EVENT CONDITION 1 is evaluated first. If it is true, then the condition on row 2 is evaluated. If condition 1 is false, then there is no need to evaluate the condition identified on row 2.

4.11   Business analysis — cross-references between perspectives

Eight components of the business analysis stage do not belong to any one perspective but provide a cross-reference between two important components, each of which has a different perspective. Such components can be referred to as cross-reference components and are presented in the following sequence:

*1.   INVOLVEMENT TYPE
 2.   BUSINESS ACTIVITY INVOLVES ENTITY TYPE
 3.   BUSINESS ACTIVITY INVOLVES ATTRIBUTE
 4.   ACTIVITY TRIGGER
 5.   BUSINESS EVENT INVOLVES ENTITY TYPE
 6.   BUSINESS EVENT INVOLVES ATTRIBUTE
 7.   CONDITION USES ENTITY TYPE
 8.   CONDITION USES ATTRIBUTE

The component marked with an asterisk is methodology dependent.

   The relationships between these components and those belonging to specific perspectives are given in Figure 4.5.

4.11.1   INVOLVEMENT TYPE

This component is methodology dependent but will be interpreted differently by different techniques. It is used to categorize the ways in which a process oriented component, such as BUSINESS ACTIVITY, or a behaviour oriented component, such as BUSINESS EVENT, could be involved with a data oriented component, such as ENTITY TYPE.

   One example is that information about the data is simply used by the BUSINESS ACTIVITY while that activity is being performed. 'Used' here implies that the BUSINESS ACTIVITY would not change the data in any way.

   If the BUSINESS ACTIVITY were to change the data, then the INVOLVEMENT TYPE component could possibly categorize the alternative ways – such as create, modify or erase.

4.11.2   BUSINESS ACTIVITY INVOLVES ENTITY TYPE

Each BUSINESS ACTIVITY is involved with one or more ENTITY TYPES. This involvement may be such that information about the ENTITY TYPES is needed as input to a BUSINESS ACTIVITY. In addition, a BUSINESS ACTIVITY may generate information about new or existing entities of a given ENTITY TYPE.

   At the same time, an ENTITY TYPE which is involved in a BUSINESS

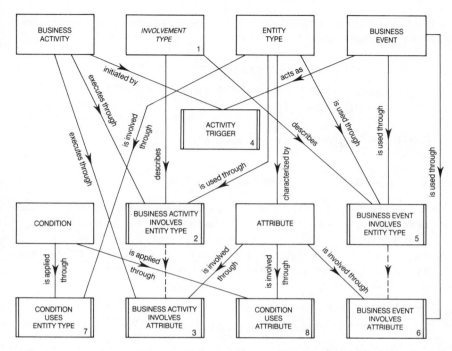

Figure 4.5 Business analysis stage – cross-references between perspectives. The component CONDITION represents the three components – ACTIVITY PRECONDITION, FLOW PRECONDITION and BUSINESS EVENT PRECONDITION as described earlier.

ACTIVITY (i.e. as input to the activity or generated as output from it) is indicated using INVOLVEMENT TYPE.

If a given BUSINESS ACTIVITY is involved with several ENTITY TYPES, it is also possible to analyse the sequence in which the ENTITY TYPES are used during the performance of the BUSINESS ACTIVITY.

4.11.3   BUSINESS ACTIVITY INVOLVES ATTRIBUTE

The cross-referencing of BUSINESS ACTIVITIES with ENTITY TYPES can be carried out in more detail by cross-referencing the BUSINESS ACTIVITIES with the ATTRIBUTES of each ENTITY TYPE.

4.11.4   ACTIVITY TRIGGER

This component captures the interrelationship between BUSINESS EVENTS and BUSINESS ACTIVITIES. A BUSINESS EVENT is an ACTIVITY TRIGGER to a BUSINESS ACTIVITY. In other words, when the BUSINESS EVENT happens – possibly outside the environment of the information system – then a given BUSINESS ACTIVITY should be performed.

If a designer chooses to analyse both BUSINESS ACTIVITIES and BUSINESS EVENTS, then three components

- ACTIVITY PRECEDENCE/SUCCEDENCE
- EVENT PRECEDENCE/SUCCEDENCE
- ACTIVITY TRIGGER

must collectively be completely consistent.

4.11.5   BUSINESS EVENT INVOLVES ENTITY TYPE

Each BUSINESS EVENT, when it happens, can 'use' information about some ENTITY TYPES or it can create new information about some ENTITY TYPES.

It may not be necessary for each ENTITY TYPE to be involved in a BUSINESS EVENT. However, if both BUSINESS EVENTS and BUSINESS ACTIVITIES are analysed, it would be expected that each ENTITY TYPE is involved with at least one of these two components.

4.11.6   BUSINESS EVENT INVOLVES ATTRIBUTE

The cross-referencing between BUSINESS EVENT and ENTITY TYPE can be analysed in detail by cross-referencing the BUSINESS EVENTS with the ATTRIBUTES of each ENTITY TYPE. This can include the logical sequences in which the ATTRIBUTES have to be evaluated.

The INVOLVEMENT TYPE on the ATTRIBUTE level of detail may be the same as that for the ENTITY TYPE to which the ATTRIBUTE belongs. On the other hand, it may be more specific than the broader categorization used on the ENTITY TYPE level.

4.11.7   CONDITION USES ENTITY TYPE

A CONDITION can usually be expressed in data oriented terms. This cross-reference indicates, for each CONDITION, the ENTITY TYPES whose data would be used to express the CONDITION.

4.11.8   CONDITION USES ATTRIBUTE

This cross-reference component supplements the previous component, namely CONDITION USES ENTITY TYPE, and allows for an analysis of the detailed definition of a CONDITION down to the level of the ATTRIBUTES of each ENTITY TYPE.

4.12 Examples of business analysis cross-references

The following tables give examples of each of the eight components defined in the previous section. The examples are based on the same inventory control application as used in the individual perspectives. Some examples are displayed as cross-reference tables, rather than the column format used to illustrate other components.

4.12.1 INVOLVEMENT TYPE

Involvement Code	Involvement Description
R	Reads information about
U	Updates information about

This table shows the complete set of alternatives for INVOLVEMENT TYPE, which is a methodology dependent component used to qualify various cross-reference components.

4.12.2 BUSINESS ACTIVITY INVOLVES ENTITY TYPE

	Activity Number				
Entity Type Name	1.1.1	1.1.2	1.2.1	1.2.2	1.3
Supplier		U	R		
Stock Item	U	R		R	R
Stock Item Type	R				
Calendar Date				R	R
Purchase Order			U	R	
Purchase Order Item				U	
Stock on Hand					R
Supplier Stock Item		U	R		

U and R indicate the INVOLVEMENT TYPE (see Section 4.12.1).

This cross-reference component indicates, for example, that the BUSINESS ACTIVITY number 1.1.2 (called 'Registration of alternative supplier') involves the three ENTITY TYPES – Supplier, Stock Item and Supplier Stock Item.

When the BUSINESS ACTIVITY takes place, information about Stock Items is used and information about Suppliers and Supplier Stock Items is generated. This indicates that the BUSINESS ACTIVITY is concerned with Suppliers of identifiable Stock Items.

4.12.3 BUSINESS ACTIVITY INVOLVES ATTRIBUTE

To illustrate this component, only BUSINESS ACTIVITY 1.1.1 (Categorization of new stock items) is used. It can be seen from the illustration in the preceding section that this activity involves two ENTITY TYPES, namely ET2, Stock Item and ET3, Stock Item Type (see Section 4.6.1). The ATTRIBUTES of these ENTITY TYPES are shown in Section 4.6.9.

Entity Type Code	Attribute	Activity Number	Involvement Code
ET2	Stock Code	1.1.1	U
ET2	Stock Item Name	1.1.1	U
ET2	Stock Item Type Code	1.1.1	U
ET3	Stock Item Type Code	1.1.1	R
ET3	Stock Item Type Description	1.1.1	R

4.12.4 ACTIVITY TRIGGER

Event Number	Event Description	Activity Number	Activity Description
1	Stock depletion	1.3	Monitoring stock levels
2	Stock below reordering level	1.2	Ordering stock required
4	Consignment received	1.1	Handling new stock
5	Consignment added to stock	1.3	Monitoring stock levels

It is noted that BUSINESS EVENT 3 (Issue purchase order) does not trigger a BUSINESS ACTIVITY. This is acceptable in terms of consistency in that it does initiate a FLOW to an EXTERNAL UNIT.

4.12.5 BUSINESS EVENT INVOLVES ENTITY TYPE

Entity Type Code	Event Number				
	1	*2*	*3*	*4*	*5*
Supplier			R	R	
Stock Item	R	R		R	
Stock Item Type	R				
Calendar Date	R	R		R	
Purchase Order			U		
Purchase Order Item			U		
Stock on Hand	U	R			U
Supplier Stock Item		R			

This cross-reference component indicates which ENTITY TYPES are involved in each BUSINESS EVENT and also the nature of the involvement. For example, BUSINESS EVENT 1, which is called Stock depletion, reads information about the ENTITY TYPES Stock Item Type, Stock Item and Calendar Date. This BUSINESS EVENT then causes the information about the ENTITY TYPE Stock on Hand to be updated.

4.12.6   BUSINESS EVENT INVOLVES ATTRIBUTE

To illustrate this component, only BUSINESS EVENT 1 (Stock depletion) is used. It can be seen from the illustration in the preceding section that this event involves three ENTITY TYPES, namely ET2 (Stock Item), ET3 (Stock Item Type) and ET4 (Calendar Date; see Section 4.6.1). The ATTRIBUTES of these ENTITY TYPES are shown in Section 4.6.9.

Entity Type Code	*Attribute Name*	*Event Number*	*Involvement Code*
ET2	Stock Code	1	R
ET2	Stock Item Name	1	R
ET2	Stock Item Type Code	1	R
ET3	Stock Item Type Code	1	R
ET3	Stock Item Type Description	1	R
ET4	Date	1	R
ET7	Stock on Hand	1	U

4.12.7   CONDITION USES ENTITY TYPE

	Condition Number	
Entity Type Name	*1*	*2*
Supplier		
Stock Item	Y	Y
Stock Item Type	Y	
Calendar Date	Y	Y
Purchase Order		
Purchase Order Item		
Stock on Hand	Y	
Supplier Stock Item		

This cross-reference component shows that CONDITION 2, which in this case is a BUSINESS EVENT CONDITION and is called 'No phase out indication given', uses information about the two ENTITY TYPES – Calendar Date and Stock Item.

4.12.8 CONDITION USES ATTRIBUTE

Attribute Name	Condition Number	
	1	*2*
Stock Code	Y	Y
Stock Item Name	Y	Y
Price		
Supplier Number		
Supplier Name		
Stock Item Type Code	Y	Y
Stock Item Type Description	Y	
Date of Purchase	Y	Y
Date of Delivery		
Purchase Order Number		
Purchase Order Item Number		

The ATTRIBUTES in this list are taken from Section 4.6.9. The recognition of CONDITION 2, namely 'No phase out indication given', brings out the fact that some kind of phase out indicator needs to be associated with each Stock Item. The need for this ATTRIBUTE was not recognized in the examples of components in the data perspective. In practice, a further iteration would be called for.

4.13   Concluding remarks on business analysis stage

This chapter has identified about 50 components associated with the business analysis stage. An illustration of the tabular representation of each of these components has been given. In addition, Appendix B presents a worked example (for a different business area) of all the business analysis components, presented in the same sequence as they appear in this chapter.

This kind of tabular representation would not (and should not) be used in practice to communicate the results of the business analysis to a user. However, for some of the components, particularly for cross-reference components, a tabular representation would be the preferred representation in many information systems methodologies. A more typical representation for most others would be diagrams.

Any methodology which is computer supported would record the results in tabular form in computerized tables and use these tables to generate the diagrams.

It must be emphasized that no business analysis methodology is expected to generate all of these components. Any attempt to do so would encounter major consistency problems – especially with a more substantive application than that used for illustrative purposes in this chapter.

However the business analysis stage is performed, the resulting components can collectively be regarded as a descriptive business model. Such a model can change during the course of time and the analyst can revise his or her early interpretations of the business area covered by the model, and reflect such changes in the model.

It is assumed that after a number of iterations, this descriptive analytic business model can be used as a basis for the prescriptive work of the system design stage.

As indicated in Section 4.4, the selection of components in this chapter was based on the typical components found in information systems methodologies that are currently in use. This has led, inevitably, to a certain amount of what might be seen as redundancy.

For example, the following aspects of data perspective components have so much in common that one might argue that they should be combined on a higher abstraction level:

1.   zero or one to one relationship,
2.   is-a relationship,
3.   one population wholly contained in another, and
4.   subtypes.

In fact, these aspects have been covered under the RELATIONSHIP TYPE component and under POPULATION OVERLAP, both of which have other aspects which are not comparable.

The abstraction level chosen in this chapter for components, and indeed in the next chapter on system design, should enable a reader with knowledge of one existing information systems methodology to place that methodology in the framework.

The way in which components are interrelated in the framework is predicated, to some extent, on design considerations in that the framework for the business analysis stage has been designed and design tends to be more precise than analysis. In addition, it is necessary to present the framework in such a way that it communicates effectively with readers.

The effect of this has been that most interrelationships between components in the business analysis stage are RELATIONSHIPS belonging to the RELATIONSHIP TYPE 'one to many', where 'many' means 'zero, one or more'. There are a few 'zero or one to many' relationships between components and one example of a unary relationship (on BUSINESS ACTIVITIES).

Needless to say, the preparation of this framework for the business analysis stage has gone through numerous iterations during the course of its preparation.

EXERCISES

A.   *Self-assessment*

4.1   Summarize the different approaches to business analysis emphasized by each of the three perspectives described in Chapter 3. (It may be useful to refer to Figures 4.1, 4.3, 4.4 and 4.5.)

4.2   The components discussed for the three perspectives are listed in Sections 4.5, 4.7 and 4.9. The entries in one list do not overlap with any entries in the other. Cross-references not belonging exclusively to a single perspective are listed in Section 4.11.

The non-overlap of the first three lists, of course, is a consequence of the differences among the perspectives. For instances of components relating to the same business area, there are several cross-references possible between pairs of components, some of which are made explicit in the items in the fourth list.

(a)   Explain the occurrence of specific components or groups of components in the three lists, each covering one perspective (for example, entity, relationship and attribute in the first, activity and flow in the second, and so on).

(b)   Paraphrase the cross-references of Section 4.11.

(c)   Identify further relationships between pairs of components, not immediately expressible in cross-reference form.

4.3   Four components are listed as 'methodology dependent' among the 16 components associated with the data perspective (RELATIONSHIP CLASS, RELATIONSHIP TYPE, VALUE CONSTRAINT TYPE and POPULATION OVERLAP TYPE). Discuss the usefulness of these in defining the other data oriented components.

4.4   Three components are indicated as 'methodology dependent' among the 22 components associated with the process perspective (INFORMATION OR MATERIAL, INVOLVEMENT TYPE and FLOW TYPE). Discuss the usefulness of these in defining the other data oriented components.

4.5   One component, BUSINESS EVENT ROLE, is indicated as 'methodology dependent' among the seven components associated with the behaviour perspective. Discuss the usefulness of this in defining the other behaviour oriented components.

B.   *Methodology related*

(for those familiar with one or more specific methodologies)

4.6 If the methodology has an explicit business analysis stage (possibly under a different name), discuss the correspondences between the components introduced in this chapter and those in the methodology.

4.7 If the methodology does not have an explicit business analysis stage corresponding to that described in this chapter, discuss the correspondences to the extent possible.

C. Case studies

In Appendix D, case studies are described for three business areas – theatre, airline and car hire. The following exercises may be carried out for any or all of these case studies. The case studies are non-trivial and several iterations may be necessary.

4.8 Work through the components identified in Chapter 4 systematically. For methodology dependent components, it is possible to designate a set of alternatives, possibly based on those shown in the text or alternatively on some methodology used in the set of 'methodology related' exercises above. For the 'analyst prescribable' components, prepare instances of each component for the case study, using the same tabular format as in the chapter.

4.9 Supplement the instances of components prepared in tabular format with diagramming techniques used in a known methodology. It is important that the results are consistent with each other and, as far as possible, with the specification given in the tabular format.

4.10 If some of the components are not applicable to the case study chosen, explain the reason for this.

4.11 Perform Exercises 4.1 and 4.2 using a computerized design aid, such as an analyst's workbench tool. Identify the instances of the methodology dependent components which are implicit in the tool. Is the user of the tool allowed to specify the instances of any of the methodology dependent components? Identify any analyst prescribable components which cannot be represented using the tool chosen and indicate whether the omission is acceptable.

5

Component analysis for the system design stage

5.1 Mapping from business analysis

The scope of a system design stage can usually be determined in terms of the area covered in the preceding business analysis stage. The system design stage may cover the same area or, typically, a part of the area covered by the business analysis stage which precedes it.

The descriptive model produced during the business analysis stage should form the basis for the system design stage. This basis may be *firm and to some extent formal* in the sense that some of the system design components can be *cross-referenced back* to business analysis components. The basis may be *loose*, in the sense that the designer studies the business analysis components and then proceeds to generate system design components in such a way that these cannot *easily be cross-referenced* back to the business analysis components.

In some cases, the system design may be the starting point in the design process. This might be because the designer feels that he or she understands the business area sufficiently and has sufficient experience to be able to proceed with a design, without generating any of the business analysis components described in the previous chapter. Another possibility is that the designer may be able to use existing analytical models.

It should not be assumed that the initiation of a system design stage after completion of a business analysis stage closes the door on the former stage. The whole design process should be regarded as evolutionary. The breakdown into business analysis and system design in this text was made partly for ease of presentation, although some existing information system methodologies do make a clear distinction between the two stages.

The approach to system design in this chapter emphasizes what the designed system is intended to do and not how it is to be built. Techniques relevant to the design of programs are regarded as part of the construction design stage which follows the system design stage in the information system life cycle outlined in Chapter 3.

5.2   Choice of presentation sequence

The presentation sequence used in this chapter differs slightly from that used in the preceding chapter for the business analysis stage components. It is as follows:

1. data oriented perspective,
2. process oriented perspective,
3. cross-references between data and process, and
4. behaviour oriented perspective and cross-references to other perspectives.

The components are first presented and then illustrated using the same example of inventory control as used for business analysis.

5.3   Overview of perspectives

5.3.1   Data oriented perspective

After ENTITY TYPES, RELATIONSHIPS and ATTRIBUTES have been identified in the business analysis stage, the system design stage calls for a mental change of attitude with regard to the data perspective. While the business analysis called for **descriptive** work, the system design stage needs to be **prescriptive**.

If the business analysis stage has gone into considerable detail with respect to the ATTRIBUTES and the various constraints which the values of these ATTRIBUTES must satisfy, then the system design stage does not need to repeat that work and the data oriented components can be adopted on a one-to-one basis as the prescriptive design components. However, if the business analysis stage was less probing, then the data design may differ from the results of the business analysis stage.

Three important kinds of CONSTRAINT were identified in the preceding chapter – uniqueness CONSTRAINTS, referential CONSTRAINTS and check CONSTRAINTS. A uniqueness CONSTRAINT will apply to one or more ATTRIBUTES of the same ENTITY TYPE and merely assert that the values of this ATTRIBUTE (or ATTRIBUTE GROUP) for any entity of the ENTITY TYPE must be different from the corresponding values for all other entities of the same ENTITY TYPE.

A referential CONSTRAINT on the values of an ATTRIBUTE or set of ATTRIBUTES of an ENTITY TYPE implies that the values are constrained by the values of another ATTRIBUTE or ATTRIBUTE GROUP which typically belong to another ENTITY TYPE. Referential CONSTRAINTS are typically closely associated with RELATIONSHIPS between ENTITY TYPES and one can choose whether to analyse referential CONSTRAINTS directly or to start by identifying the RELATIONSHIPS and then base the referential CONSTRAINTS on the RELATIONSHIPS.

Check CONSTRAINTS are a more difficult kind of CONSTRAINT. The designer can often predicate his or her design approach on the knowledge that the database management system to be used in construction can handle the referential CONSTRAINTS. Most such construction tools do not yet handle check CONSTRAINTS. Nevertheless, the identification of such CONSTRAINTS by a designer is important even if they have to be programmed into updating programs in the conventional way.

The transformation from the descriptive components (resulting from the business analysis stage) to the prescriptive components (which have to be generated in the system design stage) can be recorded as a series of interstage components.

To clarify that there may be some kind of transformation from one to the other, it is felt preferable to use different terms in each stage. For this reason the data oriented components in the system design stage are identified using what are generally regarded as 'relational' terms. This is not intended to imply that the system design stage must be predicated on the use of a relational DBMS. This use of different component names means that ENTITY TYPES are mapped to TABLES, and ATTRIBUTES and ATTRIBUTE GROUPS are mapped to COLUMNS and COLUMN GROUPS. RELATIONSHIPS and CONSTRAINTS from the business analysis are then mappable to CONSTRAINTS.

The design of EXTERNAL FORMS which are to be printed or displayed (or both) is regarded as part of the data perspective. An EXTERNAL FORM may consist of one or more EXTERNAL FORM ELEMENTS and various DISPLAY OPTIONS can be identified for each piece of data from a COLUMN in a TABLE which is to be presented on an EXTERNAL FORM.

Another aspect of the data perspective is the specification of computational procedures which are to be performed on numeric and non-numeric data. These are related in this chapter to the COLUMN in which the result of using the procedure is to be recorded. The procedure may optionally be relatable to a specific TASK and, for this reason, the component involved is described under cross-reference components.

5.3.2   Process oriented perspective

Each information system is usually designed to perform certain TASKS, where a TASK is here defined as invokable by a user from a terminal and should be relatable to one or more of the BUSINESS ACTIVITIES recorded as part of the business analysis stage. In addition, an information system will have managerial, administrative and clerical tasks. Some methodologies take these into account but they are not considered further in this text.

It is important at this stage not to confuse a TASK with a computer program of any kind. The identification of a TASK in user terms as a 'line on a lower level MENU' is recognition of the fact that most information systems currently under design are on line systems for use by non-technical users.

A line on a MENU can also identify another MENU and there are various ways of designing an interrelated set of MENUS. Finally, it should be noted that some approaches to system design allow one TASK to trigger another TASK and also for TASKS to be initiated automatically when the time on the calendar clock reaches a certain point.

TASKS can be arrived at in one of four ways. One is by decomposing BUSINESS ACTIVITIES until a detailed level is reached at which each BUSINESS ACTIVITY can be regarded as a computerizable TASK. Each TASK identified in this way can be cross-referenced to the INFORMATION SETS derivable from the INFORMATION/MATERIAL SETS of the business analysis stage described earlier.

A second approach is to perform an analysis of the TASKS needed by the different kinds of user in the business environment. This analysis would be separate from the analysis of BUSINESS ACTIVITIES for which the components were described in the previous chapter. Only subsequent to this analysis can each of the resulting TASKS be related to one, or possibly more, of the BUSINESS ACTIVITIES.

A third approach, which is possible if thorough data design has preceded task specification, is for TASKS to be created to support the updating and retrieval of each TABLE. For each TABLE, there could be TASKS to create, modify and delete rows in the TABLE, as well as several to retrieve selected rows from one or more TABLES. This approach will be clearer from the examples presented later in this chapter.

The final approach to TASK identification uses the behavioural components from the business analysis. For example, a TASK may be triggered by each BUSINESS EVENT or when a certain set of CONDITIONS is satisfied.

One problem which is common to all approaches is that of 'task granularity'. Some designers prefer many small TASKS, almost on the level of primitive operations. Other designers tend to use more all-embracing TASKS which can impact many TABLES in one execution. There may be some correlation between which of the four approaches to task identification is used and the resulting task granularity.

Whatever the preference for task granularity and for approach, the choice may be overridden by the construction tools to be used. Some transaction monitors are known to perform better with many small TASKS, while others favour a smaller number of complex ones. The design of the application programs which drive these TASKS also raises problems of granularity, but these are outside the scope of this text.

Another aspect of TASK definition is that of defining a hierarchy of TASKS, such that a TASK may trigger one or more other TASKS.

5.3.3   Cross-references between data and process perspectives

There are numerous cross-references possible in the system design stage. One is between TABLES and TASKS, and another would be between COLUMNS and TASKS. A cross-reference between COLUMNS and TASKS should result in a more detailed picture than that from TABLES and TASKS or from the business analysis stage between ENTITY TYPES and BUSINESS ACTIVITIES.

The cross-reference component should indicate that every COLUMN is created by a TASK and used by a TASK. If a TASK needs a COLUMN not in the list of COLUMNS, then the list of COLUMNS in a given TABLE may need extending.

5.3.4   Behaviour oriented perspective and cross-references to data and process perspectives

From the behaviour oriented perspective, a number of SYSTEM EVENTS are prescribed. A SYSTEM EVENT may or may not be relatable to a TABLE. Each SYSTEM EVENT may trigger one or more TASKS and each TASK may calculate the content of one or more COLUMNS of a TABLE. Associated with each SYSTEM EVENT is one or more CONDITIONS, each of which may reference certain COLUMNS of the TABLES identified as components with a data oriented perspective.

The process oriented component TASK covers the concept of processes which are initiated from a terminal by a human user. There are two further situations one needs to be able to design. The first is a calendar clock triggered SYSTEM EVENT and the second is a condition triggered SYSTEM EVENT.

A calendar clock SYSTEM EVENT is initiated at a certain time on a certain day. This would require reference to some kind of calendar clock. A condition triggered SYSTEM EVENT is triggered when a condition expressed on the data maintained by the system is satisfied. Cross-reference components between SYSTEM EVENTS and TASKS can also be prepared.

Cross-reference components which relate system design components with business analysis components are described under the perspective to which the system design component belongs. The business analysis component which is referenced usually has the same perspective.

5.4   Components of system design — data perspective

The components of the system design stage which belong to the data oriented perspective are as follows:

   1.   TABLE
 *2.   ASSIGNMENT TYPE
   3.   ENTITY TYPE TO TABLE ASSIGNMENT
 *4.   DATA TYPE
   5.   COLUMN NAME
   6.   COLUMN
   7.   ATTRIBUTE TO COLUMN ASSIGNMENT
   8.   COLUMN GROUP
   9.   COLUMN IN GROUP
*10.   CONSTRAINT TYPE
 11.   CONSTRAINT
 12.   RELATIONSHIP TO CONSTRAINT ASSIGNMENT
 13.   ROW
 14.   EXTERNAL FORM
 15.   EXTERNAL FORM ELEMENT
*16.   DISPLAY OPTION
 17.   COLUMN ON FORM ELEMENT

Components preceded by an asterisk are methodology dependent.

It should be noted that three of these components, namely

   3.   ENTITY TYPE TO TABLE ASSIGNMENT,

7.   ATTRIBUTE TO COLUMN ASSIGNMENT, and

12.   RELATIONSHIP TO CONSTRAINT ASSIGNMENT

are cross-reference components between a business analysis component and a system design component.

Figure 5.1 shows the interrelationships among the above 17 components. It also includes the following three components from the business analysis stage in order to clarify three cross-reference components:

- ENTITY TYPE,
- ATTRIBUTE, and
- RELATIONSHIP.

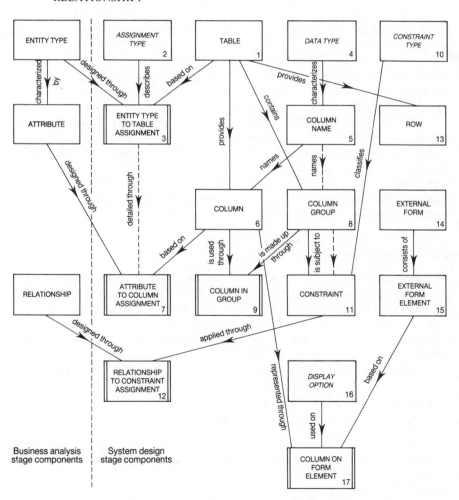

Figure 5.1   System design stage – data perspective.

It should be noted that the system design component CONSTRAINT is similar to the business analysis component VALUE CONSTRAINT. During business analysis, the analyst is recording the existence of a constraint in the business. During system design, the designer is prescribing a rule to which the information system must adhere.

5.4.1   TABLE

This component may also be referred to by other names, such as file, record type and object. A TABLE, when it is designed, is a logical data container in the same way as a file. When some content has been added, one tends to think of the TABLE as a population of ROWS. Terms such as 'record type', which are used in programming languages such as COBOL, convey the idea of type or class, rather than container or population. However, by defining the set of COLUMNS which belong to a TABLE, the designer is implicitly designating a 'row type'.

A TABLE is a two dimensional array of data values. A TABLE contains one or more COLUMNS, and zero, one or more ROWS. Each ROW in the TABLE contains as many values as there are COLUMNS in the TABLE. A value in a ROW may be required to satisfy certain CONSTRAINTS.

Each TABLE prescribed in the system design stage is usually, but not necessarily, related to one or more ENTITY TYPES resulting from the preceding business analysis stage. In the simplest case, the designer decides that an ENTITY TYPE can conveniently and usefully be designated as a TABLE. In other cases, a designer can choose to split an ENTITY TYPE into two or more TABLES. He or she can also choose to combine one or more ENTITY TYPES into one TABLE.

5.4.2   ASSIGNMENT TYPE

This component is methodology dependent and hence peculiar to a design process, rather than to a use of it. It serves to prescribe the alternative ways in which one or more ENTITY TYPES from the business analysis stage could be transformed to one or more TABLES in the system design stage. This transformation could be done on an *ad hoc* basis or according to a set of rules prescribed for the methodology in use.

The following list of basic alternatives is not intended to be exhaustive:

1.   One ENTITY TYPE to one TABLE.
2.   Two or more ENTITY TYPES to one TABLE.
3.   One ENTITY TYPE to two or more TABLES.
4.   Two or more ENTITY TYPES to two or more TABLES.

Others may be added.

5.4.3 ENTITY TYPE TO TABLE ASSIGNMENT

This component is a cross-reference from the ENTITY TYPE component from the business analysis stage to the TABLE component in the system design stage. It could contain an indication of the ASSIGNMENT TYPE. It should be noted that the mapping from ENTITY TYPE to TABLE may not be as straightforward as the alternative ASSIGNMENT TYPES in the above list may indicate.

5.4.4 DATA TYPE

This component is methodology dependent and hence peculiar to a design process, rather than to a use of it. It serves to prescribe the alternative data representations which a COLUMN in a TABLE may use.

The following list of DATA TYPES is intended to be illustrative rather than exhaustive:

1. character,
2. numeric,
3. date, and
4. logical.

The DATA TYPES used in a given design process may be based on those supported by a database management system or programming language which is planned for use as a construction tool.

5.4.5 COLUMN NAME

The component COLUMN NAME is intended to identify a kind of COLUMN which will be used in one or more TABLES. The reason for identifying COLUMN NAME as a different component from COLUMN is that the same name is often used to identify two or more COLUMNS in a corresponding number of TABLES.

A design process may associate a DATA TYPE with each COLUMN NAME or it may associate it with each individual COLUMN.

5.4.6 COLUMN

Each TABLE consists of one or more COLUMNS and each COLUMN belongs, by definition, to one TABLE. Each COLUMN has a COLUMN NAME but the same COLUMN NAME may be used by several COLUMNS, provided these belong to different TABLES.

A COLUMN may have the same DATA TYPE as that prescribed for its COLUMN NAME or it may be possible for different COLUMNS with the same COLUMN NAME to have different DATA TYPES.

5.4.7   ATTRIBUTE TO COLUMN ASSIGNMENT

Each ATTRIBUTE from the business analysis stage will typically be treated as a COLUMN in one of the TABLES prescribed in the system design phase. This will usually depend on the ENTITY TYPE TO TABLE ASSIGNMENT for the ENTITY TYPE to which the ATTRIBUTE belongs, although more complex assignments may need to be allowed for.

A design process may require the ENTITY TYPE TO TABLE ASSIGNMENT to be identified in the ATTRIBUTE TO COLUMN ASSIGNMENT, although in the case of more complex assignments, this may not be feasible.

5.4.8   COLUMN GROUP

This component is used to associate two or more COLUMNS in the same TABLE in such a way that a CONSTRAINT can be expressed on them collectively. The order of COLUMNS in a COLUMN GROUP is important.

5.4.9   COLUMN IN GROUP

This is a cross-reference component between COLUMN and COLUMN GROUP, indicating which COLUMNS belong to which COLUMN GROUPS. A COLUMN can belong to more than one COLUMN GROUP even if they are in the same TABLE. A COLUMN GROUP consists of two or more COLUMNS from the same TABLE.

5.4.10   CONSTRAINT TYPE

This component is methodology dependent and is used to categorize the different kinds of CONSTRAINT which may be expressed using a given design process.

The following list is intended to be illustrative but not exhaustive:

1.   null values not allowed,
2.   uniqueness constraint,
3.   referential constraint, and
4.   check constraint.

These will each be described in turn. A CONSTRAINT on a COLUMN GROUP consisting of one or more COLUMNS, which asserts that null values are not allowed, means that all values in any of the COLUMNS must be non-null values.

A uniqueness CONSTRAINT on a COLUMN GROUP means that the set of values on a given row in the COLUMNS in the COLUMN GROUP must be different from the set of values on any other row.

The simplest and most common kind of referential CONSTRAINT on a COLUMN GROUP means that the values of the set of COLUMNS on a given row in the COLUMNS in the COLUMN GROUP must be equal to the values for another COLUMN GROUP in the same or, more typically, a different TABLE.

A much less common kind of referential CONSTRAINT could require that the values in the COLUMN GROUP on which the CONSTRAINT is expressed are less than the values in the COLUMN GROUP referred to.

A check CONSTRAINT is a CONSTRAINT expressed on the values which are allowed in the COLUMNS of one or more TABLES. The CONSTRAINT expresses a condition which must be satisfied at all times by the values in all the TABLES collectively. It is different from a referential CONSTRAINT which refers to a set of values in one TABLE, whereas a check CONSTRAINT may refer to one or more TABLES other than the one on which the condition is expressed.

It should be noted that this component CONSTRAINT TYPE in the system design stage is similar to the component VALUE CONSTRAINT TYPE in the business analysis stage. In the earlier stage, the business analyst should recognize the relevance of a CONSTRAINT. In the system design stage, the designer may choose to define similar CONSTRAINTS in terms of the TABLES and COLUMNS he or she is prescribing.

5.4.11 CONSTRAINT

This component prescribes the rules which values in the COLUMNS of the TABLES are required to satisfy. A CONSTRAINT may apply to one or more COLUMNS in a TABLE, except for a check CONSTRAINT which may apply to values in several TABLES collectively.

The constructor may choose a construction tool for the information system which enables the direct expression of such rules. Alternatively, the constructor may choose to prepare programs to evaluate and enforce the rules. The system design stage is not intended to specify which approach is preferred.

5.4.12 RELATIONSHIP TO CONSTRAINT ASSIGNMENT

This component is a cross-reference from the RELATIONSHIP component of the business analysis stage to the CONSTRAINT component in the system design stage.

An approach to data analysis which called for a definition of CONSTRAINTS in the business analysis stage, would probably not analyse RELATIONSHIPS as well. In such a case, the analysis CONSTRAINTS may need to be mapped to design CONSTRAINTS when the designer decides to use something other than a one-to-one mapping from ENTITY TYPES to TABLES.

5.4.13   ROW

Each TABLE contains zero, one or more ROWS, where a ROW consists of a set of values corresponding to the COLUMNS defined for the TABLE. A system designer could prescribe all ROWS in some of the TABLES if such ROWS are an inherent part of the design.

5.4.14   EXTERNAL FORM

An EXTERNAL FORM is typically either a printed report or a screen display format. This component covers both. Each EXTERNAL FORM has a prescribable width and contains one or more EXTERNAL FORM ELEMENTS.

5.4.15   EXTERNAL FORM ELEMENT

An EXTERNAL FORM ELEMENT is a type of element on an EXTERNAL FORM which is to be printed or displayed (or both) by the system being designed. An element may be a line of characters or a vertical column of characters.

5.4.16   DISPLAY OPTION

A DISPLAY OPTION is a methodology dependent component. It is an option available for printing or displaying a value or character string on an EXTERNAL FORM ELEMENT. It may be a character font, an underlining option, reverse video (on a screen) or a colour option.

5.4.17   COLUMN ON FORM ELEMENT

This cross-reference component indicates which COLUMNS are to be displayed on an EXTERNAL FORM ELEMENT and with which DISPLAY OPTION.

5.5   Examples of system design components from the data perspective

This section gives examples for eight of the 11 components defined in the previous section. The following four components are example independent. The examples given for these could be relevant to any application area.

2.   ASSIGNMENT TYPE

4.   DATA TYPE

10.   CONSTRAINT TYPE

16.   DISPLAY OPTION

The examples are based on the same inventory control application as used for the business analysis stage. The sequence is the same as for the component description.

Figure 5.2 illustrates a data structure diagram of the same kind as used to indicate the interrelationships among components. It shows only the ten TABLES and the ten referential CONSTRAINTS.

5.5.1 TABLE

The following table gives a list of ten TABLES. Each is given a number for future reference.

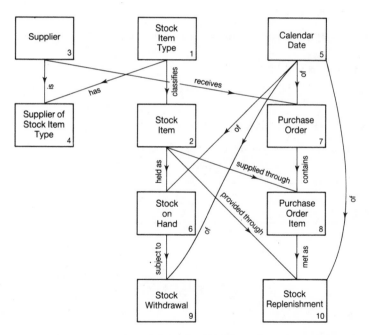

Figure 5.2 Inventory control example. The figure is used to illustrate various components. Tables are shown as rectangles and referential CONSTRAINTS as arrowed lines. The referential CONSTRAINT is expressed on COLUMNS in the TABLE to which the arrow is pointing. Since the names of the components are designated in upper case (for example, TABLE), the names of instances of components are shown using initial capitals only.

Table Number	Table Name
1	Stock Item Type
2	Stock Item
3	Supplier
4	Supplier of Stock Item Type
5	Calendar Date
6	Stock on Hand
7	Purchase Order
8	Purchase Order Item
9	Stock Withdrawal
10	Stock Replenishment

It should be noted that the designer has chosen to make some changes to the results of the business analysis stage (see Figure 4.2). These will be clarified further in subsequent components.

5.5.2 ASSIGNMENT TYPE

The following codes are used in the next component:

1. One ENTITY TYPE to one TABLE
2. One ENTITY TYPE to two or more TABLES

5.5.3 ENTITY TYPE TO TABLE ASSIGNMENT

This component is illustrated in the form of a cross-reference table:

Entity Type Code	Table Number									
	1	2	3	4	5	6	7	8	9	10
ET1			1							
ET2		1								
ET3	1									
ET4					1					
ET5							1			
ET6								1		
ET7						1				
ET8										

It should be noted that this example indicates that the designer has decided not to include one of the analyst's ENTITY TYPES, namely ET8 which was Supplier of Stock Item (possibly on the basis that it is impossible to keep such information up-to-date). The designer has included three TABLES not resulting from the business analysis as follows:

4.   Supplier of Stock Item Type
9.   Stock Withdrawal
10. Stock Replenishment

5.5.4 DATA TYPE

The following codes are used to illustrate the next component:

C   Character
D   Date
N   Numeric

5.5.5 COLUMN NAME

The following list of COLUMN NAMES consists of ATTRIBUTE NAMES from Section 4.6.8 plus others necessitated by the introduction of the three TABLES which do not derive from the results of the business analysis stage:

- Stock Code
- Stock Item Name
- Delivery
- Issue
- Price
- Supplier Number
- Supplier Name
- Stock Item Type Code
- Stock Item Type Description
- Date of Purchase
- Date of Delivery
- Date of Withdrawal
- Purchase Order Number
- Purchase Order Item Number
- Quantity of Stock
- Date

5.5.6 COLUMN

Each COLUMN must belong to a TABLE. This means that each of the above COLUMN NAMES should be assignable to one of the ten TABLES already identified. It may transpire that some of these COLUMN NAMES cannot be assigned to a TABLE. The following cross-reference table indicates the initial assignments:

Column Name	1	2	3	4	5	6	7	8	9	10
				Table Number						
Stock Code		X				X		X	X	X
Stock Item Name		X								
Delivery										X
Issue									X	
Price								X		
Supplier Number			X	X			X			
Supplier Name			X							
Stock Item Type Code	X	X		X						
Stock Item Type Description	X									
Date of Purchase							X			
Date of Delivery										X
Date of Withdrawal									X	
Purchase Order Number							X	X		
Purchase Order Item Number								X		
Quantity of Stock						X		X	X	X
Date					X	X				

5.5.7   ATTRIBUTE TO COLUMN ASSIGNMENT

The 20 ATTRIBUTES identified by an 'X' in the cross-reference table in Section 4.6.9 may be cross-referenced to the 29 COLUMNS shown in the cross-reference table in Section 5.5.6.

It can be seen from the cross-reference table in Section 5.5.6 that eight of the nine extra COLUMNS are necessary because of the two extra TABLES which have been added for design purposes. These two TABLES are:

9   Stock Withdrawal

10   Stock Replenishment

The COLUMN Quantity of Stock has also been added to the TABLE:

6   Stock on Hand

8   Purchase Order Item

making two extra COLUMNS.

A new COLUMN called Price has been added to the TABLE 8, Purchase Order Item. The business analysis stage shows Price as an ATTRIBUTE of the ENTITY TYPE ET8, Supplier Stock Item.

The ATTRIBUTES of ENTITY TYPE ET4, namely Calendar Date in Section 4.6.9, have been combined into one COLUMN in the TABLE Calendar Date in Section 5.5.6.

The replacement of ENTITY TYPE ET8, Supplier Stock Item by TABLE 4, Supplier of Stock Item Type means that one ATTRIBUTE, namely Stock Code, of ENTITY TYPE ET8, is replaced by one COLUMN, namely Stock Item Type Code while Price is omitted. The net increase in the number of COLUMNS over the corresponding ATTRIBUTES is hence nine.

Preparation of the full cross-reference table for a large application is usually difficult because of the size involved. However, a check of the kind indicated in this section serves to give an audit trail.

5.5.8 COLUMN GROUP

The need for COLUMN GROUPS is based on the requirement to be able to specify the CONSTRAINTS which are to be imposed on the values in the COLUMNS.

The first COLUMN GROUP consists of the following two COLUMNS:

- Purchase Order Number
- Purchase Order Item Number

These two will be necessary to identify each occurrence of a Purchase Order Item.

The second COLUMN GROUP consists of the following two COLUMNS:

- Supplier Number
- Stock Item Type Code

These two COLUMNS will be necessary to identify each entry in the cross-reference table Supplier of Stock Item.

The third COLUMN GROUP consists of the following two COLUMNS:

- Stock Code
- Stocktaking Date

These two COLUMNS identify the level of a Stock Item on a given DATE.

5.5.9 COLUMN IN GROUP

This example uses three COLUMN GROUPS, each of which contains two COLUMNS, as illustrated in the preceding section. In a more comprehensive application, in which many COLUMN GROUPS would be needed, and in which it may be necessary for a COLUMN of a TABLE to belong to more than one COLUMN GROUP of that TABLE, a cross-reference table may be useful.

5.5.10 CONSTRAINT TYPE

There are four CONSTRAINT TYPES identified in Section 5.4.10. The example illustrates uniqueness CONSTRAINTS and referential CONSTRAINTS in the next section.

5.5.11 CONSTRAINT

There should be at least one uniqueness CONSTRAINT defined for each of the ten TABLES. Each such CONSTRAINT is expressed either for a single COLUMN or for a COLUMN GROUP of that TABLE. The uniqueness CONSTRAINTS for the ten TABLES are as follows:

Table Name	Column Name	Constraint Type
Stock Item Type	Stock Item Type Code	U
Stock Item	Stock Item Code	U
Supplier	Supplier Number	U
Supplier of Stock Item Type	Supplier number Stock Item Type Code	U
Calendar Date	Date	U
Stock on Hand	Stock Item Code Stocktaking Date	U
Purchase Order	Purchase Order Number	U
Purchase Order Item	Purchase Order Number Purchase Order Item Number	U
Stock Withdrawal	Stock Item Code Date of Withdrawal Withdrawal Number	U
Stock Replenishment	Stock Item Code Date of Delivery Replenishment Number	U

Each of the 14 arrows depicted in Figure 5.2 represents a referential CONSTRAINT. Each of these represents a CONSTRAINT on the values of one or more COLUMNS in one of the TABLES.

These COLUMNS to which the CONSTRAINTS apply are always 'matchable' with the values of COLUMNS in the other TABLE at the tail of the arrow. The following table indicates the TABLE and the constrained COLUMNS for each of the 14 CONSTRAINTS:

Table Number	Constraint Type	Column Name	Referred Table Number	Column Name
2	R	Stock Item Type Code	1	Stock Item Type Code
4	R	Supplier Number	3	Supplier Number
4	R	Stock Item Type Code	1	Stock Item Type Code
6	R	Stock Item Code	2	Stock Item Code
6	R	Stocktaking Date	5	Date
7	R	Supplier Number	3	Supplier Number
7	R	Date of Purchase	5	Date
8	R	Purchase Order Number	7	Purchase Order Number
8	R	Stock Item Code	2	Stock Item Code
9	R	Date of Withdrawal	5	Date
9	R	Stock Item Code	2	Stock Item Code
10	R	Date of Delivery	5	Date
10	R	Stock Item Code	2	Stock Item Code
10	R	Purchase Order Number	8	Purchase Order Number
		Purchase Order Item Number	8	Purchase Order Item Number

It should be noted that the first 13 of the above list of referential CONSTRAINTS are based on individual COLUMNS. The last one is based on a COLUMN GROUP. All 14 referential CONSTRAINTS are based on value equality. It would also be possible to add one or more extra columns to the above table in which to record various kinds of cardinality, most typically the maximum permitted. For example, there might be only ten Purchase Order Items allowed on any Purchase Order. This would constrain the number of Purchase Order Numbers in TABLE 8 which are equal to any given number in TABLE 7.

As an example, the CONSTRAINT on TABLE 8 (Purchase Order Item) implies that the value in the COLUMN called Purchase Order Number in the TABLE Purchase Order Item must correspond to an extant value in the COLUMN also called Purchase Order Item, but in TABLE 7 (Purchase Order).

It should also be noted that there are no referential CONSTRAINTS on TABLES 1, 3 and 5. It will be seen in Figure 5.2 that these three TABLES, namely:

1.   Stock Item Type
3.   Supplier
5.   Calendar Date

are not dependent on any other TABLES.

5.5.12   RELATIONSHIP TO CONSTRAINT ASSIGNMENT

The following table shows which of the 14 referential CONSTRAINTS listed in Section 5.5.11 are relatable to the nine RELATIONSHIPS identified in Section 4.6.6:

Table Number	Column Name	Referred Table Number	Column Name	Relationship Number
2	Stock Item Type Code	1	Stock Item Type Code	1
4	Supplier Number	3	Supplier Number	
4	Stock Item Type Code	1	Stock Item Type Code	
6	Stock Item Code	2	Stock Item Code	7
6	Stocktaking Date	5	Date	4
7	Supplier Number	3	Supplier Number	6
7	Date of Purchase	5	Date	3
8	Purchase Order Number	7	Purchase Order Number	2
8	Stock Item Code	2	Stock Item Code	5
9	Date of Withdrawal	5	Date	—
9	Stock Item Code	2	Stock Item Code	—
10	Date of Delivery	5	Date	—
10	Stock Item Code	2	Stock Item Code	
10	Purchase Order Number	8	Purchase Order Number	—
	Purchase Order Line Number	8	Purchase Order Line Number	

It should be noted that two of the RELATIONSHIPS, namely numbers 8 and 9, have not been represented as referential CONSTRAINTS in the design.

This is due to the introduction of the new TABLE called Supplier of Stock Item Type. Seven of the 14 CONSTRAINTS can be related to RELATIONSHIPS while the other seven cannot.

5.5.13   ROW

Of the ten TABLES listed in Section 5.5.1, none would require the content of any of the ROWS to be prescribed by the designer.

5.5.14   EXTERNAL FORM

One example of an EXTERNAL FORM for inventory control is a Purchase Order. This would consist of information extracted from the following four TABLES:

- Supplier
- Purchase Order
- Stock Item
- Purchase Order Item

This EXTERNAL FORM would be designed for printing in hard copy but it would also need to be displayed on a screen on demand.

Another example of an EXTERNAL FORM is a Stock Breakdown which would give a list of all the Stock Items of a selected Stock Item Type. This would need to be designed as a screen display format.

5.5.15   EXTERNAL FORM ELEMENT

The following is a set of possible elements on a printed Purchase Order form:

1. heading line
2. footing line
3. item line
4. column heading.

The first two of these EXTERNAL FORM ELEMENTS would be repeating lines, of which zero, one or more would be defined for each form. An item line would be a variable, possibly repeating, such that each line on the same form showed a different value. A column heading would be a partial line, and there may be several column headings on a single line of each form.

5.5.16   DISPLAY OPTION

The alternative DISPLAY OPTIONS are independent of any specific example. The following examples are related to printing and are used to illustrate the possibilities:

1.   bold print
2.   expanded print
3.   compressed print.

   Other examples which are related to screen displays are:

4.   normal
5.   reverse video
6.   flashing.

5.5.17   COLUMN ON FORM ELEMENT

The following cross-reference table indicates which of the COLUMNS listed in Section 5.5.6 are used in an EXTERNAL FORM and in which of the four ways each COLUMN is used.

| Column Name | External Form Element | | | |
	1	*2*	*3*	*4*
Stock Code			Y	Y
Stock Item Name			Y	Y
Delivery				
Issue				
Price			Y	Y
Supplier Number				
Supplier Name	Y			
Stock Item Type Code			Y	Y
Stock Item Type Description			Y	Y
Date of Purchase				
Date of Delivery			Y	Y
Date of Withdrawal				
Purchase Order Number			Y	Y
Purchase Order Item Number			Y	Y
Quantity of Stock			Y	Y
Date				

   This cross-reference table shows that the Supplier Name is to be included in the heading for the EXTERNAL FORM, that no COLUMN NAME is included in the footing, and that nine of the sixteen possible designated COLUMNS are included in the body of the EXTERNAL FORM, both as column headings and as values.

5.6 Components of system design — process perspective

The components of the system design stage which belong to the process oriented perspective are as follows:

*1. ON LINE OR BATCH

*2. TASK CATEGORY

*3. HOMING IN OR OUT-OF-THE-BLUE

*4. MENU-DRIVEN OR FAST TRACK

*5. INITIATION MEANS

6. TASK

7. MENU

8. MENU HIERARCHY

9. TASK IN MENU

10. ACCESS CONTROL CLASS

11. TASK IN ACCESS CONTROL CLASS

*12. TASK TO TASK INITIATION TYPE

13. TASK TO TASK INITIATION

Components preceded by an asterisk are methodology dependent.

Figure 5.3 shows the interrelationships among the 13 components. It also includes the component BUSINESS ACTIVITY from the business analysis stage process perspective, in order to illustrate the relationship between the system design components and the business analysis components.

The first five components in the above list each provide a way of categorizing a TASK. It is intended that these five ways are mutually exclusive. Most, but not all, combinations of the alternatives are meaningful. For example, the combination of batch and fast track is not meaningful.

5.6.1 ON LINE OR BATCH

This component provides a categorization scheme which may be used to classify each TASK in terms of its urgency when initiated. The component is hence peculiar to the design process rather than to the use of it. The following list of alternatives is not intended to be exhaustive:

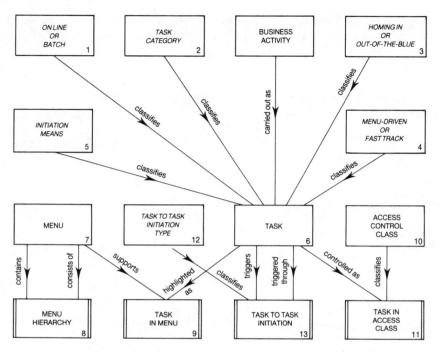

Figure 5.3   System design stage – process perspective and cross-reference.

1.   On line interactive, immediate response needed at place of initiation.
2.   Initiated on line, no immediate urgency in response needed.
3.   Initiated from batch job stream for background processing.

Others may be added.

5.6.2   TASK CATEGORY

This component provides a categorization scheme which may be used to classify each TASK in terms of the kind of processing to be performed on the TABLES that will be accessed when the TASK is initiated. The component can be used to provide a coarse categorization of the TASK as a whole. A more detailed categorization of the kind of processing to be performed on each TABLE processed by the TASK is covered under the cross-reference components.

One categorization of TASKS has the following two alternatives:

1.   retrieval
2.   update.

It is assumed that an update TASK would normally need to retrieve data from the TABLES being updated.

Alternatively, the categorization of updating could be broken down more finely as follows:

1.   add one or more rows to a table
2.   modify one or more rows in a table
3.   delete one or more rows from a table.

The processing of each specific TABLE processed by a TASK is discussed in the section on cross-references.

5.6.3   HOMING IN OR OUT-OF-THE-BLUE

This categorization focuses on the information that the user at the terminal has to have available at the time that he or she initiates the TASK. In some cases, the user may have the value of an important identifier (such as a Customer Number), which will enable the system to access a row in a specific TABLE (such as a Customer table) and to display the content of that row at the terminal. This means that the TASK is an 'out-of-the-blue' TASK which requires the system to make an 'out-of-the-blue' access to data in the database.

Other TASKS assume that the user needs to be able to 'home in' on the information required by entering a series of prompts in response to displayed data screens. Such a TASK would be categorized as a 'homing in' TASK.

Other alternatives, such as browsing, may be possible.

5.6.4   MENU-DRIVEN OR FAST TRACK

This component provides a categorization scheme which may be used to classify each TASK in terms of the way in which a user at a terminal is expected to want to initiate the TASK. Three alternatives are possible.

The first alternative is that the user will be prepared to pick out the TASK by going through a set of MENUS containing the TASKS which he or she is authorized to initiate.

The second alternative is that some users use the TASK with considerable regularity and hence should not be expected to browse through a set of MENUS each time they wish to initiate the TASK. This means that they need a 'fast track' to initiating the TASK. This could be by entering a TASK identification or by hitting a special key at the terminal.

A third alternative is that some users will need to do a menu search to pick out a TASK, while others require fast track facilities.

5.6.5 INITIATION MEANS

There are several ways in which a TASK can be initiated independently of any
other TASK. The following list identifies four alternatives:

1.   person entering a prompt at a terminal,
2.   calendar clock setting,
3.   condition on data values being satisfied, and
4.   real time interrupt from external source.

The different ways in which a TASK can be initiated by another TASK are
covered later in this section.

5.6.6 TASK

The TASK component is central to the process perspective of the system design
stage. A TASK is a piece of work, performable by the system being designed,
which is meaningful to some or all of the users of the information system. A
TASK is not a 'construction block' such as an application program or the
equivalent in terms of facilities available in construction tools, such as
'fourth generation languages'. The word TASK is used here in the sense of a
prescribable type and not in the sense of an executing instance.

Each TASK should be relatable to one BUSINESS ACTIVITY derived in the
business analysis stage, in the sense that the TASK is intended to support the
performance of that BUSINESS ACTIVITY.

The business analysis stage provides for a hierarchical decomposition
of BUSINESS ACTIVITIES. This decomposition may be achieved in several
ways, one of which might mean that the BUSINESS ACTIVITIES on the lowest
level of decomposition are equivalent to those TASKS which need to be
identified in the system design stage.

However, the hierarchical decomposition of BUSINESS ACTIVITIES may
also be carried out in such a way that the individual TASKS cannot relate to the
lowest level of BUSINESS ACTIVITIES, because some of the TASKS can be seen
to support more than one bottom level BUSINESS ACTIVITY.

Another class of approaches to TASK definition is based on the TABLES
which have been identified as a data oriented component of the system design
stage. One member of this class would generate the TASKS from the data by
requiring update TASKS to add, modify and delete rows from each table. In
addition, one or more retrieval TASKS would be required to retrieve rows
from each TABLE according to various criteria.

Some approaches to TASK definition rely on utilizing both BUSINESS
ACTIVITY information and TABLE information, in order to determine which
TABLES are input to certain TASKS and which TABLES are output from certain
TASKS.

A design problem with the definition of TASKS is the granularity. Some methodologies indicate an approach leading to many small TASKS and others lead to fewer more encompassing TASKS. The approach to be taken may be influenced by the construction tool to be used, if this is already known when work on the system design stage is in progress.

Irrespective of the way in which the TASKS may be identified, it is also possible to categorize each TASK in various ways. The preceding five components have attempted to indicate five ways of doing so.

5.6.7 MENU

A MENU is a list of TASKS or a list of other MENUS. In a large system, there may be three or four levels of MENU (or even more) with the TASKS on the lowest level.

MENUS are prevalent in modern computerized information systems. There are, however, different ways of designing the configuration of MENUS and TASKS. In some approaches MENUS for TASK selection need to be 'gone through' prior to the handling of a TASK. In other approaches, MENUS of TASKS can be included in the data screens which are displayed in the middle of a TASK.

5.6.8 MENU HIERARCHY

This component is included to allow for a hierarchical structure of MENUS such that one MENU can be accessed from another. The structure in Figure 5.3, in fact, allows for a network of MENUS such that any MENU can be accessed from one or more other MENUS and the subject MENU can, in turn, provide access to one or more other MENUS. Even cyclic MENU structures are possible.

5.6.9 TASK IN MENU

This component is a cross-reference component between TASKS and MENUS. A MENU contains zero, one or more TASKS and each TASK may be included on zero, one or more MENUS.

5.6.10 ACCESS CONTROL CLASS

This component allows the designer to group TASKS together for the purpose of access control (or security). In a system with a fairly large number of TASKS, the designer may wish to identify groups of several TASKS, all of which require a user to have the same authority to initiate them.

The designer may designate mutually exclusive ACCESS CONTROL CLASSES, such that each TASK is in only one ACCESS CONTROL CLASS. Alternatively, he or she may find it convenient to designate partially overlapping ACCESS CONTROL CLASSES or a hierarchy of classes such that each class is completely contained in a higher class.

5.6.11 TASK IN ACCESS CONTROL CLASS

This component is a cross-reference which indicates which TASK is in which ACCESS CONTROL CLASS and vice versa.

5.6.12 TASK TO TASK INITIATION TYPE

This framework prescribed component categorizes the different ways in which TASKS can be interrelated with other TASKS. Some possible alternatives are:

1. TASK A automatically initiates TASK B on completion.
2. TASK A conditionally initiates TASK B.
3. Successful completion of TASK A is necessary to enable initiation of TASK B.

5.6.13 TASK TO TASK INITIATION

This component is used to indicate the possible associations between different TASKS. An executing instance of one TASK can trigger the initiation of another, separately identified, TASK which could itself be initiated independently in the same way as the first TASK.

5.7 Examples of system design components from the process perspective

The following sections give examples, based on the inventory control application, for the 13 components defined in the previous section. The six methodology dependent components are as follows:

1. ON LINE OR BATCH
2. TASK CATEGORY
3. HOMING IN OR OUT-OF-THE-BLUE
4. MENU-DRIVEN OR FAST TRACK
5. INITIATION MEANS
12. TASK TO TASK INITIATION TYPE

These would always need to be prescribed for a given design process and could then be used with any application. In order to illustrate the TASK component, a set of alternatives is shown for each of these components. These alternatives are illustrative only.

5.7.1 ON LINE OR BATCH

L   On line

B   Batch

5.7.2 TASK CATEGORY

R   Retrieval

U   Update

5.7.3 HOMING IN OR OUT-OF-THE-BLUE

H   Homing in

O   Out-of-the-blue

N   Neither

5.7.4 MENU-DRIVEN OR FAST TRACK

M   Menu-driven

F   Fast track

B   Both menu-driven and fast track

5.7.5 INITIATION MEANS

P   Person at terminal

C   Calendar clock

V   Value related condition

R   Real time interrupt

5.7.6 TASK

The following TASKS are identified for each of the lowest level BUSINESS ACTIVITIES listed in Section 4.8.1. The five categorizations for each TASK are as defined in the previous five subsections.

Each TASK is given a number which is an extension of that assigned in Section 4.8.1 to the BUSINESS ACTIVITY. Each TASK is then related to one and only one of these BUSINESS ACTIVITIES. The coded categorizations for each TASK are given after the TASK description, in the sequence in which the five codes are presented above. The number and name of each BUSINESS ACTIVITY is also included for clarity.

Task Code	Description		Task Categorization
1.1.1	Categorization of new stock items		
	Task 1.1.1.1	Create new stock item type	LUHMP
	Task 1.1.1.2	Display available stock item types	LRHMP
	Task 1.1.1.3	Create new stock item	LUHMP
1.1.2	Registration of alternative supplier		
	Task 1.1.2.1	Produce list of suppliers	BRNMP
	Task 1.1.2.2	Create new supplier	LANMP
1.2.1	Select supplier		
	Task 1.2.1.1	Produce list of suppliers of a given stock item	LRHMP
1.2.2	Send purchase order		
	Task 1.2.2.1	Prepare a purchase order	LANFV
	Task 1.2.2.2	Display completed purchase order to a given supplier	LRHFP
	Task 1.2.2.3	Print out day's purchase orders	BRNMP
1.3	Monitoring stock levels		
	Task 1.3.1	Display stock on hand for given stock item	LROFP
	Task 1.3.2	List stock items below reorder level	BRNMP
	Task 1.3.3	Display stock on hand for all stock items of a given type	LRNMP

It should be noted that this list of TASKS should be extended to handle the extension in terms of extra TABLES made from the results of the business analysis stage (see Section 5.5.3). The above list could also be illustrated in tabular form, as was done with the components in the data perspective. It should be noted that all of the TASKS except one have an INITIATION MEANS of P.

5.7.7   MENU

The 12 TASKS listed in the preceding section are not sufficient to illustrate more than three MENUS. The top level MENU might appear as follows:

TOP LEVEL MENU

---

1. Change static data in system
2. Day-to-day operations

The two second level MENUS would then contain the TASKS assigned to each of these two lines on the top level MENU.

MENU FOR CHANGING STATIC DATA IN SYSTEM

---

1. Create new stock item type
2. Create new stock item
3. Create new supplier

MENU FOR DAY-TO-DAY OPERATIONS

---

1. Display available stock item types
2. Produce list of suppliers
3. Produce list of suppliers of a given stock item
4. Prepare a purchase order
5. Display completed purchase order to a given supplier
6. Print out day's purchase orders
7. Display stock on hand for given stock item
8. List stock items below reorder level
9. Display stock on hand for all stock items of a given type

5.7.8 MENU HIERARCHY

This component can be illustrated in two ways. The first is as a normal table:

Calling Menu	*Called Menu*
Top	1
Top	2

The second is as a cross-reference table:

Calling Menu	*Top*	*1*	*2*
Called Menu			
Top		Y	Y
1			
2			

This presentation gives a clearer picture and is more effective for more complex menu structures.

5.7.9   TASK IN MENU

This cross-reference between TASK and MENU is illustrated in the following table:

Task	Menu		
	Top	1	2
1.1.1.1		Y	
1.1.1.2			Y
1.1.1.3		Y	
1.1.2.1			Y
1.1.2.2		Y	
1.2.1.1			Y
1.2.2.1			Y
1.2.2.2			Y
1.2.2.3			Y
1.3.1			Y
1.3.2			Y
1.3.3			Y

In this example, each TASK is assigned to only one MENU. It can be seen from the previous component that these MENUS (1 and 2) are both 'bottom level' MENUS. Other ways of designing MENUS and assigning TASKS to MENUS can also be represented using the components MENU, MENU HIERARCHY and TASK IN MENU.

5.7.10   ACCESS CONTROL CLASS

As an illustration of this component, it is proposed to allow four partially overlapping ACCESS CONTROL CLASSES. In order to give these some meaning, the following list indicates the kinds of individual who would be allowed to initiate the TASKS in each of the classes.

A   Data administrator

B   Purchasing manager

C   Purchasing department clerks

D   Warehouse personnel

In a more complex example, the design of the ACCESS CONTROL CLASSES would be more involved.

5.7.11   TASK IN ACCESS CONTROL CLASS

This is a cross-reference component which indicates the assignment of TASKS to ACCESS CONTROL CLASSES. The assignment of the 12 TASKS in the example to the four ACCESS CONTROL CLASSES is indicated in the following cross-reference table:

Task	Access Control Class			
	A	B	C	D
1.1.1.1	Y			
1.1.1.2			Y	Y
1.1.1.3		Y		
1.1.2.1		Y	Y	
1.1.2.2		Y		
1.2.1.1		Y	Y	
1.2.2.1			Y	
1.2.2.2			Y	
1.2.2.3			Y	
1.3.1		Y	Y	Y
1.3.2			Y	Y
1.3.3			Y	Y

This shows that each TASK is assigned to one, two or three ACCESS CONTROL CLASSES.

5.7.12   TASK TO TASK INITIATION TYPE

A   TASK A automatically initiates TASK B on completion

C   TASK A conditionally initiates TASK B

S   Successful completion of TASK A is necessary to enable initiation of TASK B.

5.7.13   TASK TO TASK INITIATION

The following table is not intended to be exhaustive but attempts to illustrate some examples of this component:

Initiating Task	Initiated Task	Initiation Type
1.1.1.1	1.1.2.1	S
1.1.1.3	1.3.1	S

5.8   Components of system design — cross-references between data and process perspectives

In the system design stage, the interaction between the data and the processes to be performed on the data is of paramount importance. For this reason, the components which represent the cross-references between the two are presented here.

The components are identified as follows:

*1.   ACCESS PATH NODE TYPE

*2.   TASK DATA USAGE TYPE

3.   TASK USES TABLE

4.   TASK USES COLUMN

5.   ALGORITHM

6.   ALGORITHM REFERENCES COLUMN

7.   TASK USES ALGORITHM

*8.   FORM USAGE CLASS

9.   TASK USES EXTERNAL FORM

Components preceded by an asterisk are methodology dependent.

Figure 5.4 includes the following components from the data and process perspectives, in order to clarify the cross-reference components:

- TABLE
- COLUMN
- EXTERNAL FORM
- TASK.

5.8.1   ACCESS PATH NODE TYPE

Every TASK will need to be able to access one or more TABLES when it is initiated. At the most basic level, it is useful to identify which TABLES are accessed by a given TASK. Going somewhat further, it is also possible to indicate whether the TABLE is accessed by the TASK for update or for retrieval (see Section 5.6.2). This categorization can be handled using the component TASK CATEGORY from the process oriented perspective.

With a more complete approach to system design, the concept of an 'access path' (or information path) for each TASK can be designated by defining and using appropriate ACCESS PATH NODE TYPE alternatives to classify each TABLE used by a TASK.

An 'access path' is a set of one or more TABLES which are accessed in a given sequence by a TASK. Each TABLE along the access path for a TASK plays

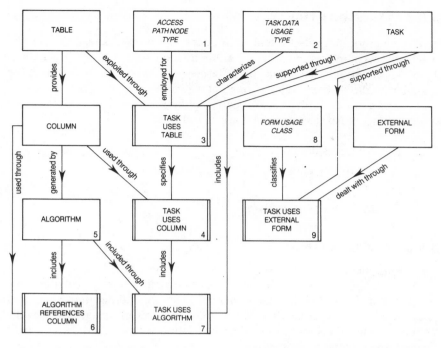

Figure 5.4 System design stage – cross-references between data and process.

a given type of role, with respect to the access path. The types of role are identified in this component ACCESS PATH NODE TYPE.

It can be seen that there are many different ACCESS PATH NODE TYPES. The following list gives some possibilities but these should not be regarded as exhaustive. A code value for each alternative is introduced and these codes will be used subsequently in the examples.

     S   Starting point

     P   Intermediate point along straight path

     I   Inflection point

     T   Target point

Other alternatives are possible. An access path must have at least one starting point and at least one target. However, if the path consists of only one TABLE, that TABLE should be classed as a starting point. There will need to be at least three TABLES for any of them to be classed as an intermediate point or as an inflection point.

5.8.2   TASK DATA USAGE TYPE

This is a methodology dependent component. It is used to categorize the way in which a TASK makes use of data – either a TABLE or a COLUMN in a TABLE. The categorization scheme may be different for each case. For example, the designer might wish to make a rough categorization of how a TASK uses a TABLE and a more detailed categorization of how a TASK uses a COLUMN in a TABLE. Some illustrative examples are as follows:

R   Retrieves data
A   Adds new data
D   Deletes data
M   Modifies existing data

5.8.3   TASK USES TABLE

This component is a cross-reference between TASK and TABLE, with each cross-reference categorized in two ways. The first is in terms of the TASK DATA USAGE TYPE. This indicates whether the TASK updates the TABLE (and possibly how) or whether the TASK merely retrieves information from the TABLE. The second is in terms of the role of the TABLE along the access path through the database.

It should be recalled that the component TABLE is intended to cover the concept of conventional sequential files, as might be processed in a conventional COBOL program. The design of conventional systems can be represented by an appropriate interpretation of ACCESS PATH NODE TYPE as a way of categorizing the way a TASK uses such a file.

5.8.4   TASK USES COLUMN

This component is a cross-reference between TASK and COLUMN, with each cross-reference categorized in one way. This categorization is in terms of the TASK DATA USAGE TYPE. This indicates whether the TASK updates the COLUMN in a TABLE (and possibly how) or whether the TASK merely retrieves information from the COLUMN.

When the cross-reference between TASKS and COLUMNS is used as well as that between TASKS and TABLES, then the two cross-references would need to be consistent with each other.

5.8.5   ALGORITHM

An ALGORITHM is a computational procedure, using numeric or non-numeric values recorded in one or more COLUMNS in one or more TABLES, to generate a further value to be recorded in a specific COLUMN in a specific TABLE.

5.8.6 ALGORITHM REFERENCES COLUMN

Each ALGORITHM may reference one or more COLUMNS in the same or different TABLES as the quantity being calculated. This component allows for the cross-referencing between ALGORITHM and COLUMN.

5.8.7 TASK USES ALGORITHM

A TASK may use one or more ALGORITHMS to generate the content of a COLUMN. The same ALGORITHM may be used by more than one TASK.

5.8.8 FORM USAGE CLASS

This component is used to categorize the possible ways in which a TASK makes use of an EXTERNAL FORM. The following list shows three possible alternatives:

1. input to task
2. output from task
3. input and output.

5.8.9 TASK USES EXTERNAL FORM

This cross-reference shows which EXTERNAL FORMS (if any) are used by a given TASK and which TASK or TASKS use each external form. The way that the TASK uses the EXTERNAL FORM is categorized in terms of the FORM USAGE TYPE.

5.9 Examples of system design components for the data and process perspectives

This section gives examples of the components defined in the previous section. Of the nine components, three are methodology dependent. The other six are specific to the example of inventory control used throughout this chapter. These six components are as follows:

3. TASK USES TABLE
4. TASK USES COLUMN
5. ALGORITHM
6. ALGORITHM REFERENCES COLUMN
7. TASK USES ALGORITHM
9. TASK USES EXTERNAL FORM

5.9.1   ACCESS PATH NODE TYPE

This component is methodology dependent.

Node Type Code	Description
S	Starting point
P	Intermediate point along straight path
T	Target point

The inflection point option has been deliberately omitted in this example.

5.9.2   TASK DATA USAGE TYPE

This component is methodology dependent.

Date Usage Type	Description
R	Retrieves data
A	Adds new data
D	Deletes data
M	Modifies existing data

5.9.3   TASK USES TABLE

In order to illustrate this component, the set of ten TABLES from Section 5.5.1 is used. It should be recalled that the TASKS identified in Section 5.7.6 were derived from the BUSINESS ACTIVITIES and not from the data. It was pointed out in Section 5.6.6 that there were different approaches to deriving the TASKS, one of which called for identifying the TASKS in terms of the TABLES. This approach will be used in the examples here. The table on page 161 shows the TASKS that are needed for each of the ten TABLES.

The table representing this component identifies 25 different TASKS. It should be noted that Purchase Order and Purchase Order Item are processed by the same TASKS on the basis that every Purchase Order is required to have at least one Purchase Order Item. It is not meaningful to add a Purchase Order without adding at least one Purchase Order Item. Furthermore, any retrieval TASK which accesses one of these two TABLES will also access the other.

It is also possible to categorize each of these 25 TASKS in the same way as the 12 TASKS in the example in Section 5.7.6.

The table on page 162 illustrates the component TASK USES TABLE with the categorization of each TABLE used by a TASK in terms of its ACCESS PATH NODE TYPE.

Table Number	Description	Data Usage Type			
		Add	*Delete*	*Modify*	*Retrieve*
1	Stock Item Type	1		2	3
2	Stock Item	4		5	6
3	Supplier	7		8	9
4	Supplier of Stock Item				
	Type	10			11, 12
5	Date	13			
6	Stock on Hand	14		15	16, 17
7	Purchase Order	18, 19			20, 21
8	Purchase Order Item	19			20, 21
9	Stock Withdrawal	22			23
10	Stock Replenishment	24			25

The codes used in this cross-reference table are as given in Sections 5.9.1 and 5.9.2. These indicate, respectively, the ACCESS PATH NODE TYPE and the TASK DATA USAGE TYPE.

This table provides a compact and highly codified definition of the access paths to be used by the 25 TASKS. It shows which TABLES each TASK needs to access. The sequence is defined in terms of the starting points and end point (target) for each access path.

As a simple example, TASK 5 accesses two TABLES, namely Stock Item Type and Stock Item. The TASK uses Stock Item Type as a starting point and Stock Item as a target. It retrieves data from Stock Item Type and then modifies Stock Item.

As a more complex example, TASK 14 can be described in detail. It accesses the following four TABLES:

Starting points:	Date, Stock Item Type
Intermediate point:	Stock Item
Target point:	Stock on Hand.

This TASK homes in on a Stock Item from a Stock Item Type. The terminal user specifies a Date (or the system takes the date from the calendar clock). The Stock on Hand is then updated.

These examples do not cover all the aspects of the design of TASKS. Some TASKS, such as 21 and 23, will need to perform numeric computation in order to modify the content of a TABLE.

5.9.4 TASK USES COLUMN

For each of the 25 TASKS identified in the previous section, the table on pages 164–5 indicates which COLUMNS in each TABLE are used when that TASK is performed and the TASK DATA USAGE TYPE for each case.

Table Name	Task	Stock Item Type	Stock Item	Supplier	Supplier of Stock Item Type	Date	Stock on Hand	Purchase Order	Purchase Order Item	Stock Withdrawal	Stock Replenishment
Stock Item Type	1	AS									
	2	MS									
	3	RS									
Stock Item	4	RS	AT								
	5	RS	MT								
	6		RS								
Supplier	7			AS							
	8			MS							
	9			RS							
Supplier of Stock Item Type	10	RS			AT						
	11	RS			RT						
	12		RS		RT						
Date	13					AS					
Stock on Hand	14	RS	RI			RS	AT				
	15	RS	RI			RS	MT				
	16	RS	RI			RS	RT				
	17		RS			RS	RT				
Purchase Order	18			RS		RS		AT	AT		
	19					RS		AT	AT		
	20							RS	RT		
	21					RS		RI	RT		
Purchase Order Item											
Stock Withdrawal	22	RS	RI			RS	MT			AT	
	23	RS	RI			RS	RI			RT	
Stock Replenishment	24	RS	RI			RS	MT				AT
	25	RS	RI			RS	RI				RT

5.9.5 ALGORITHM

It can be seen from the table for the preceding section that TASK 22 and TASK 24 cause a modification to the COLUMN called Quantity on Hand in the Stock on Hand TABLE. TASK 22 is performed to record the fact that stock has been withdrawn and TASK 24 is performed to indicate that stock has been replenished by the receipt of a delivery of stock ordered on a given Purchase Order.

The ALGORITHM identified as X and used by TASK 22 is as follows:

New Quantity on Hand in Stock on Hand = ·

        Old Quantity on Hand in Stock on Hand
   – Quantity Withdrawn in Stock Withdrawal

The ALGORITHM identified as Y and used by TASK 24 is as follows:

New Quantity on Hand in Stock on Hand =

        Old Quantity on Hand in Stock on Hand
   + Quantity Added in Stock Replenishment.

It is also possible to have ALGORITHMS which are used by several TASKS.

5.9.6 ALGORITHM REFERENCES COLUMN

Table Number	Column	Algorithm
6 (Stock on Hand)	Quantity of Stock	X
9 (Stock Withdrawal)	Quantity of Stock	X
6 (Stock on Hand)	Quantity of Stock	Y
10 (Stock Replenishment)	Quantity of Stock	Y

5.9.7 TASK USES ALGORITHM

Task	Algorithm
22	X
24	Y

5.9.8 FORM USAGE CLASS

This component is methodology dependent.

Task Number

Table Number	Table Name / Column Name	1	2	3	4	5	6	7	8	9	10	11	12	13	14	15	16	17	18	19	20	21	22	23	24	25
1	**Stock Item Type**																									
	Stock Item Type Code		A	R	R	R					R	R			R	R	R						R	R	R	R
	Stock Item Type Description		A	M	R	R					R	R			R	R	R						R	R	R	R
2	**Stock Item**																									
	Stock Item Type Code				A	R	R						R		R	R	R	R					R	R	R	R
	Stock Code				A	M	R						R		R	R	R	R					R	R	R	R
	Stock Item Name				A	M	R						R		R	R	R	R					R	R	R	R
3	**Supplier**																									
	Supplier Number							A	R	R																
	Supplier Name							A	M	R																
4	**Supplier of Stock Item Type**																									
	Stock Item Type Code										A	R	R													
	Supplier Number										A	R	R													
5	**Date**																									
	Calendar date													A	R	R	R			R		R				
6	**Stock on Hand**																									
	Stock Code														A	R	R	R					R	R	R	R
	Stocktaking Date														A	R	R	R					R	R	R	R
	Quantity of Stock														A	M	R	R					M	R	M	R

Task Number

Table Number	Table Name / Column Name	1	2	3	4	5	6	7	8	9	10	11	12	13	14	15	16	17	18	19	20	21	22	23	24	25
7	Purchase Order																									
	Purchase Order Number																			A	R	R				
	Date of Purchase																			A	R	R				
	Supplier Number																			A	R	R				
8	Purchase Order Item																									
	Purchase Order Number																			A	R	R				
	Purchase Order Item Number																			A	R	R				
	Stock Code																			A	R	R				
	Price																			A	R	R				
	Quantity Ordered																			A	R	R				
9	Stock Withdrawal																									
	Stock Code																					A	R			
	Withdrawal Date																						A	R		
	Quantity Withdrawn																						A	R		
10	Stock Replenishment																									
	Stock Code																								A	R
	Replenishment Date																								A	R
	Quantity Added																								A	R
	Purchase Order Number																								A	R
	Purchase Order Item Number																								A	R

1. input to task
2. output from task
3. input and output.

5.9.9 TASK USES EXTERNAL FORM

Two examples of an EXTERNAL FORM were described in Section 5.5.14. One of these was a Purchase Order form. This would be used as an output form from TASK 20.

5.10   Components of system design — behaviour perspective

This section covers not only the behaviour components, but also the cross-reference components between behaviour components and components already presented as part of the other two perspectives.

The nine components presented in this section are as follows:

1.   SYSTEM EVENT
*2.   TRIGGER CATEGORY
3.   BUSINESS EVENT TRIGGERS SYSTEM EVENT
4.   SYSTEM EVENT PRECEDENCE/SUCCEDENCE
5.   CONDITION
6.   CONDITION REFERENCES COLUMN
*7.   CONDITION ROLE
8.   CONDITION ROLE FOR SYSTEM EVENT
9.   SYSTEM EVENT TRIGGERS TASK

Components preceded by an asterisk are methodology dependent.

Figure 5.5 shows the interrelationships among the above nine components. In addition, four components from the data oriented perspective and the process oriented perspective are included in order to show the cross-references between the behaviour oriented components and components from other perspectives.

5.10.1 SYSTEM EVENT

A SYSTEM EVENT is prescribed by the designer to take place in the computerized system which is under design. A SYSTEM EVENT may be the result of an interaction between the computerized system and its users. However, it is important to distinguish between the interaction itself, which is here categorized as an invocation of a TASK and the effect or result, which is what is here categorized as a SYSTEM EVENT. A SYSTEM EVENT can also be

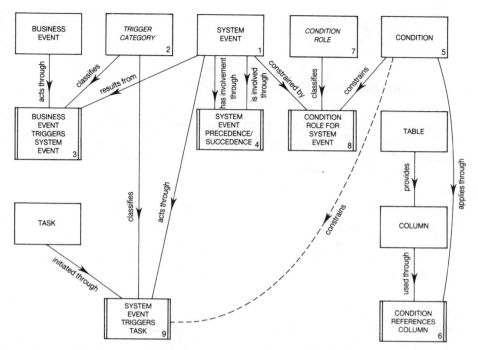

Figure 5.5 System design stage – behaviour perspective and cross-references to data and process perspectives.

dependent on the time as given by a calendar clock or it may occur when a particular state of the computerized system has been achieved. An example of the second possibility is that the numeric value stored in a COLUMN in a TABLE passes a prescribed value following the initiation of an updating TASK.

Another example of a SYSTEM EVENT is where a signal of a certain kind is received from a source external to the computerized system, which then triggers a TASK that would need to have been assigned the appropriate INITIATION MEANS (see Section 5.6.5).

When a SYSTEM EVENT occurs, it is usually necessary to initiate one or more TASKS.

5.10.2 TRIGGER CATEGORY

This methodology dependent component is used to categorize the different ways in which a BUSINESS EVENT, as recognized during the business analysis stage, can trigger a SYSTEM EVENT to take place while the computerized information system is in operation.

One possibility is that there is some kind of automated device used by the person or persons involved in the BUSINESS ACTIVITY which causes the BUSINESS EVENT to happen. When the BUSINESS EVENT occurs, the SYSTEM EVENT is then triggered.

Another possibility is that the nature of the BUSINESS ACTIVITY is such that the BUSINESS EVENT and the SYSTEM EVENT are essentially the same event.

5.10.3 BUSINESS EVENT TRIGGERS SYSTEM EVENT

This cross-reference component relates a BUSINESS EVENT from the business analysis stage with the SYSTEM EVENT in the system design stage.

A SYSTEM EVENT may or may not be triggered by a BUSINESS EVENT. If it is, then the way in which it is triggered could be categorized in terms of a prescribed TRIGGER CATEGORY.

5.10.4 SYSTEM EVENT PRECEDENCE/SUCCEDENCE

In some information systems with a large number of possible SYSTEM EVENTS, there may be constraints on the sequence in which they should be allowed to occur. Such constraints on the permitted sequence can be expressed as a network of SYSTEM EVENTS using this component.

5.10.5 CONDITION

This component is used to identify any CONDITIONS which are either necessary for a given SYSTEM EVENT to take place or which must hold after the SYSTEM EVENT has occurred. The former are usually called 'preconditions' and the latter are called 'postconditions'. It may be necessary to specify a triggering CONDITION to establish exactly the basis on which a SYSTEM EVENT may trigger a transition of the computerized information from one state to another. The SYSTEM EVENT PRECEDENCE/SUCCEDENCE determines the permitted ordering of such state transitions.

A CONDITION of either kind can be expressed in textual terms or, more definitively, in terms of COLUMNS in TABLES.

5.10.6 CONDITION REFERENCES COLUMN

This cross-reference component makes it possible to define a CONDITION in terms of the COLUMNS in various TABLES.

5.10.7 CONDITION ROLE

This component is used to categorize the two possible roles a CONDITION can play with respect to a SYSTEM EVENT. These two roles are as a precondition or as a postcondition.

5.10.8 CONDITION ROLE FOR SYSTEM EVENT

This cross-reference component indicates which CONDITION is involved with each SYSTEM EVENT and, furthermore, which of the two CONDITION ROLES it plays. Theoretically, a given CONDITION can have one CONDITION ROLE with respect to one SYSTEM EVENT and another CONDITION ROLE with respect to another SYSTEM EVENT.

5.10.9 SYSTEM EVENT TRIGGERS TASK

A given SYSTEM EVENT will typically trigger one, or possibly more, TASKS. It is also possible for one TASK to be triggered by zero, one or more SYSTEM EVENTS. The triggering of TASKS by SYSTEM EVENTS is separate and distinct from the initiating of TASKS by users at terminals.

The triggering of a TASK by a SYSTEM EVENT may be dependent on a CONDITION and, furthermore, the way in which the TASK is triggered may be categorized in terms of a TRIGGER CATEGORY.

5.11 Examples of system design components from the behaviour perspective

The following sections give examples based on the inventory control application for the nine components defined in the previous section. The sequence used is the same as in the previous section.

5.11.1 SYSTEM EVENT

System Event Number	Description
1	Stock is depleted
2	Stock below reordering level
3	Stock is empty
4	New consignment added to stock
5	Purchase order issued

These examples of SYSTEM EVENTS are events which can take place within the computerized information system.

5.11.2 TRIGGER CATEGORY

Trigger Category Code	Description
A	Automatic
M	Manual intervention

This is a methodology dependent component.

5.11.3 BUSINESS EVENT TRIGGERS SYSTEM EVENT

Business Event Number	System Event Number	Trigger Category Code
1 (Stock depletion)	1 (Stock is depleted)	M
1 (Stock depletion)	3 (Stock is empty)	A
2 (Stock below reordering level)	2 (Stock below reordering level)	A
3 (Issue purchase order)	5 (Purchase order issued)	M
4 (Consignment received)	4 (New consignment added to stock)	M
5 (Consignment added to stock)	4 (New consignment added to stock)	M

Two of the rows in this table represent situations where the SYSTEM EVENT is automatic: the system knows about the event before it is realized in the business system.

5.11.4 SYSTEM EVENT PRECEDENCE/SUCCEDENCE

Preceding System Event Number	Succeeding System Event Number
2 (Stock below reordering level)	1 (Stock is depleted)
3 (Stock is empty)	2 (Stock below reordering level)
5 (Purchase order issued)	2 (Stock below reordering level)

This table illustrates the precedence/succedence relationship for some of the SYSTEM EVENTS.

5.11.5 CONDITION

Condition Number	Condition Description
1	Quantity on hand below reorder level
2	Quantity on hand is zero or less

The two rows in this table illustrate conditions which are used in determining whether a SYSTEM EVENT shall take place.

5.11.6   CONDITION REFERENCES COLUMN

Condition Number	Table Name	Column Name
1	Stock on hand	Quantity of stock
2	Stock on hand	Quantity of stock

The CONDITION identified in Section 5.11.5 references the COLUMN (see Section 5.5.6) named 'Quantity of stock' in TABLE 6, which has the Table Name 'Stock on Hand'.

5.11.7   CONDITION ROLE

Condition Role	Condition Description
B	Precondition
A	Postcondition

This is a methodology dependent component. The table shows the two possible CONDITION ROLES.

5.11.8   CONDITION ROLE FOR SYSTEM EVENT

System Event Number	Condition Number	Condition Role
2 (Stock below reordering level)	1	A

The role of the CONDITION 'Quantity on hand below reorder level' is a precondition for the SYSTEM EVENT 'Generate purchase order'.

5.11.9   SYSTEM EVENT TRIGGERS TASK

System Event Number	Task Number	Trigger Category	Condition Number
1 (Stock is depleted)	15	A	—
2 (Stock below reordering level)	19	A	—
3 (Stock is empty)	19	A	—
4 (New consignment added to stock)	15	M	—
5 (Purchase order issued)	19	A	—

This component is a cross-reference between SYSTEM EVENT and TASK. For example, TASK 15 can be triggerd by SYSTEM EVENTS 1 and 4.

5.12   Conclusions on system design

This chapter has identified and illustrated 48 components which could result from a system design stage. As with the business analysis stage, any attempt to produce all of these would cause considerable consistency problems, even for an information system of modest complexity. Appendix C contains a worked example of all the system design components.

One could refer to a set of components generated in the system design stage collectively as a design product or as a prescriptive system model. It is the basis for the next stage in the information system life cycle, namely construction design. Many methodologies have been developed to tackle the problems of construction design.

At the conclusion of Chapter 4, the problems of the abstraction level of the components identified in that chapter as part of the reference framework for business analysis were discussed. It was pointed out that the framework was, in fact, the result of a design exercise.

While similar problems can be identified in connection with the components comprising the reference framework for system design, it is also important to note that the system designer producing instances of some of these system design components will inevitably have an analogous problem in choosing an appropriate abstraction level for the TABLE and TASKS which will be the cornerstones in his or her design product.

If the designer chooses a low abstraction level, there will be a large number of components which will prove more expensive in the ensuing construction stage. In the system design phase, however, the problem of having to communicate with users is not as critical as in the business analysis stage.

The user's view of the system will be the TASKS on the MENUS. These must be specified in such a way that the system user understands them. If this means more TASKS, rather than fewer, then this should be an acceptable price to pay. The abstraction level of the TABLES need not be so visible to the user, and minimizing the number of TABLES (without necessarily minimizing the number of TASKS which are available to process such TABLES) may be a worthwhile strategy.

It is important to note that the system design stage has not concerned itself with programming design problems and issues. As indicated earlier, these are regarded as part of construction design and are not considered in detail in this text.

EXERCISES

A. Self-assessment

5.1   Summarize the significance of the data oriented perspective, the process oriented perspective, the behaviour oriented perspective and their cross-references, as applicable to the system design stage. (It may be useful to refer to Figures 5.1, 5.3, 5.4 and 5.5.)

5.2   Section 5.4 lists 17 components of the system design stage which belong to the data oriented perspective, three of which are cross-reference components with corresponding business analysis components.

Prepare a two column list comparing the system design data oriented components with the business analysis data oriented components.

Discuss the significance of the similarity between the system design stage and the business analysis stage, as far as data aspects are concerned.

5.3   Section 5.6 lists 13 process oriented components and Section 5.8 lists an additional nine data and process perspective cross-reference components. Discuss why the latter number is twice as high as in the corresponding case for the business analysis components (where there is involvement of entity types and activities with business activity and use of the same in activity preconditions).

5.4   The number of methodology dependent components belonging to the data oriented and process oriented perspectives is higher than in the corresponding cases in the business analysis stage. Discuss whether this is suggestive of the need to consider the practical application in more precise detail.

5.5   Section 5.10 lists the nine components belonging to the behaviour oriented perspective. Figure 5.5 shows the interrelationships involving these components, together with the interrelationships with four components from the data and process perspectives. Discuss the closer connection between the perspectives as one gets closer to the actual system specification.

B. Methodology related

(for those familiar with one or more specific methodologies)
It should be noted that many methodologies use the term 'system design' or

'system development' to refer to the stage described in Chapter 3 as construction design. This may cause difficulties when trying to apply these exercises to such methodologies.

5.6   If the methodology has a clearly identified system design stage (possibly under a different name), discuss the correspondences between the components introduced in this chapter and those in the methodology.

5.7   If the methodology does not have an explicit system design stage corresponding to that described in this chapter, discuss the correspondence to the extent possible.

5.8   In the methodology, to what extent are the data oriented, process oriented and behaviour oriented components supported in the system design stage?

C.   Case studies

In Appendix D, case studies are described for three business areas – theatre, airline and car hire. The following exercises may be carried out for any or all of these case studies. It will be necessary to establish relationships with some of the components from the business analysis stage. It is also advisable that anyone attempting these exercises should have a good understanding of the principles of data normalization.

5.9   Work through the components identified in Chapter 5 systematically. For each methodology dependent component, a set of instances should be designated, possibly based on those shown in the text or, alternatively, on some methodology used in the set of 'methodology related' exercises above. For the 'designer prescribed' components, prepare instances of each component for the case study, using the same tabular format as used in the chapter.

5.10   Supplement the instances of components prepared in tabular format with diagramming techniques used in a known methodology. It is important that the results are consistent with each other and with the specifications in the tabular format.

5.11   If some of the components are not applicable to the case study chosen, explain the reason for this.

5.12   Perform Exercises 5.1 and 5.2 using a computerized design aid, such as an analyst's workbench tool. Identify the instances of the methodology dependent components which are implicit in the tool. Is the user of the tool allowed to specify the instances of any of the methodology dependent components? Identify any designer prescribable components which cannot be represented using the tool chosen and indicate whether this omission is acceptable.

6

Illustrations of design processes and design products

6.1 Introduction

This chapter presents several examples of design processes and the resulting design products. Each example contains a series of steps from one or two stages. These steps collectively comprise a design process. Furthermore, for each step, the resulting components (if any) are identified. Each component is one of those identified in the previous two chapters. Some of the components may be from the business analysis stage and some from the system design stage.

A distinction must be made between a component, such as ENTITY TYPE, which is part of a design process, and the instances of that component, such as Supplier and Purchase Order, both of which are instances of the component ENTITY TYPE and produced by use of the design process.

The aim of this chapter is to show how design processes and the components they generate are different. The instances of components are taken from the inventory control application used in the preceding chapters. No attempt is made to illustrate that when two different design processes produce the same component, the instances of that component may be different. In practice, this would tend to be the case.

Some of the existing methodologies only cover one of these two stages, but not both. An analysis methodology would contain only components from the business analysis phase and it may be slightly confusing to refer to these collectively as a design product. However, the term 'design process' is used here to identify a sequence of steps which collectively cover some part of the two stages presented, and hence produce some of the components which, for consistency, are referred to as a design product.

Some existing methodologies generate components which, in the presentation of this text, are covered in the information systems planning stage (see Chapter 7). Other methodologies generate components as part of their system design which would here be categorized as belonging to the construction design stage in the system life cycle (see Section 3.2.4).

While the illustrations in this chapter are based on an understanding of numerous existing methodologies, any attempt to relate the illustrations to any specific methodology is deliberately avoided. Furthermore, there is no implication that these illustrations are adequate or complete in any way. A major problem in trying to identify the steps in some existing methodologies is that the documentation does not give a structured step breakdown, although the different techniques used indicate an implicit step breakdown.

The examples in this chapter are as follows:

A   A first analysis methodology
B   A mainly analysis methodology including data design
C   A second analysis methodology
D   A comprehensive methodology covering both stages

These examples do not cover the information systems planning stage which is presented in Chapter 7. A methodology which covers that stage would often generate an early iteration of some of the components used in these examples.

6.2   Example A: analysis methodology only

The design process contains the following abstraction steps, all of which belong to the business analysis stage:

1.   Business activity analysis
2.   Activity precedence analysis

3.   Organization study

4.   Entity relationship analysis.

These four steps will be discussed in more detail and the components generated by each step will be identified.

6.2.1   Example A: Step 1. Business activity analysis

This step consists of an analysis of the BUSINESS ACTIVITIES performed in the business area under consideration. For each BUSINESS ACTIVITY, an evaluation is made of the INFORMATION/MATERIAL SETS it requires as input to the activity and which it generates as output from the activity.

In addition to distinguishing between the two ways in which an INFORMATION/MATERIAL SET is involved in a BUSINESS ACTIVITY, the step also distinguishes between INFORMATION/MATERIAL SETS which represent physical objects, that is to say 'material sets', and others which represent intangible information required to perform the activity (or generated by the activity).

The components generated by performing this abstraction step are as follows:

- BUSINESS ACTIVITY
- INFORMATION/MATERIAL SET
- ACTIVITY USES SET

The third of these three is a cross-reference between the first two.

Two methodology dependent components described in Section 4.7 are specific to a use of this step but are not generated by performing the step. These components are:

- INFORMATION OR MATERIAL
- INVOLVEMENT TYPE

This step uses an approach to business activity analysis which is usually carried out by preparing a set of diagrams. Figure 6.1 shows an activity graph for the example data from Sections 4.8.1, 4.8.6 and 4.8.10.

6.2.2   Example A: Step 2. Activity precedence analysis

Given the output from Step 1, a step can be performed which could be classified as a checking step. The step consists of analysing the permitted sequences in which the BUSINESS ACTIVITIES may be performed based on the INFORMATION/MATERIAL SETS needed by each and those generated by each.

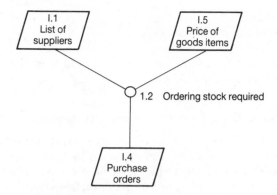

Figure 6.1 Simple activity graph for ordering stock required. Each
INFORMATION/MATERIAL SET is represented by a parallelogram. The BUSINESS
ACTIVITY is represented by a small circle. The number on the top line in each box
refers to the INFORMATION/MATERIAL SET number assigned in Section 4.8.6. The
BUSINESS ACTIVITY has number 1.2 in Section 4.8.1.

If one BUSINESS ACTIVITY generates an INFORMATION/MATERIAL SET
which is needed as input to another BUSINESS ACTIVITY, then it is clear that
these two BUSINESS ACTIVITIES must be performed in a given sequence. It
often happens that for one given BUSINESS ACTIVITY to be performed, two or
more other BUSINESS ACTIVITIES must precede it.

This step is classified as a control step because it provides a means of
checking the consistency of the preceding business activity analysis step and
possibly causes the output from that step to be revised. The component
ACTIVITY PRECEDENCE/SUCCEDENCE is generated by this step.

This can be displayed as a cross-reference table or as a graph. The
presentation form used in Section 4.8.4 would be difficult to read with a large
number of BUSINESS ACTIVITIES.

6.2.3 Example A: Step 3. Organization study

Given the list of BUSINESS ACTIVITIES from Step 1, the next step in the design
process is to identify who is responsible for performing each BUSINESS
ACTIVITY.

The business area may or may not have clearly identified ORGANIZA-
TION UNITS and, in the worst case, it may be necessary to carry out an analysis
of the groups involved in the business area under consideration and to break
these groups down into appropriately sized ORGANIZATION UNITS.

The two components resulting from this step would be as follows:

- ORGANIZATION UNIT
- ACTIVITY RESPONSIBILITY

Organization Unit Name	Activity Number		
	1.1	*1.2*	*1.3*
Purchasing		X	
Warehouse			X
Goods receiving	X		

Figure 6.2 Results of organization study for inventory control.

The results can be depicted as a simple cross-reference table between BUSINESS ACTIVITY and ORGANIZATION UNITS, such as that shown in Figure 6.2. This is based on the examples from Sections 4.8.13 and 4.8.14.

When the results of Step 3 are taken together with those from Steps 1 and 2, they should present a good definition of what goes on in the business area under consideration. It should be noted that, so far, these three steps have considered only those components with a process perspective.

6.2.4 Example A: Step 4. Entity relationship analysis

This step does not use any of the output from the first three steps. It involves identifying the ENTITY TYPES which are of interest in the business area and, furthermore, what RELATIONSHIPS exist between pairs (or possibly groups) of ENTITY TYPES.

The methodology dependent components RELATIONSHIP CLASS and RELATIONSHIP TYPE are important in this step. The alternatives used are as follows:

- RELATIONSHIP CLASS – binary only
- RELATIONSHIP TYPE – one to many
    many to many

The terms 'one' and 'many' are not precisely defined. 'One', for example, could mean either 'exactly one' or 'zero or one'.

The components generated by this abstraction step are as follows:

- ENTITY TYPE
- RELATIONSHIP
- ENTITY TYPE IN RELATIONSHIP

The results of this step can be depicted in some kind of data structure diagram, such as those used in Chapters 4 and 5, to show the interrelationships between components. Figure 6.3 gives an illustration of a data structure diagram for the inventory control example. This is identical to Figure 4.2. There are other styles of data structure diagram in use. These use different conventions for representing RELATIONSHIPS.

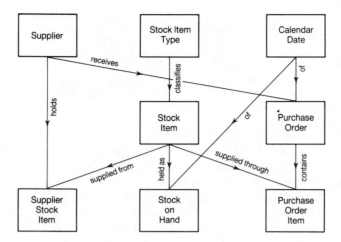

Figure 6.3   Data structure diagram for inventory control. ENTITY TYPES are represented by rectangles and RELATIONSHIPS by arrowed lines connecting two ENTITY TYPES. The component ENTITY TYPE IN RELATIONSHIP is implicitly represented by the two ENTITY TYPES at the ends of each RELATIONSHIP.

6.3   Review of Example A

Figure 6.4 shows the 12 components from the business analysis stage which are produced by this design process. The number in each rectangle indicates the step in which the components are generated. The absence of a number indicates that the component is methodology dependent and hence defined independently of any specific use of this design process. The absence of any interrelationship between the four data oriented components and the process oriented components is a feature of the design process and is indicated graphically in Figure 6.4 by the wavy line.

6.4   Example B: mainly analysis methodology including data design

This design process consists of five steps as follows:

1.   Business activity decomposition
2.   Organization study
3.   Entity relationship analysis
4.   Activity/entity cross-reference
5.   Relational database design

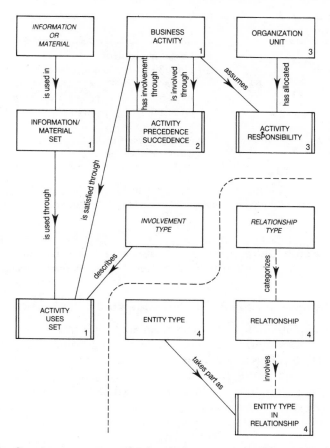

Figure 6.4 Components generated using design process A. The number in a rectangle indicates the step in the design process during which the component was generated. Absence of a number indicates that the component is methodology dependent.

The first four steps are part of the business analysis stage and the last one belongs to the system design stage.

These five steps will be discussed in more detail and the components generated by each step will be identified.

6.4.1 Example B: Step 1. Business activity decomposition

The first step in this design process consists of identifying a number of top level BUSINESS ACTIVITIES. Each BUSINESS ACTIVITY is then decomposed into one (or usually more) lower level BUSINESS ACTIVITIES.

Depending on the size of the business area being analysed, this

Activity Number	Description
1	Inventory control
1.1	Handling new stock
1.1.1	Categorization of new stock items
1.1.2	Registration of alternative supplier
1.2	Ordering stock required
1.2.1	Select supplier
1.2.2	Send purchase order
1.3	Monitoring stock levels

Figure 6.5   Business activities for inventory control. (The hierarchy of these activities is defined in the structure of the numbering system used.)

decomposition process can be continued to further levels. The two components produced by this step are BUSINESS ACTIVITIES and BUSINESS ACTIVITY HIERARCHY. Figure 6.5 illustrates the results from this step.

6.4.2   Example B: Step 2. Organization study

Given the list of BUSINESS ACTIVITIES from Step 1, the next step in the design process is to identify who is responsible for performing each BUSINESS ACTIVITY. The business area may or may not have clearly identified ORGANI-ZATION UNITS and, in the worst case, it may be necessary to carry out an analysis of the groups involved in the business area under consideration and to break these groups down into appropriately sized ORGANIZATION UNITS.

The two components resulting from this step would be as follows:

- ORGANIZATION UNIT
- ACTIVITY RESPONSIBILITY

The results can be depicted as a simple cross-reference table between BUSINESS ACTIVITY and ORGANIZATION UNITS of the form shown for design process A in Figure 6.2.

6.4.3   Example B: Step 3. Entity relationship analysis

This step does not use any of the output from the first two steps. It involves identifying the ENTITY TYPES which are of interest in the business area and, furthermore, what RELATIONSHIPS exist between pairs (or possibly groups) of ENTITY TYPES.

The component RELATIONSHIP CLASS is an important input to this step and there are many different choices of RELATIONSHIP CLASS possible, depending on the preference of the analyst.

The components generated by this abstraction step are as follows:

- ENTITY TYPE
- RELATIONSHIP
- ENTITY TYPE IN RELATIONSHIP

The results of this step are usually depicted in the same kind of data structure diagram as in Figure 6.3.

6.4.4 Example B: Step 4. Activity/entity cross-reference

Having identified both BUSINESS ACTIVITIES and ENTITY TYPES in the earlier steps, Step 4 is a checking step which produces a cross-reference component, BUSINESS ACTIVITY INVOLVES ENTITY TYPE, cross-referencing the two components.

If the result of Step 1 is a hierarchical breakdown into four or five levels, then there will normally be an optimum level between the top and the bottom level which is to be used for cross-referencing with the ENTITY TYPES.

The cross-reference component indicates how a BUSINESS ACTIVITY 'uses' each ENTITY TYPE. Data about the ENTITY TYPE can be input to the BUSINESS ACTIVITY. Alternatively, the BUSINESS ACTIVITY can generate data about the ENTITY TYPE. Which of these two is applicable is indicated by the methodology dependent component INVOLVEMENT TYPE.

Entity Type Name	Activity Number				
	1.1.1	*1.1.2*	*1.2.1*	*1.2.2*	*1.3*
Supplier		U	R		
Stock Item	U	R		R	R
Stock Item Type	R				
Calendar Date				R	R
Purchase Order			U	R	
Purchase Order Item				U	
Stock on Hand					R
Supplier Stock Item		U	R		

Figure 6.6 Cross-reference table for ENTITY TYPES and BUSINESS ACTIVITIES. U (update) and R (retrieval) indicate the INVOLVEMENT TYPE.

On completion, the cross-reference component BUSINESS ACTIVITY USES ENTITY TYPE can be checked for consistency. All ENTITY TYPES should be used by at least one BUSINESS ACTIVITY.

Furthermore, each ENTITY TYPE should be generated by at least one BUSINESS ACTIVITY. Any exceptions to this should be examined carefully and the output from Steps 1, 2 and 3 revised as necessary.

An illustration of the results generated by this step is shown in Figure 6.6.

6.4.5   Example B: Step 5: Relational database design

The last step in this design process is a prescriptive step based on the results of the preceding analysis steps. The aim of this step is to define a relational database in terms of the following eight components, those with an asterisk being methodology dependent:

1.   TABLE
*2.   DATA TYPE
3.   COLUMN NAME
4.   COLUMN
5.   COLUMN GROUP
6.   COLUMN IN GROUP
*7.   CONSTRAINT TYPE
8.   CONSTRAINT

This design process chooses to designate a uniqueness CONSTRAINT on each TABLE but does not concern itself with referential CONSTRAINTS. Furthermore, there is no cross-reference maintained between the data oriented com-

Table Number	Description
1	Stock Item Type
2	Stock Item
3	Supplier
4	Supplier of Stock Item Type
5	Calendar Date
6	Stock on Hand
7	Purchase Order
8	Purchase Order Item
9	Stock Withdrawal
10	Stock Replenishment

Figure 6.7   TABLES resulting from relational database design.

Stock Code	Supplier Name
Stock Item Name	Stock Item Type Code
Consignment	Stock Item Type Description
Delivery	Date of Purchase
Issue	Date of Delivery
Price	Purchase Order Number
Supplier Number	Purchase Order Item Number
Withdrawal Number	Replenishment Number

Figure 6.8   COLUMN NAMES resulting from relational database design.

ponents from the business analysis phase and those generated in the system design phase.

The ten TABLES which make up the design are listed in Figure 6.7. The 16 different COLUMN NAMES used are shown in Figure 6.8. The COLUMNS in each of the ten TABLES are shown in Figure 6.9

Column Name	Table Number									
	1	2	3	4	5	6	7	8	9	10
Stock Code		I				I		X	X	X
Stock Item Name		X								
Delivery										X
Issue									X	
Price								X		
Supplier Number			I	I			X			
Supplier Name			X							
Stock Item Type Code	I	X		I						
Stock Item Type Description	X									
Date of Purchase							X			
Date of Delivery										X
Date of Withdrawal									X	
Purchase Order Number							I	I		
Purchase Order Item Number								I		
Quantity of Stock						X		X	X	X
Date					I	I				
Withdrawal Number									I	
Replenishment Number										I

Figure 6.9 COLUMNS and uniqueness CONSTRAINTS for each TABLE. A letter I indicates that the COLUMN is all or part of the unique identifier for the TABLE. An X indicates that the table has a COLUMN with that COLUMN NAME.

6.5 Review of Example B

Figure 6.10 shows the nine components from the business analysis stage and the eight from the system design stage which are involved in this design process. The number in each rectangle indicates the step in which the components are generated. The absence of a number indicates that the component is a methodology dependent component defined independently of any specific use of this design process.

The absence of any interrelationship between the business analysis data oriented components and the system design data oriented components is a feature of the design process in this example.

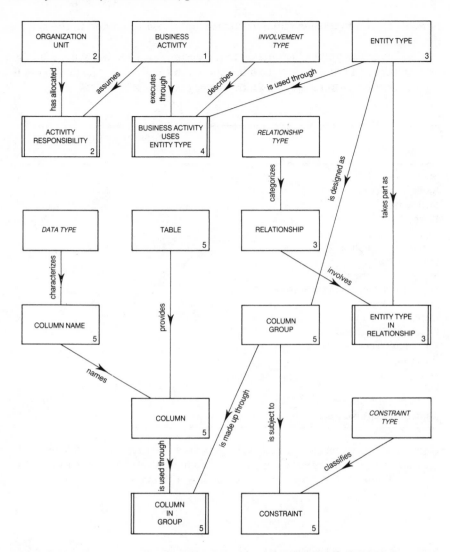

Figure 6.10 Components generated using design process B. The number in most of the rectangles indicates the step in the design process in which the component was generated. Absence of a number indicates that the component is prescribed for the design process.

6.6 Example C: second purely analysis methodology

The design process in this example contains five steps as follows:

1. Information flow
2. Business activity analysis

3.   Information needs

4.   Organization study

5.   Information flow and activities

These five steps are all from the business analysis stage. They will be discussed in more detail and the components generated by each step will be identified.

6.6.1   Example C: Step 1. Information flow

This step consists of analysing the FLOW of information between ORGANIZA-TION UNITS and between ORGANIZATION UNITS and EXTERNAL UNITS in both directions. Each FLOW is either between two ORGANIZATION UNITS or between one ORGANIZATION UNIT and one EXTERNAL UNIT.

It should be noted that this step merely analyses the existence of a FLOW and does not examine the nature of the information which is transmitted.

The components generated by this step are as follows:

- ORGANIZATION UNIT
- EXTERNAL UNIT
- FLOW

The results of this step are usually depicted in some kind of flow diagram such as the one depicted in Figure 6.11.

6.6.2   Example C: Step 2. Business activity analysis

This step consists of identifying the BUSINESS ACTIVITIES performed in the business area under consideration and analysing how they interrelate in terms of sequence.

The two components resulting from this step are as follows:

- BUSINESS ACTIVITY
- ACTIVITY PRECEDENCE/SUCCEDENCE

6.6.3   Example C: Step 3. Information needs

This abstraction step consists of analysing the information needed as input to each BUSINESS ACTIVITY and the information generated as output from each BUSINESS ACTIVITY. The analysis is also repeated for physical objects needed by each BUSINESS ACTIVITY.

Both information and physical objects are represented by the component INFORMATION/MATERIAL SET. The four components generated by this step are as follows:

- INFORMATION/MATERIAL SET
- SET NAME
- INFORMATION/MATERIAL SET USES NAME
- ACTIVITY USES SET

The component ACTIVITY USES SET is a cross-reference between BUSINESS ACTIVITY and INFORMATION/MATERIAL SET.

The results of this step can be depicted in an enhanced flow diagram based on those produced in Step 1.

6.6.4   Example C: Step 4. Organization study

Given the list of BUSINESS ACTIVITIES from Step 2, the next step in the design process is to identify who is responsible for performing each BUSINESS ACTIVITY. The business area may or may not have clearly identified ORGANIZATION UNITS and, in the worst case, it may be necessary to carry out an analysis of the groups involved in the business area under consideration and to break these groups down into appropriately sized ORGANIZATION UNITS.

The two components resulting from this step would be as follows:

- ORGANIZATION UNIT
- ACTIVITY RESPONSIBILITY

The results can be depicted as a simple cross-reference table between BUSINESS ACTIVITY and ORGANIZATION UNITS. An example has been shown for design process A in Figure 6.2.

6.6.5   Example C: Step 5. Information flow and activities

This control step consists of cross-referencing the component ACTIVITY USES SET from Step 3 with the FLOWS identified in Step 1 of this design process. Each FLOW between two units (ORGANIZATION UNITS or EXTERNAL UNITS) should be part of one or more BUSINESS ACTIVITIES.

Furthermore, when a BUSINESS ACTIVITY generates an INFORMATION/MATERIAL SET which is needed by another BUSINESS ACTIVITY for which a different ORGANIZATION UNIT has ACTIVITY RESPONSIBILITY, then a FLOW between the two ORGANIZATION UNITS should have been identified.

6.7   Review of Example C

Figure 6.11 shows the 16 components from the business analysis stage which are involved in this design process. The number in each rectangle indicates the

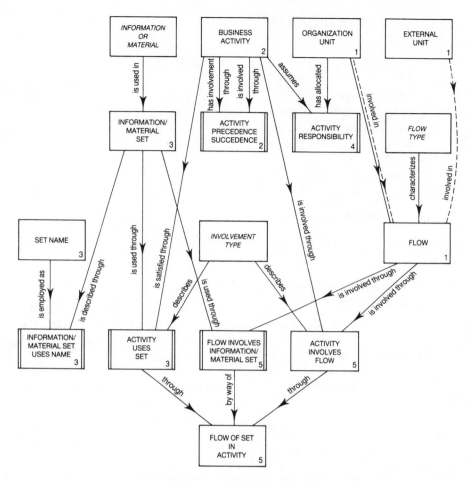

Figure 6.11 Components generated using design process C.

step in which the components are generated. The absence of a number indicates that the component is a methodology dependent component defined independently of any specific use of this design process. The absence of any data oriented components is a feature of the design product in this example.

6.8 Example D: comprehensive methodology covering both stages

The design process in this example covers both business analysis and system design. It also generates components in the system design stage which, in the reference framework, are identified only in the business analysis stage.

The steps are identified as follows:

Business analysis:

1. Data flow analysis
2. Entity relationship analysis
3. Entity life history analysis
4. Relational data analysis

System design:

5. Composite logical data design
6. Process design
7. Dialogue design

These steps will now be described in more detail.

6.8.1   Example D: Step 1. Data flow analysis

This step consists of analysing the 'existing system' which may or may not be computerized. In the case that there is no existing computerized system, the step would be an analysis of a business area, involving the preparation of a set of data flow diagrams. This case is considered here.

    The approach chosen considers both information FLOWS and material FLOWS, using a different graphic representation for each. Each diagram relates to a BUSINESS ACTIVITY and shows the FLOWS among lower level BUSINESS ACTIVITIES which are part of the subject BUSINESS ACTIVITY. This allows for a set of hierarchically related diagrams. Each diagram covers a BUSINESS ACTIVITY on a higher level and each BUSINESS ACTIVITY in the diagram may be further decomposed into two or more BUSINESS ACTIVITIES, the flows between which may be shown on a diagram on the next level down.

    A diagram on a given level contains the following components:

- INFORMATION/MATERIAL SET
- BUSINESS ACTIVITY
- ACTIVITY USES SET
- FLOW
- ACTIVITY INVOLVES FLOW
- FLOW INVOLVES INFORMATION/MATERIAL SET
- ORGANIZATION UNIT
- ACTIVITY RESPONSIBILITY
- EXTERNAL UNIT

The EXTERNAL UNITS are 'external' relative to the diagram on which they are used. This means that something might be an ORGANIZATION UNIT on the diagram for one BUSINESS ACTIVITY but an EXTERNAL UNIT on one or more of the diagrams on the next level down.

Furthermore, the component INFORMATION/MATERIAL SET is used in two ways. The first is in the sense of a 'data store' which is accessed and maintained by the various BUSINESS ACTIVITIES. The second is in the sense of a FLOW which identifies the information or physical resource flowing into or out of a 'data store' or into or out of an EXTERNAL UNIT. The sets used in the second way are those recorded in the cross-reference component FLOW INVOLVES INFORMATION/MATERIAL SET.

The results of this step are represented in the form of data flow diagrams. Various symbols are used in data flow diagrams to represent the components of a data flow analysis. Those used in this chapter are shown in Figure 6.12.

An example of a data flow diagram covering inventory control and using the symbols of Figure 6.12 is presented in Figure 6.13.

6.8.2 Example D: Step 2. Entity relationship analysis

This step in the design process of Example D is very similar to Step 4 in the design process shown in Example A (see Section 6.2.4). There are typical differences between one kind of entity relationship analysis and another and these are detectable in terms of the following methodology dependent components:

- RELATIONSHIP CLASS
- RELATIONSHIP TYPE

In Example D, the following alternatives are applicable:

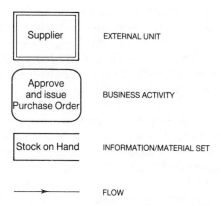

Figure 6.12 Symbols used in data flow diagrams.

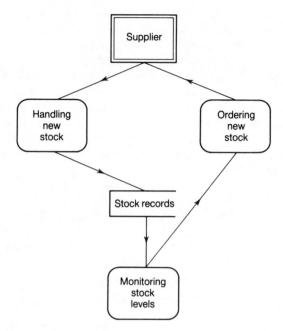

Figure 6.13   Data flow diagram for inventory control.

- RELATIONSHIP CLASS   – unary relationships
                          binary relationships
- RELATIONSHIP TYPE   – unary or recursive
                          binary: one to many
                          binary: one to one
                          binary: many to many

The exact interpretation of the words 'one' and 'many' for the methodology dependent component RELATIONSHIP TYPE in Example D depends on whether a RELATIONSHIP is classified as 'optional'. The use of the 'optional' concept means that the number of binary RELATIONSHIP TYPES which may be used is more than the three in the above list. In terms of the list shown in Section 4.5.5, this means that all ten RELATIONSHIP TYPES are permitted.

In addition, it is possible to designate two or more RELATIONSHIPS which involve the same subordinate ENTITY TYPE as mutually exclusive. This means that only one of those defined can hold at any time. (This can only be meaningful in the case that the RELATIONSHIPS are optional with respect to the subordinate ENTITY TYPE.)

The concept of entity modelling includes the identification of a primary key, which means that a VALUE CONSTRAINT of the VALUE

CONSTRAINT TYPE 'uniqueness' (see Section 4.5.13) is associated with an ATTRIBUTE GROUP of each ENTITY TYPE.

The entity relationship analysis step is actually divided into six discrete substeps, each of which would itself be regarded as a step in the terminology of the reference framework. These six substeps may be identified as follows, together with the components generated (if any):

Select initial set of ENTITY TYPES

The only component generated is ENTITY TYPE.

Interrelationships

This substep is performed using a matrix with a list of the ENTITY TYPES along each dimension. If an ENTITY TYPE is considered to have a RELATIONSHIP with another ENTITY TYPE, then this results in a cross in the matrix at that intersection. It should be noted that, at this level of analysis, there may be seen to be more than one RELATIONSHIP between the same two ENTITY TYPES, which would imply more than one cross at the intersection.

The components generated in this substep are as follows:

- RELATIONSHIP
- ENTITY TYPE IN RELATIONSHIP

Each cross at an intersection in the above matrix implies two components of the type ENTITY TYPE IN RELATIONSHIP.

Prepare entity relationship diagrams

The next substep is to prepare an entity relationship diagram (such as that in Figure 6.3) from the matrix of the previous substep. This substep does not produce any new components but does result in each binary RELATIONSHIP being assigned a RELATIONSHIP TYPE. This substep is an example of the step category referred to 'form conversion' in Section 3.5.3.

Validate diagram

This substep consists of checking the diagram against an initial set of BUSINESS ACTIVITIES, as identified in the first data flow analysis step.

The aim of this step is to ensure that the entity relationship diagram covers the business area. There are different ways of carrying out this substep, one of which might result in the component BUSINESS ACTIVITY INVOLVES ENTITY TYPE.

This substep is an example of a step in the step category 'checking' as described in Section 3.5.2.

Rationalize structure diagram

This substep is based on the entity relationship diagram of the previous substep. The diagram is reviewed and any cases of duplicate access paths to an ENTITY TYPE are possibly, but not necessarily, eliminated.

The substep is a further example of the step category 'checking' (see Section 3.5.2). It may result in the creation of further ENTITY TYPES and further RELATIONSHIPS.

Revalidate structure

This substep is basically a reiteration of substep 4 in order to take into account any effects caused by substep 5.

6.8.3   Example D: Step 3. Entity life history

The first part of an entity life history analysis step consists of identifying the set of BUSINESS EVENTS that can happen to each ENTITY TYPE which has resulted from the previous step. An example of the BUSINESS EVENTS is shown in Figure 6.14.

Part of this step consists of interrelating the BUSINESS EVENTS such that it can be seen which BUSINESS EVENT has to precede some other BUSINESS EVENT. This part of the step results in the generation of the component EVENT PRECEDENCE/SUCCEDENCE.

A BUSINESS EVENT can have a number of different effects on an ENTITY TYPE and these effects would be categorized in the framework in terms of INVOLVEMENT TYPES. Basically, a BUSINESS EVENT can create, modify or eliminate an entity of a given ENTITY TYPE.

The components created by this abstraction step are BUSINESS EVENT and BUSINESS EVENT INVOLVES ENTITY TYPE. The latter is a typical cross-reference component between two components with different perspectives and would be represented in a cross-reference table as shown in Figure 6.15.

An R in Figure 6.15 indicates that the BUSINESS EVENT needs information about the ENTITY TYPE when it happens. An I in the table indicates that

Event Number	Description
1	Stock depletion
2	Stock below reordering level
3	Issue purchase order
4	Consignment received
5	Consignment added to stock

Figure 6.14   Examples of BUSINESS EVENTS.

Entity Type Name	\ Event Number \ 1	2	3	4	5
Supplier			R	R	
Stock Item	R	R		R	
Stock Item Type	R				
Calendar Date	R	R		R	
Purchase Order			I		
Purchase Order Item			I		
Stock on Hand	M	M		M	M
Supplier Stock Item		R			

Figure 6.15 Entity life history cross-reference.

the BUSINESS EVENT creates (inserts) an entity of the ENTITY TYPE when the BUSINESS EVENT happens and an M means that the BUSINESS EVENT modifies an entity of the ENTITY TYPE when it happens. The codes I, M and R represent the methodology dependent component INVOLVEMENT TYPE described in Section 4.12.1.

The cross-reference table can be checked to ensure that there is consistency between the ENTITY TYPES and the list of BUSINESS EVENTS. For example, the creation of each ENTITY TYPE should be triggered by some BUSINESS EVENT or other.

6.8.4   Example D: Step 4. Relational data analysis

The aim of this step is to ensure that the data is presented in a form, usually referred to as 'third normal form'. It is a step which follows on from Step 2 (an entity relationship analysis) and which uses the components that it has generated as input.

A set of ATTRIBUTES is identified for each ENTITY TYPE and the resulting structures are analysed and modified in such a way that the resulting data is structured in third normal form.

The following business analysis components result from this step:

- ATTRIBUTE NAME
- ATTRIBUTE
- ATTRIBUTE GROUP
- ATTRIBUTE IN GROUP
- VALUE CONSTRAINT

Two VALUE CONSTRAINT TYPES are considered. The first is 'uniqueness constraints' which are identified in such a way that each ATTRIBUTE GROUP to which a uniqueness CONSTRAINT applies is regarded as a primary key of the ENTITY TYPE. The second is 'referential constraints' which are identified in such a way that each ATTRIBUTE GROUP to which a referential CONSTRAINT applies is regarded as a foreign key of the ENTITY TYPE.

A number of consistency checks are included as part of this step which aim at ensuring that the data resulting from the analysis is adequately normalized.

6.8.5   Example D: Step 5. Composite logical data design

The aim of this step is to combine the results of Steps 2 and 4 and to apply a set of prescribed rules in order to achieve an optimum and consistent data design.

These rules result in a series of substeps which involve reviewing the various ATTRIBUTE GROUPS designated in order to specify primary and foreign keys for each ENTITY TYPE. As a result of carrying out these substeps, some sets of two or more ENTITY TYPES may be combined into one TABLE. Such design decisions can be represented in the component ENTITY TYPE TO TABLE ASSIGNMENT (see Section 5.4.3).

As a result of this step, the following components from the system design stage are created:

- TABLE
- ENTITY TYPE TO TABLE ASSIGNMENT
- COLUMN NAME
- COLUMN
- COLUMN GROUP
- COLUMN IN GROUP
- CONSTRAINT

The composite logical data design consists of all of the above components, except the second, which is generated in order to check that the results of the entity relationship analysis in Step 2 have been completely handled.

6.8.6   Example D: Step 6. Process design

This step consists of developing a series of 'process outlines' each of which is categorized as either a logical update or a logical enquiry.

A process outline represents the processing required, in logical terms, to support a single BUSINESS EVENT. The operations specified in a process outline are translated into a program design in the construction design stage following system design.

The process outlines are based on the components generated in earlier steps, specifically Steps 2, 3 and 4. This means that the processes are defined in terms of the normalized TABLES. Each 'process outline' relates to a BUSINESS EVENT identified in Step 3. Each process is essentially a TASK component, as discussed in Section 5.6.6.

For update TASKS, this step is broken down into four substeps as follows:

1. Identify access paths
2. Identify how TASK is initiated
3. Complete the outline for the TASK
4. Validate against earlier components

Each of these will be discussed in turn.

Identify access paths

This substep results in the generation of the following components:

*   TASK
*   TASK USES TABLE

Each TASK is related to a BUSINESS EVENT from Step 3. There is also an appropriate qualification of each occurrence of TASK USES TABLE in terms of the methodology dependent component ACCESS PATH NODE TYPE and in terms of whether the TASK updates the TABLE or merely retrieves information from it.

Identify how TASK is initiated

This substep categorizes each TASK in terms of the methodology dependent component INITIATION MEANS (see Section 5.6.5).

Complete the outline for the TASK

This substep gives further qualification to the component TASK USES TABLE. In addition, the following components are generated:

*   EXTERNAL FORM
*   EXTERNAL FORM ELEMENT
*   TASK USES EXTERNAL FORM
*   TASK USES COLUMN
*   ALGORITHM

- ALGORITHM REFERENCES COLUMN
- TASK USES ALGORITHM

Validate against earlier components

This is a checking substep which ensures consistency of the process outlines with the other components generated in Steps 1, 2, 3 and 4.

6.8.7 Example D: Step 7. Dialogue design

This step is used to specify the logical design of the dialogue associated with each TASK. Each dialogue will use a number of screen formats which are represented in the framework by the system design components MENU and EXTERNAL FORM.

The following components are generated by this step:

- MENU
- MENU HIERARCHY
- EXTERNAL FORM
- TASK IN MENU
- COLUMN ON FORM ELEMENT

6.9 Review of Example D

Figure 6.16 shows the business analysis components with a process perspective which are produced in Step 1 of the design process illustrated in Example D. For each component produced, the number on the right hand side of the rectangle indicates the number of the step in which the component is produced. Methodology dependent components used by the design process are included in the figure and the number of the step in which they are used is also indicated.

Figure 6.17 shows the business analysis components with a data perspective which are either produced or (in the case of methodology dependent components) used in Steps 2, 3 and 4 of the design process illustrated in Example D. The number of the step involved is again indicated. In the same way, Figure 6.18 shows the system design components which are either produced or used in Steps 5, 6 and 7 of the design process illustrated in Example D.

This example illustrates a fairly comprehensive methodology covering both business analysis and system design. Seven steps are used, some of which can be broken down into further substeps. The total number of components generated is 35 and these are in each of the three perspectives – data, process and behaviour.

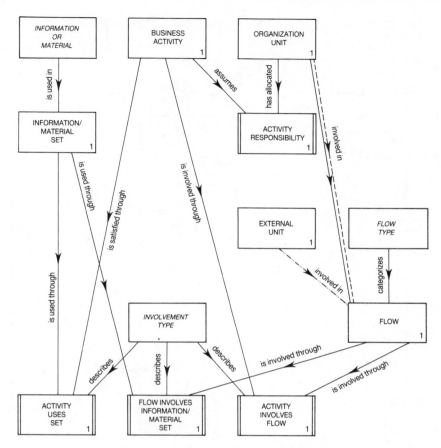

Figure 6.16 Components generated in Step 1 using design process in Example D. The numbers in each rectangle correspond to the step in which generated.

6.10 Conclusions on design processes

This chapter has illustrated four different design processes, varying from a fairly simple analysis methodology to a comprehensive analysis and design methodology. The examples are based, to some extent, on extant methodologies, although it should be noted that many of these develop components which are here seen as belonging to the construction design stage in the information system life cycle.

The examples have varying numbers of steps, use different techniques and generate different sets of components. An attempt has been made to illustrate how the sequence of steps can vary from one example to another, with a given component, such as BUSINESS ACTIVITIES, being generated in an early step in one example and in a later step in another. It is not only the

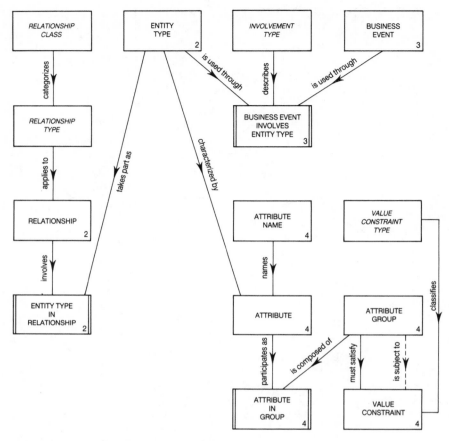

Figure 6.17   Components generated using Steps 2, 3 and 4 in design process for Example D.

generation of the components which is significant but also whether the relationships between the components are generated.

The components generated in the four examples vary, although there is some overlap. This variation is intended to illustrate the disparity among extant methodologies. There are many ways of going through the process of analysis and design and, by the same token, there are many ways of representing a design product. Those selected for inclusion in this chapter are chosen for illustration purposes only and should not be considered to be given any kind of endorsement or approval.

It is important to note that these examples do not illustrate the information systems planning stage which is discussed in Chapter 7. As already indicated, this book does not analyse the components found in the construction design stage. Many extant methodologies are wholly or partially

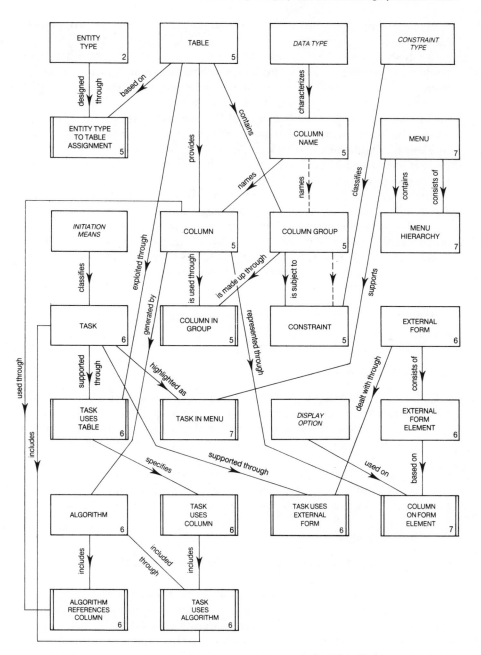

Figure 6.18 Components generated using Steps 5, 6 and 7 in design process for Example D.

dedicated to the problems of how best to construct a suite of programs to meet a set of requirements.

It should now be clear that the number of different components which could be generated by any information systems methodology is reasonably finite. Chapter 4 identified 53 for the business analysis stage, nine of which are classed as methodology dependent, leaving a maximum of 44 to be generated by an analyst. Chapter 5 identified 48 components for the system design stage, 15 of which are classed as methodology dependent, leaving a maximum of 33 to be generated by a designer.

Given these 77 components to be generated by analyst and designer, plus considerable degrees of freedom in the specification of some 24 methodology dependent components by a methodology designer, it can be seen that a virtual infinity of different methodologies could exist.

The important thing to remember is that the number of components is much more modest. An understanding of the more important of these components and how they are interrelated is fundamental to an understanding of information systems methodologies.

EXERCISES

A. Self-assessment

6.1 Prepare a comparative evaluation of the four illustrations presented in this chapter. Show which techniques are used in more than one illustration. Indicate feasible alternative step sequences for the examples and discuss the advantages and disadvantages of such alternatives.

6.2 Discuss the different step categories illustrated in this chapter. Some are not illustrated. For each illustration suggest additional decision and review steps which could be interspersed with those steps shown.

B. Methodology related

(for those familiar with one or more specific methodologies)

It should be noted that many methodologies cover what is referred to here as the construction design stage. In some cases, the methodology concentrates exclusively on construction design. In others, there is also some coverage of the two stages presented in Chapters 4 and 5. This should be borne in mind when tackling these exercises.

6.3 For the methodology chosen, identify the steps in the methodology and the step category of each step. Identify the instances of each methodology dependent component relevant to the methodology.

6.4 Prepare data structure diagrams, such as those indicated in this chapter, and indicate the step in which each component is generated. If there are difficulties in identifying the interrelationships between some of the components generated by the methodology, discuss the problems this could create when using the methodology in question.

6.5 Discuss the perceived shortcomings of the framework in representing selected methodologies.

6.6 Discuss the perceived shortcomings of a selected existing methodology, based on the understanding of information systems methodologies acquired by studying this framework.

7

Component analysis for the information systems planning stage

7.1 Introduction

This chapter presents a description of many components which are used in the strategic planning of computerized information systems. Most of these are specific to information systems planning, and to understand their purpose it is first necessary to understand the context within which information systems planning takes place and also the major topics with which it usually deals. That context, and the topics within the scope of information systems planning, are the subjects of this section.

7.1.1   Planning context

Most enterprises require a substantial number of information systems. The number is so great that it is impractical to consider developing them all simultaneously. Information systems planning is therefore concerned with creating a plan which shows how the limited resources available should, in the medium term, be allocated to stages of the systems life cycle. For such planning to be possible it is first necessary to be able to identify projects for incorporation in the plan and then to determine priorities for developing them. The plan is therefore for projects which will lead to the set of systems to be built and should include a clear view of how to progress from the current set of systems to the future required set of systems.

Information systems planning takes place in the context of other forms of planning practised within the enterprise. These may exist on several levels and may differ according to the style of the enterprise. Figure 7.1 illustrates a structure for plans which is typical of many enterprises.

To be successful, the information systems plan and its derivatives (the systems development plan and the technology development plan, for example) must take related plans into account. It must therefore be seen to be contributing to the achievement of the higher level plans and it must combine with plans on the same level to provide a balanced deployment of the enterprise's resources. This means that, in the ideal information systems planning process, it is necessary to understand the other plans, to make allowance for them and even to orient the information systems plan in such a way that it will contribute to the success of the other plans.

For these reasons, a number of components are introduced in this chapter which do not contribute directly to the design of any information system. Instead, they contribute to an understanding of the context for the information systems and therefore to establishing the priorities for building them.

Throughout this chapter the term 'information system' is used in a way which is slightly different from that used in other chapters. The concept

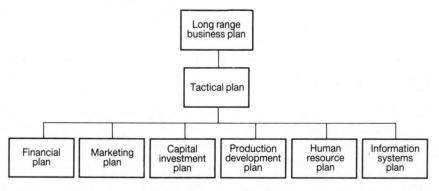

Figure 7.1   Common types of plan.

of an information system at the information systems planning stage is both broader and less well formed than it will be later in the design process. At this point, no decision has been taken as to whether the information system (or which parts of it) will be given automated support. The general concept is that of a business information system. Subsequent stages will refine and define what this means and prescribe what it is to become.

7.1.2 Information systems planning scope

Prior to conducting an information systems planning project, a preliminary scoping exercise is often undertaken. The aims are two-fold:

1.   to clarify the boundaries of the project, and
2.   to limit the scope so that an acceptable result can be achieved within a reasonable time, with acceptable expenditure of resources.

Many enterprises are so large that a global investigation and a single, comprehensive information systems plan cannot readily be developed. The scoping effort is therefore concerned with identifying parts of the enterprise with sufficient autonomy or uniqueness of identity to justify a separate plan. If such units cannot be found then scoping is used to identify those aspects of the enterprise that are sufficiently unimportant to be safely omitted from the current round of planning.

Information systems planning can be a very broadly based process. If it is assumed that almost every activity of an enterprise may be given systems support then there is an argument in favour of exploring every activity during the planning study. In practice this is too expensive, so methodologies focus on topics that are currently believed, by decision takers in the enterprise, to provide the best indicators of direction for information systems planning and that can also be used to determine what systems are required. These topics are then examined in only just enough detail to make adequate planning decisions. Figure 7.2 illustrates the principal topics that can be explored by information systems planning. No methodology incorporates them all.

The topics relevant to the enterprise, which are shown in Figure 7.2, would commonly be characterized as follows:

- **Business plan** would typically cover issues such as objectives, goals and critical success factors. Information systems planning based on this would seek to promote systems which would help to achieve the business plan through the provision of information needed to support it.
- **Finance** would typically cover investment in various parts of the enterprise and the returns expected, together with the corresponding current investments in information systems. Information systems

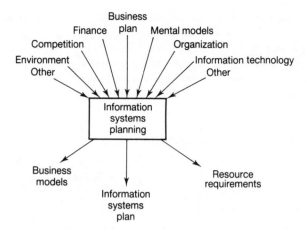

Figure 7.2   The scope of information systems planning.

planning would seek to use systems to improve either specific or overall financial returns.

- **Mental models** would typically deal with the enterprise in terms such as those used in this text to develop data, process and behaviour oriented business models. Information systems planning would seek to develop a logically derived set of systems providing complete support for the mental models.

- **Competition** would typically deal with markets, competitors, products/services, channels and sources of added value. Information systems planning would seek to use systems to improve competitive standing and to enhance returns on value-adding activities.

- **Organization** would typically deal with organization units, interest groups, problems and possibilities for change within the enterprise. Information systems planning would seek systems which would promote change to ease problems and to improve the organization's overall effectiveness.

- **Environment** would typically cover government, regulatory bodies, sources of influence and geographical locations. Information systems planning would seek to provide systems to manage environmental elements to ensure that they did not impede progress for the enterprise.

- **Information technology** would typically deal with developments in hardware, software and communications capability and their potential impact within relevant sectors of industry. Information systems planning would seek systems which could exploit new technology to the benefit of the enterprise.

- **Other** covers any additional relevant topics which could be used to guide information systems planning. However, those described above illustrate the current state-of-the-art.

Figure 7.2 also illustrates the principal products of information systems planning. Information systems planning is conducted in two phases. The first phase contains analytic steps, generally concerned with gathering information and creating some sort of model of the business and identifying relative priorities for components. The second contains prescriptive steps, creating a plan for projects to undertake analyses on areas of the business in priority order and defining the resources required.

This chapter does not attempt to explore all possible components of information systems planning (to do so would require another book); instead it concentrates on those most commonly used which tie in, in the most straightforward manner, with concepts used elsewhere in this text. The components described and the processes illustrated in Sections 7.4 and 7.5 deal only with business planning, mental models and organization.

7.2 Presentation sequence

As in previous chapters, the presentation sequence is tutorial (see Section 3.9). An overview is followed by descriptions of two processes to illustrate typical patterns of approach. Components of these different processes have then been consolidated in subsequent discussion on the subject. Each component is, however, described in its own right as before.

Information systems planning requires that the plan should provide systems that clearly support the relevant topics chosen by the enterprise. The descriptions and illustrations of components have therefore been organized into two groups:

1. one which describes components from analytic steps when dealing with the business plan, organization and mental modelling topics; and
2. one which describes components from prescriptive steps when dealing with the information systems plan and which also describes cross-references to the components from the analytic steps.

7.3 Overview of illustrative approaches

Approaches to information systems planning vary significantly but, nonetheless, show substantial areas of overlap. Information systems planning has to demonstrate a need for information system support before a project can be incorporated in the plan. Each approach focuses on different topics chosen by the enterprise for its estimation of need. The effect is that they have different starting points for their investigations and follow different pathways to achieve their results.

This overview describes two processes, either of which might be used for information systems planning (although neither is in sufficient detail to be practical). These provide examples of how the stage can be approached and provide a context for components which are typical of this kind of activity. They are based on an understanding of several existing methodologies but each is more limited in scope (for tutorial purposes) than any current approach. As in Chapter 6, there is no attempt to relate them, or the illustrations in subsequent paragraphs, to any specific methodology.

The first process to illustrate information systems planning is based on an analysis of business problems, followed by the identification of changes to information systems and business activities which will improve the business situation. It can be viewed as primarily organization driven, since it concentrates on understanding current business problems, what changes are needed to improve them, and what information systems should support these changes.

The second illustration is based on an analysis of the objectives and information needs of the enterprise, followed by the definition of an ideal set of systems to support them. It, by contrast, is business plan and mental model driven.

7.4   Planning process A — organization driven

This process provides an approach in which information systems planning is aimed at improving the enterprise in relation to identifiable business problems. It consists of the following steps (with step categories shown in parentheses):

1.	Analyse business problems	(abstraction).
2.	Identify needs for change	(abstraction).
3.	Identify information systems	(abstraction).
4.	Propose change alternatives and new information systems	(form conversion).
5.	Analyse benefits and costs	(abstraction).
6.	Evaluate change alternatives	(checking).
7.	Prepare plan	(decision).

These steps are now discussed in more detail and the components they generate are identified.

7.4.1   Step 1. Analyse business problems

Conduct an analysis of the BUSINESS PROBLEMS which have been encountered in the environment. The intention is to focus attention on ways of supporting improvement in the enterprise through INFORMATION SYSTEMS aimed at the changes needed for dealing with these BUSINESS PROBLEMS. Each BUSINESS PROBLEM will affect one or more BUSINESS ACTIVITIES and it is often valuable to pin down which INTEREST GROUPS are concerned with a given BUSINESS PROBLEM. An INTEREST GROUP will often be relatable to an ORGANIZATION UNIT.

7.4.2   Step 2. Identify needs for change

Establish the OBJECTIVES of the enterprise and identify any likely NEEDS FOR CHANGE required if the enterprise is to achieve its OBJECTIVES.

A NEED FOR CHANGE must clearly be relatable to a BUSINESS PROBLEM in the sense that any proposal to deal with the problem will cause a NEED FOR CHANGE. Each NEED FOR CHANGE can also relate to more than one OBJECTIVE since it may have been established specifically to meet various OBJECTIVES.

7.4.3   Step 3. Identify information systems

Identify the existing and planned INFORMATION SYSTEMS and relate each to the BUSINESS ACTIVITIES which it supports. INFORMATION SYSTEMS can also be cross-referenced to INFORMATION/MATERIAL SETS to give a record of which (clearly only INFORMATION SETS) is handled by which INFORMATION SYSTEM.

7.4.4   Step 4. Propose change alternatives and new information systems

Use the information now available on BUSINESS PROBLEMS, NEEDS FOR CHANGE and INFORMATION SYSTEMS to propose CHANGE ALTERNATIVES indicating what changes can be envisaged to the organization and its systems. Where necessary, this can include proposals for new INFORMATION SYSTEMS.

7.4.5   Step 5. Analyse benefits and costs

Once the nature of each INFORMATION SYSTEM and CHANGE ALTERNATIVE has been established it is then possible to analyse BENEFITS which the enterprise is seeking from introducing the changes (BENEFITS will, in many cases, be a paraphrased version of OBJECTIVES). An INFORMATION SYSTEM (planned or existing) should provide one or more BENEFITS. Likewise, a broad estimate of COSTS is made for the development of new systems and for

the modification of existing ones in the light of the various CHANGE
ALTERNATIVES.

7.4.6   Step 6. Evaluate change alternatives

It is now possible to evaluate the various CHANGE ALTERNATIVES to show
those which are preferable. Each CHANGE ALTERNATIVE can be related
to supporting INFORMATION SYSTEMS and, furthermore, to BUSINESS
ACTIVITIES affected.

7.4.7   Step 7. Prepare plan

At this point, it becomes possible to prepare a strategic plan. One approach is
to list a number of CHANGE ALTERNATIVES and to relate each CHANGE
ALTERNATIVE to the already perceived NEEDS FOR CHANGE in order to assess
which CHANGE ALTERNATIVE meets which NEED FOR CHANGE. The CHANGE
ALTERNATIVES can also be cross-referenced to the BENEFITS sought in order
to assess which CHANGE ALTERNATIVES provide which BENEFIT.

From this, a ranking is developed which provides the basis for
sequencing in the INFORMATION SYSTEMS PLAN.

7.5   Planning process B — business plan and mental model driven

This process provides an approach in which the principal information needs
of the enterprise are identified and planning is aimed at supporting them all
(in time). It consists of the following steps (with step categories shown in
parentheses):

1.	Identify business plan components and information needs	(abstraction).
2.	Develop business model (from a data perspective)	(abstraction).
3.	Identify information systems and business areas	(form conversion).
4.	Analyse priorities	(abstraction).
5.	Prepare plan	(decision).

These steps are now discussed in more detail and the components they
generate are identified.

7.5.1   Step 1. Identify business plan components and information needs

The analysis starts by identifying the OBJECTIVES of the enterprise and of its
major ORGANIZATION UNITS and BUSINESS ACTIVITIES. The intention is to

focus attention on ways of supporting the OBJECTIVES and other business planning concepts of the enterprise through INFORMATION SYSTEMS that provide their information needs. Measurable GOALS are determined for each OBJECTIVE to show how it will be achieved and CRITICAL SUCCESS FACTORS are highlighted to emphasize what must go right if the OBJECTIVES and GOALS are to be met. The information needed in support of all these is then established and recorded as INFORMATION/MATERIAL SETS.

7.5.2   Step 2. Develop business model

Having identified the major INFORMATION/MATERIAL SETS it then becomes possible to develop a more formal, high level (global) data model for the enterprise. This is described in terms of ENTITY TYPES and the RELATIONSHIPS which associate them.

7.5.3   Step 3. Identify information systems and business areas

Following this modelling, each BUSINESS ACTIVITY's use of data is illustrated in an entity type/business activity cross-reference component. These cross-reference components can be reordered to show groupings of data shared between groupings of BUSINESS ACTIVITIES. Combinations of these groupings are viewed as potential INFORMATION SYSTEMS.

7.5.4   Step 4. Analyse priorities

A logical sequence for developing the INFORMATION SYSTEMS is then established based on their dependencies on other systems for information. This sequence is modified by soliciting business PRIORITIES, by a COST/BENEFIT evaluation and by estimates of the transition effort required in moving from the current systems.

7.5.5   Step 5. Prepare plan

A further grouping of INFORMATION SYSTEMS is carried out to create BUSINESS AREAS which provide the scope for subsequent business analysis projects. The relative importance of each BUSINESS AREA is taken from the accumulated PRIORITIES of its components. The INFORMATION SYSTEMS PLAN is then constructed as a sequenced collection of PLAN PROJECTS, each of which is to analyse either a BUSINESS AREA or (to understand subsequent migration requirements) an INFORMATION SYSTEM whose DEVELOPMENT STATUS is 'extant'.

7.6   Consolidation of components of information systems planning

Figure 7.3 shows, in a consolidated form, the major components required for processes A and B. All of these components could potentially be used in information systems planning.

It should be noted that while most of these components are new, some do already appear in Chapters 4 and 5 while others are just cross-references to these known components.

Figure 7.3 is, in fact, a summary of the content of Figures 7.4 and 7.5. It has, however, been simplified by removing all cross-reference components and replacing them by many to many relationship lines. These are shown by using a convention of two opposing arrowheads on the line. As a further simplification, no relationship names have been included – but these can all be found in Figures 7.4 and 7.5.

Figure 7.3 is also divided into two areas, as described in Section 7.2. These divisions relate to the analytic and prescriptive steps of information systems planning and are used here as convenient units for presentation purposes. They deal with:

- analytic components related to the business plan, organization and mental modelling, and
- prescriptive components related to the information systems plan, together with cross-references.

Each division is detailed in the sections which follow.

7.7   Components of the analytic steps of information systems planning — business plan, organization and mental model related

The business plan, organization and mental model related components of the analytic steps of information systems planning are:

1.   BUSINESS PROBLEM
2.   ORGANIZATION UNIT
3.   UNIT IN ORGANIZATION
4.   INTEREST GROUP
5.   ORGANIZATION UNIT INVOLVED WITH INTEREST GROUP
6.   OBJECTIVE
7.   PROBLEM FOR OBJECTIVE
8.   GOAL

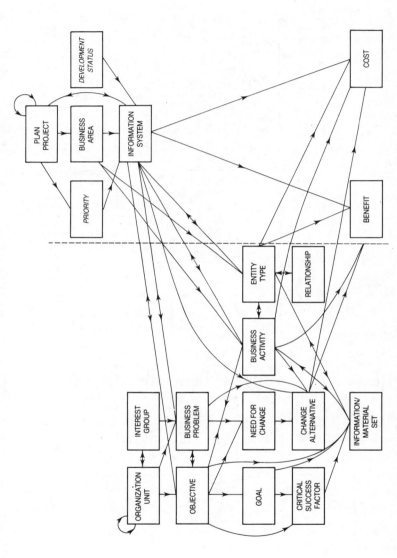

Figure 7.3 Information systems planning – consolidation of major components. This diagram employs many to many relationships as a means of summarizing its content. These are replaced by cross-reference components in subsequent diagrams.

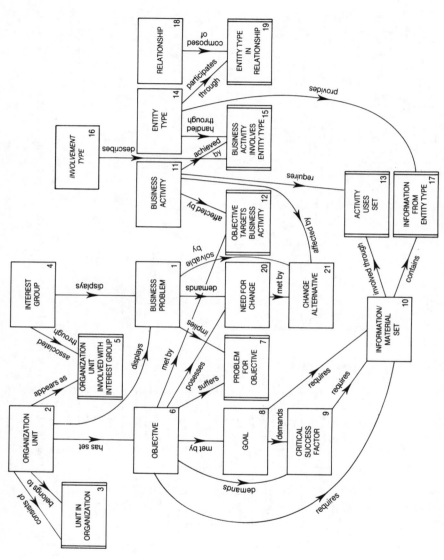

Figure 7.4 Information systems planning – analytic steps' components related to business plans, organizations and mental models. The numbers in the boxes refer to the sequence of description of the components in Section 7.7.

9. CRITICAL SUCCESS FACTOR
10. INFORMATION/MATERIAL SET
11. BUSINESS ACTIVITY
12. OBJECTIVE TARGETS BUSINESS ACTIVITY
13. ACTIVITY USES SET
14. ENTITY TYPE
15. BUSINESS ACTIVITY INVOLVES ENTITY TYPE
*16. INVOLVEMENT TYPE
17. INFORMATION FROM ENTITY TYPE
18. RELATIONSHIP
19. ENTITY TYPE IN RELATIONSHIP
20. NEED FOR CHANGE
21. CHANGE ALTERNATIVE

The component preceded by an asterisk is methodology dependent.

Each of these is presented in turn. The interrelationships between them are depicted in Figure 7.4.

In some cases, an adequate description of a component has already been given in Chapter 4 so only a section reference is provided here. Some components may have already been described but are employed in a somewhat different manner for information systems planning purposes. In these cases, the unique usage is described and a cross-reference given.

7.7.1 BUSINESS PROBLEM

A BUSINESS PROBLEM is a difficulty being experienced with some aspect of the functioning of the enterprise or its information systems. It is not related to regular algorithm-solving types of problem but highlights areas of potential improvement in the enterprise. Its initial expression may be somewhat subjective but, by cross-referencing it to the areas that it affects, its nature can be clarified and effective change analysis can be made.

7.7.2 ORGANIZATION UNIT

This component is already described in Section 4.7.13.

7.7.3 UNIT IN ORGANIZATION

UNIT IN ORGANIZATION is a cross-reference component which serves to describe the reporting structure among ORGANIZATION UNITS. It describes associations both where they report to others and where they have others reporting to them; thus both hierarchical and matrix organizations can be described in this manner.

7.7.4   INTEREST GROUP

An INTEREST GROUP is a category of people affected by a BUSINESS PROBLEM. They share an interest in the BUSINESS PROBLEM and, as a group, can be expected to have broadly similar requirements of any INFORMATION SYSTEM they use in common. In attempting to resolve their BUSINESS PROBLEMS, it will be found that each INTEREST GROUP will then have some bearing on the final choice of what is implemented.

7.7.5   ORGANIZATION UNIT INVOLVED WITH INTEREST GROUP

The people making up an INTEREST GROUP may all belong to the same ORGANIZATION UNIT but they could, equally well, be from several ORGANIZATION UNITS, or be external to the enterprise but affected by its INFORMATION SYSTEMS (a tax authority, for example). ORGANIZATION UNIT INVOLVED WITH INTEREST GROUP is a cross-reference component used to highlight cases where there is some commonality of concern.

7.7.6   OBJECTIVE

An OBJECTIVE is a broad result that an enterprise wishes to achieve in furthering its corporate mission. It is a cause of action and specifies a point or state which is to be reached by deploying corporate resource and effort.

The way in which an OBJECTIVE (or group of OBJECTIVES) is to be tackled is set out in one or more strategies and it is implemented through action plans. OBJECTIVES may be established for the enterprise as a whole or for individual ORGANIZATION UNITS.

7.7.7   PROBLEM FOR OBJECTIVE

A PROBLEM FOR OBJECTIVE is a cross-reference component which shows those cases where an identified BUSINESS PROBLEM may inhibit or (at least) add difficulty to the achieving of some OBJECTIVE set by the enterprise.

7.7.8   GOAL

A GOAL is a significant defined point or condition resulting from actions leading towards an OBJECTIVE. There must be no subjectivity or ambiguity in stating a GOAL. This means that INFORMATION SYSTEMS should be capable of carrying the information needed to determine whether a GOAL has been reached.

7.7.9   CRITICAL SUCCESS FACTOR

A CRITICAL SUCCESS FACTOR is one of those (small number of) factors which must go right if the enterprise is to achieve its OBJECTIVES and GOALS. In a sense, they represent conditions which must be satisfied. Each CRITICAL SUCCESS FACTOR is related either to an OBJECTIVE as a whole or to one of the GOALS through which the OBJECTIVE is to be achieved.

7.7.10   INFORMATION/MATERIAL SET

This component is already described in Section 4.7.6. In the information systems planning context this component is also used to define information requirements of OBJECTIVES, GOALS and CRITICAL SUCCESS FACTORS. Their INFORMATION SETS will be influential in the choice of INFORMATION SYSTEMS, especially those aimed at supporting business direction.

7.7.11   BUSINESS ACTIVITY

A BUSINESS ACTIVITY describes *what* has to be done within an enterprise rather than *how* it is done. It provides a conceptual view of the nature of the enterprise. This is particularly important in planning since the INFORMATION SYSTEMS PLAN should be relatively insensitive to the usual levels (frequent) of organizational change.

BUSINESS ACTIVITIES have already been described in Section 4.7.1 as components in the business analysis stage. It is important to note that information systems planning is concerned only with the higher levels of BUSINESS ACTIVITY which give a global view of the enterprise.

7.7.12   OBJECTIVE TARGETS BUSINESS ACTIVITY

Strictly speaking, OBJECTIVES are set to define requirements for achievement by ORGANIZATION UNITS. However, it is only possible to understand what the ORGANIZATION UNIT must do, by first identifying which of the underlying BUSINESS ACTIVITIES is affected by each OBJECTIVE. This cross-reference component therefore highlights the consequence of the OBJECTIVE.

7.7.13   ACTIVITY USES SET

This cross-reference component has already been described in Section 4.7.10.

7.7.14   ENTITY TYPE

ENTITY TYPES have already been described for business analysis in Section 4.5.1. During information systems planning, only major ENTITY TYPES are identified as satisfying the principal information needs of relatively high level BUSINESS ACTIVITIES. The resulting model is therefore described as 'high level' and, if its scope is the whole enterprise, it is commonly called 'global'.

7.7.15 BUSINESS ACTIVITY INVOLVES ENTITY TYPE

This is a cross-reference component described earlier in Section 4.11.2.

7.7.16 INVOLVEMENT TYPE

INVOLVEMENT TYPE was described earlier in Section 4.7.9. In this context, it provides a methodology dependent component to indicate the nature of an involvement between a BUSINESS ACTIVITY and an ENTITY TYPE.

7.7.17 INFORMATION FROM ENTITY TYPE

This cross-reference component indicates which ENTITY TYPES must be available to provide the information required to establish an INFORMATION SET needed by the enterprise in support of its OBJECTIVES, GOALS, CRITICAL SUCCESS FACTORS and BUSINESS ACTIVITIES.

7.7.18 RELATIONSHIP

RELATIONSHIPS have been described earlier in Section 4.5.6. However, since information systems planning develops a high level entity model, the RELATIONSHIPS are not always precisely categorized in terms of a RELATIONSHIP TYPE. They will sometimes appear in place of a missing, minor entity type and its more explicit RELATIONSHIPS. A high proportion of the RELATIONSHIPS may therefore be of the RELATIONSHIP TYPE many to many.

7.7.19 ENTITY TYPE IN RELATIONSHIP

This cross-reference component has already been described in Section 4.5.7. In essence, an occurrence of this component serves to describe the nature of the involvement of one of the two ENTITY TYPES in a RELATIONSHIP and whether it is the dependent or the independent member of the pair.

7.7.20 NEED FOR CHANGE

A NEED FOR CHANGE is a statement of something which must be improved in order to resolve a particular BUSINESS PROBLEM. It is determined by examining BUSINESS PROBLEMS in relation to OBJECTIVES, to see where the problem situation might most profitably be tackled in order to alleviate the immediate BUSINESS PROBLEM and to satisfy future requirements. A NEED FOR CHANGE commonly appears as a reformulation of a BUSINESS PROBLEM.

7.7.21 CHANGE ALTERNATIVE

A CHANGE ALTERNATIVE is a proposed new way of doing things in an INFORMATION SYSTEM or a BUSINESS ACTIVITY, in order to deal with some

BUSINESS PROBLEM or NEED FOR CHANGE. The production of CHANGE ALTERNATIVES is a creative process so the number generated in response to any BUSINESS PROBLEM or NEED FOR CHANGE is limited only by the imagination of the analyst.

7.8 Examples of business plan, organization and mental model components in information systems planning

The following tables give examples of each of the 21 components defined in Section 7.7. The sequence is the same as for the component descriptions. These examples are from a variety of sources rather than a single case study. In some cases, an example of a particular component appears in an earlier chapter so a reference to the appropriate section is given though the example is duplicated for ease of reference.

7.8.1 BUSINESS PROBLEM

Problem ID	Problem Description
P1	Poor order preparation procedure
P2	Incorrect invoices
P3	Late arrival of distribution instructions
P4	Outdated office equipment
P5	No loading bay
P6	Inconsistent material quality
P7	Low morale among stock controllers

The description is informal and reflects statements gathered while interviewing. Each description is, however, generally accepted by the members of at least one INTEREST GROUP.

7.8.2 ORGANIZATION UNIT

Organization Unit Code	Organization Unit Name
E	Enterprise
P	Purchasing
W	Warehouse and Distribution
G	Goods Receiving Unit
A	Accounting
M	Marketing

This example is taken from Section 4.8.13, but has been extended slightly to make it consistent with later examples.

7.8.3 UNIT IN ORGANIZATION

Belongs to Organization Unit Code	Consists of Organization Unit Code
—	M
—	A
E	W
E	P
M	G
W	—

This cross-reference contains pairs of Organization Unit Codes that each show a reporting relationship within the organization structure.

7.8.4 INTEREST GROUP

Interest Group ID	Interest Group Name
I1	Stock Controllers
I2	Head Office Clerical Staff
I3	Warehouse Foremen
I4	Main Board Directors
I5	Shareholders
I6	Branch Sales Managers
I7	Auditors
I8	Raw Material Suppliers
I9	Information Systems Staff
I10	Trade Union

The name is the one generally accepted within the user community and by members of the INTEREST GROUP.

7.8.5 ORGANIZATION UNIT INVOLVED WITH INTEREST GROUP

Organization Unit Code	I1	I2	I3	I4	I5	I6	I7	I8	I9	I10
E				X	X					X
P	X	X						X		X
W	X		X							X
G	X									X
A		X		X			X			
M				X		X				

This cross-reference table shows some entries from Sections 7.8.2 and 7.8.4. In practice, there will be cases where there is no cross-reference, that is, where the INTEREST GROUP lies entirely outside the enterprise.

7.8.6 OBJECTIVE

Objective ID	Organization Unit Code	Objective Name
O1	W	Economic maintenance of high service levels directly from stock
O2	M	Become market leader with principal branded product
O3	P	Improved responsiveness to customer demands

The name of an OBJECTIVE is just a statement of the OBJECTIVE. It may also have longer descriptions, but these are typically explanatory and outline the circumstances of the OBJECTIVE. OBJECTIVES have no independent existence and so must be associated with an ORGANIZATION UNIT at some level.

7.8.7 PROBLEM FOR OBJECTIVE

	Objective ID		
Problem ID	O1	O2	O3
P1	X		X
P2		X	
P3	X		
P4			X
P5	X		
P6		X	
P7	X		

This cross-reference illustrates the many to many relationship between BUSINESS PROBLEMS and OBJECTIVES. It would also be possible for it to show the degree to which a BUSINESS PROBLEM might be tackled through an OBJECTIVE.

7.8.8   GOAL

Goal ID	Objective ID	Goal Description
G1	O1	95% of requests for goods satisfied from stock at a minimum total inventory holding value
G2	O2	Achieve 27% market share for 'Zoom' product by 4th quarter
G3	O3	Improve sales of 'Zoom' by 3% each quarter
G4	O4	Introduce new order handling system within 15 months
G5	O5	Despatch 98% of demands for goods within 24 hours of receipt

GOALS are expressions of intent to carry out actions to ensure that an OBJECTIVE is reached. Each Goal Description should be seen to quantify and convey a target for achieving some aspect of an OBJECTIVE.

7.8.9   CRITICAL SUCCESS FACTOR

CSF ID	Goal ID	Objective ID	CSF Description
CSF 1		O3	Ability to measure demand accurately
CSF 2		O3	Ability to forecast demand variations
CSF 3		O1	Supplier performance in terms of both quality and lead time
CSF 4	G1		Reliability of stock records

As with GOALS, a CSF Description is likely to tie back to some vital feature of a GOAL or OBJECTIVE.

7.8.10   INFORMATION/MATERIAL SET

Set Type Code	Set Number	Description	Plan Component ID
I	1	List of suppliers	G1
I	2	List of items stocked	G1
M	1	Stocks of goods	G1
I	3	Reorder levels	G1
I	4	Purchase orders	O3
I	5	Price of goods items	O2
I	5	Missed supply-by dates	CSF3

This example is based on that in Section 4.8.6 but has the additional attribute Plan Component ID. This is the identifier of the OBJECTIVE, GOAL or CRITICAL SUCCESS FACTOR for which the information is necessary. It may be null for those INFORMATION SETS associated only with BUSINESS ACTIVITIES.

7.8.11 BUSINESS ACTIVITY

Activity Number	Activity Description
1	Inventory control
1.1	Handling new stock
1.2	Ordering stock required
1.3	Monitoring stock levels

This example is taken from Section 4.8.1 but includes only the higher level activities that might be relevant for planning purposes.

7.8.12 OBJECTIVE TARGETS BUSINESS ACTIVITY

	Activity Number		
Objective ID	1.1	1.2	1.3
O1	X	X	X
O2			
O3		X	

This cross-reference is one of the principal links between the business plan and the information (mental) model. It is useful in calculating priorities for information systems developments.

7.8.13 ACTIVITY USES SET

Activity Number	Involvement	Set Type Code	Set Number
1.1	U	M	1
1.1	U	I	2
1.2	U	I	4
1.2	R	I	5
1.2	R	I	1
1.3	R	I	3
1.3	R	I	2

This example is taken from Section 4.8.10.

7.8.14   ENTITY TYPE

Entity Type Code	Entity Type Description
ET1	Supplier
ET2	Stock Item
ET5	Purchase Order
ET7	Stock on Hand

This example is taken from Section 4.6.1 but includes only major ENTITY TYPES of the sort that might be relevant for planning purposes.

7.8.15   BUSINESS ACTIVITY INVOLVES ENTITY TYPE

	Activity Number		
Entity Type Description	1.1	1.2	1.3
Supplier	U	R	
Stock Item	U	R	R
Purchase Order		U	
Stock on Hand			R

This example is based on that in Section 4.12.2 but treats the involvement at a higher level.

7.8.16   INVOLVEMENT TYPE

Involvement Type Code	Involvement Description
R	Information set input to activity which uses set
U	Information set output from activity which updates set

This example is taken from Section 4.8.9. R is the abbreviation of 'retrieves' (and implies usage) and U is the abbreviation of 'updates'.

7.8.17   INFORMATION FROM ENTITY TYPE

	Entity Type Code		
Set Number	ET1	ET2	ET5
1	X		
2		X	
3		X	
4			X
5		X	

This cross-reference is the principal link, at the data level, between the business plan and the information (mental) model.

7.8.18 RELATIONSHIP

Relationship Number	Relationship Type	Relationship Description
6	M1	Supplier receives purchase order
7	M1	Stock item held as stock on hand
10	MM	Stock item supplied from supplier
11	MM	Stock item replenished through purchase order

This example is partly taken from Section 4.6.6, modified to match the high-level entity model implied in Section 7.8.14.

7.8.19 ENTITY TYPE IN RELATIONSHIP

Relationship Number	Entity Type Code	Dependency Code
6	ET1	I
6	ET5	D
7	ET2	I
7	ET7	D
10	ET1	—
10	ET2	—
11	ET2	—
11	ET5	—

This is taken partly from the example in Section 4.6.7 and added to from Section 7.8.18. At this level, relationships may be viewed as symmetrical, especially when described as many to many, so there may be no dependencies. Note: the Dependency Codes indicate whether the ENTITY TYPE is the dependent (D) or the independent (I) one of the pair of ENTITY TYPES involved in the RELATIONSHIP (see also Section 4.6.7).

7.8.20 NEED FOR CHANGE

Problem ID	Need ID	Need For Change Name	Need For Change Description
P1	N1	Better order processing	Simpler, faster, more accurate acceptance of requests for goods
P2	N2	More accurate invoicing	Correct notification, accumulation and billing of all items despatched and proper notification of returns credited
P3	N3	Better stock controller morale	Improved rate of response and level of accuracy in handling requests for goods and dealing with receipts of goods

Key words from Problem Descriptions and Objective Names may also appear in the names and descriptions of NEEDS FOR CHANGE in order to highlight their close association.

7.8.21 CHANGE ALTERNATIVE

Problem ID	Need ID	Change ID	Change Name	Change Description
P1	N1	C0	Acceptance by van driver	The current approach
	N1	C1	Telephone order	Take calls from the customer and input them through an on line facility
	N1	C2	Telephone order soliciting	Call customer and suggest what his or her requirement might be by extrapolation from known depletion rates
	N1	C3	Direct ordering by customer	Give customer on line access to the order processing system

Each CHANGE ALTERNATIVE is associated with a NEED FOR CHANGE and also with the original PROBLEM in order to group all of the options for that PROBLEM in a simple manner.

7.9 Components of the prescriptive steps of information systems planning — information systems plan and cross-references

The information systems plan and cross-reference components of the information systems planning stage are:

1. INFORMATION SYSTEM
*2. DEVELOPMENT STATUS
3. ACTIVITY ALLOCATION TO SYSTEM
4. ENTITY TYPE ALLOCATION TO SYSTEM
5. BUSINESS AREA
6. PLAN PROJECT
7. INFORMATION SYSTEMS PLAN
*8. PROJECT STATUS
9 PROJECT PRECEDENCE/SUCCEDENCE
10. INFORMATION SYSTEM IN PLAN PROJECT
11. INFORMATION SYSTEMS SUPPORT FOR OBJECTIVE
12. PROBLEM INVOLVES INFORMATION SYSTEM
13. COST
14. BENEFIT
*15. PRIORITY
16. PRIORITILIZATION CRITERION

Components preceded by an asterisk are methodology dependent.

Each of these is presented in turn and the interrelationships between them are depicted in Figure 7.5.

In some cases, an adequate description of a component has already been given in an earlier chapter so only a section reference is provided here. Some components may have already been described but are employed in a somewhat different manner for information systems planning purposes. In these cases, the unique usage is described and a cross-reference given.

7.9.1 INFORMATION SYSTEM

An INFORMATION SYSTEM, in the broad sense used in this chapter of a business information system, is a means of recording and communicating

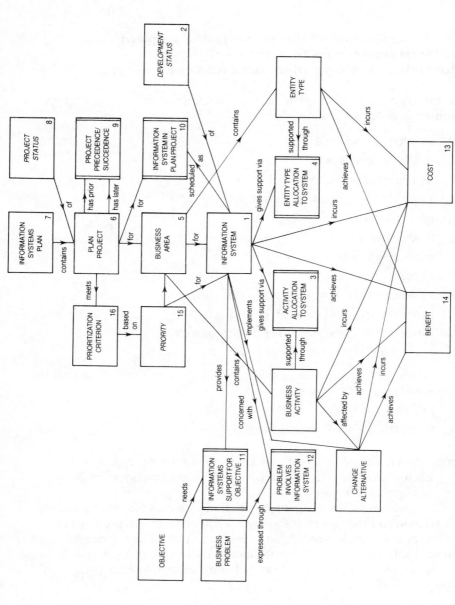

Figure 7.5 Information systems planning – prescriptive steps' components for the information systems plan and cross-references. The numbers in the boxes refer to the sequence of description of the components in Section 7.9.

information to satisfy the requirements of all its users, the BUSINESS ACTIVITIES they are engaged in and the OBJECTIVES established for them. An INFORMATION SYSTEM therefore supports a BUSINESS ACTIVITY (or group of them) by providing the information it needs or by automating some or all of it. It also must contain (or have access to) data about entities of (one or a group of) ENTITY TYPES on which it must provide information to enable the BUSINESS ACTIVITIES.

7.9.2 DEVELOPMENT STATUS

DEVELOPMENT STATUS is a methodology dependent component which allows the planner to indicate whether the INFORMATION SYSTEM being dealt with is one which already exists or whether it is newly conceived. To express this, the DEVELOPMENT STATUS provides two values:

1.   extant, and
2.   envisaged.

Each INFORMATION SYSTEM is associated with one of these. If it is 'envisaged', no decision will yet have been taken as to whether, or how extensively, computerized support should be provided.

7.9.3 ACTIVITY ALLOCATION TO SYSTEM

This cross-reference component indicates which INFORMATION SYSTEMS give support to which BUSINESS ACTIVITIES. If the INFORMATION SYSTEM is 'extant' then the allocation describes a current situation; if it is 'envisaged' then the allocation describes a possibility which will only come about once the INFORMATION SYSTEM is implemented.

7.9.4 ENTITY TYPE ALLOCATION TO SYSTEM

This cross-reference component indicates which INFORMATION SYSTEMS give support to or make use of which ENTITY TYPES. If the INFORMATION SYSTEM is 'extant' then the allocation describes a current situation; if it is 'envisaged' then the allocation describes a possibility which will only come about once the INFORMATION SYSTEM is implemented.

7.9.5 BUSINESS AREA

A BUSINESS AREA is a collection of INFORMATION SYSTEMS each with a DEVELOPMENT STATUS of 'envisaged'. It is the subject of a business analysis project and is typically defined with a scope that is sufficiently large to ensure that any systems built subsequently will be able to achieve a high level of data sharing.

7.9.6   PLAN PROJECT

A PLAN PROJECT is a project to which resources may be allocated. A PLAN PROJECT may either be for business analysis to be conducted on a BUSINESS AREA or may be for the examination of an INFORMATION SYSTEM whose DEVELOPMENT STATUS is 'extant', either to obtain a clear understanding of any subsequent transition requirements when developing future systems or to determine how best that system can be improved. It should be noted that this last may require renovation techniques, as described in Chapter 8.

7.9.7   INFORMATION SYSTEMS PLAN

The INFORMATION SYSTEMS PLAN is a collection of PLAN PROJECTS for analysing BUSINESS AREAS or for developing INFORMATION SYSTEMS. It includes the interdependencies between these projects, when they should be undertaken, and what resources are likely to be required in carrying them out.

7.9.8   PROJECT STATUS

PROJECT STATUS simply provides a methodology dependent code to indicate whether any particular PLAN PROJECT is concerned with extant or envisaged components. It has two categories:

1.   new development, and
2.   enhancement.

7.9.9   PROJECT PRECEDENCE/SUCCEDENCE

PROJECT PRECEDENCE/SUCCEDENCE is a cross-reference component which captures the intended sequence of PLAN PROJECTS. One or more PLAN PROJECTS may be necessary precursors to any given PLAN PROJECT and one or more may follow it.

7.9.10   INFORMATION SYSTEM IN PLAN PROJECT

This is a cross-reference component describing the project by which an INFORMATION SYSTEM is developed in the context of the INFORMATION SYSTEMS PLAN. For those which are extant, the project may involve no more than some enhancement or bridge-building work; for those newly envisaged, the project may proceed through all stages of the framework described in this report.

7.9.11 INFORMATION SYSTEMS SUPPORT FOR OBJECTIVE

If the INFORMATION SYSTEMS PLAN is to satisfy the strategic planning requirements of the enterprise, then it must ensure that there will be systems providing the kinds of information needed to support the enterprise as it moves towards its OBJECTIVES. The INFORMATION SYSTEMS SUPPORT FOR OBJECTIVE cross-reference component defines those strategic INFORMATION SYSTEMS intended to support the OBJECTIVES.

7.9.12 PROBLEM INVOLVES INFORMATION SYSTEM

This cross-reference component provides information about the association between BUSINESS PROBLEMS and INFORMATION SYSTEMS. In the case of extant systems they will be among the sources of the problem while an association with a planned system indicates that the new system is expected to alleviate the problem.

7.9.13 COST

A COST is a depletion of resource in an enterprise, associated with the implementation of an INFORMATION SYSTEM or CHANGE ALTERNATIVE. COSTS are commonly represented in monetary terms, although these may be derived from indirect sources, such as the loss of business opportunities during the cutover to a new system (should such a cutover ever be necessary).

7.9.14 BENEFIT

A BENEFIT is an improved or new contribution to the enterprise by an INFORMATION SYSTEM or CHANGE ALTERNATIVE or by the inclusion in one or the other of these of a particular BUSINESS ACTIVITY or ENTITY TYPE. Evaluation of BENEFITS provides a case for implementing either the INFORMATION SYSTEM or the CHANGE ALTERNATIVE, and may provide a basis upon which they may be ranked for planning purposes. Conventionally, benefits may be classed as tangible or intangible. In either case, a monetary value may be associated with them though, of course, this is more readily achieved in the former case.

7.9.15 PRIORITY

A PRIORITY is simply a methodology dependent ranking measure applied to envisaged INFORMATION SYSTEMS and BUSINESS AREAS. It indicates a desired relative order in which PLAN PROJECTS to implement or enforce them should be tackled. This order may, however, be altered in the final INFORMATION SYSTEMS PLAN to take account of significant technical interdependencies between components.

7.9.16   PRIORITIZATION CRITERION

A PRIORITIZATION CRITERION is a basis for determining a PRIORITY. It may be:

- a rule governing the prioritization process,
- a statement of business policy,
- an algorithm for assessing the merits of ranking positions, or
- some other feature of a particular methodology.

There are many ways of deriving PRIORITIES. These often involve the consolidation and weighting of other components, such as OBJECTIVES, GOALS, CRITICAL SUCCESS FACTORS, CHANGE ALTERNATIVES, PROBLEMS, BUSINESS ACTIVITIES or ENTITY TYPES. COSTS and BENEFITS are usually major factors influencing the final PRIORITIES and thus feature prominently among the PRIORITIZATION CRITERIA.

7.10   Examples of information systems plan and cross-reference components in information systems planning

The following tables give examples of each of the 16 components defined in Section 7.9. The sequence is the same as for the component descriptions. These examples are from a variety of sources rather than a single case study. In some cases, an example of a particular component appears in an earlier chapter so a reference to the appropriate section is given. The example is then duplicated for ease of reference.

7.10.1   INFORMATION SYSTEM

System Code	System Name
ICP	Inventory Control and Purchasing
OPD	Order Processing and Distribution
CAM ˙	Computer Aided Manufacturing
MRP	Material Requirements Planning
BACS	Bankers Automated Clearing System
MSR	Monthly Sales Reporting
SA	Statutory Accounts
MA	Market Analysis
CC	Customer Care
OT	Order Taking
AR	Accounts Receivable
PP	Production Planning

The System Name is likely to contain key words from the names of principal BUSINESS ACTIVITIES it supports.

7.10.2 DEVELOPMENT STATUS

This simply provides two code values, extant and envisaged, as described in Section 7.9.2. It is methodology dependent.

7.10.3 ACTIVITY ALLOCATION TO SYSTEM

System Code	Activity Number
ICP	1.1
ICP	1.2
ICP	1.3

This is a simple cross-reference component. Where the activity is supported through several systems, occurrences can exist, each of which allocates the same BUSINESS ACTIVITY to a different INFORMATION SYSTEM.

7.10.4 ENTITY TYPE ALLOCATION TO SYSTEM

System Code	Entity Type Code
ICP	ET1
ICP	ET2
ICP	ET5
ICP	ET7

This is a simple cross-reference component. Where the ENTITY TYPE is handled in several systems, occurrences can exist, each of which allocates the same ENTITY TYPE to a different INFORMATION SYSTEM.

7.10.5 BUSINESS AREA

Business Area ID	Name	System Code
BA1	Marketing	MSR
		MA
		CC
BA2	Sales and Inventory	ICP
		OT
BA3	Finance	SA
		AR
BA4	Production	CAM
		MRP
		PP

BUSINESS AREA is a collective term including activities and data for the INFORMATION SYSTEMS it includes. It is often named after a major BUSINESS ACTIVITY but may be named after a major ENTITY TYPE if development is oriented towards developing core databases for the enterprise.

7.10.6   PLAN PROJECT

Project ID	Project Description	Start Month
BA1A	Marketing and Customer analysis	1
BA2A	Sales and Inventory analysis	4
OPDT	Order Processing and Distribution transition	4
BA3A	Finance analysis	7
BACST	BACS transition	9

In the final plan, the projects which are mounted may require the development of several INFORMATION SYSTEMS together to satisfy the information needs of the enterprise.

7.10.7   INFORMATION SYSTEMS PLAN

IS Plan ID	Plan Description	Period	Start Date
'89–93 Plan	IS 5-year plan	1989–1993	1 Jan 1989

The INFORMATION SYSTEMS PLAN provides a collection point at which all PLAN PROJECTS are grouped.

7.10.8   PROJECT STATUS

This provides codes for two categories of development – new development and enhancement, as given in Section 7.9.8. It is methodology dependent.

7.10.9   PROJECT PRECEDENCE/SUCCEDENCE

Succeeding Plan Project	Preceding Plan Project
BA1A	—
BA2A	BA1A
OPDT	—
BA3A	BA2A
BA3A	OPDT

This cross-reference component identifies dependencies within PLAN PROJECTS, and so is an important element in scheduling within the PROJECT PLAN.

7.10.10 INFORMATION SYSTEM IN PLAN PROJECT

System Code	Project ID
OPD	OPDT
MSR	BA1A
MA	BA1A
CC	BA1A
ICP	BA2A
OT	BA2A

This component is a simple cross-reference.

7.10.11 INFORMATION SYSTEMS SUPPORT FOR OBJECTIVE

System Code	Objective ID		
	O1	O2	O3
ICP	X		
OPD		X	
MSR			X

This cross-reference is important in determining PRIORITIES when there is a general desire to provide INFORMATION SYSTEMS as support to achieving the OBJECTIVES of the business plan.

7.10.12 PROBLEM INVOLVES INFORMATION SYSTEM

System Code	Business Problem				
	P1	P3	P5	P6	P7
ICP					X
OPD	X	X	X		
MRP				X	

This component is a simple cross-reference.

7.10.13   COST

Cost ID	Cost Description
C1	5 man-year development project
C2	Doubled MIPS* in central hardware
C3	Terminals for 52 branch offices
C4	New international advertising campaign
C5	10 week training requirement for 138 staff

* MIPS = million instructions per second.

Further detail can be added to this component by providing financial quantification and also by categorizing each COST item as direct or indirect and as capital or expense.

7.10.14   BENEFIT

Benefit ID	Benefit Description
B1	10% increase in likelihood of achieving each sale
B2	Better risk management
B3	50% reduction in maintenance
B4	Improved international corporate identity
B5	6% increase in production line throughput

Further detail can be added to this component by providing financial quantification and also by categorizing each BENEFIT as tangible or intangible.

7.10.15   PRIORITY

System Code	System Name	Priority
OPD	Order Processing and Distribution	1
MSR	Monthly Sales Reporting	2
ICP	Inventory Control and Purchasing	3

This methodology dependent component is essentially a list arranged in rank order following the prioritization procedure.

7.10.16 PRIORITIZATION CRITERION

Criterion ID	Criterion Description
PC1	Planning systems take precedence over all others
PC2	Support for a CRITICAL SUCCESS FACTOR is 1.5 times as important as for a GOAL
PC3	An ENTITY TYPE used by 30% or more of BUSINESS ACTIVITIES receives a PRIORITY of 1

The description of each PRIORITIZATION CRITERION is an informally stated rule to be applied in the prioritization procedure.

7.11 Linking to the business analysis stage

The principal product of information systems planning is the INFORMATION SYSTEMS PLAN. A major element in that plan is the identification of BUSINESS AREAS for which business analysis projects should be mounted. Precisely how this is done and how the results are presented is methodology specific. For tutorial reasons, however, this section indicates how, within the context of the framework presented in this text, a link can be established between information systems planning and business analysis. The principal link is in terms of components created during information systems planning which are common to the business analysis stage. These components are:

- ORGANIZATION UNIT
- BUSINESS ACTIVITY
- ENTITY TYPE
- BUSINESS ACTIVITY INVOLVES ENTITY TYPE
- RELATIONSHIP
- ENTITY TYPE IN RELATIONSHIP

The definition of these components in information systems planning may be less precise, and the identification of properties less complete, than will be achieved in business analysis. However, they provide a 'starter set' for the analysis and they can assist in the definition of the scope of an analysis project by saying which of them are within the PLAN PROJECT's area of responsibility.

Other links are established as a result of identifying potential INFORMATION SYSTEMS. These provide a baseline of expectation against which progress on analysis and design projects can be assessed.

Further important links are provided through components viewed by the enterprise as especially important within the topics they chose as their principal indicators of business relevance in information systems planning. In this chapter these components are:

- OBJECTIVE
- INFORMATION SYSTEMS SUPPORT FOR OBJECTIVE
- GOAL
- CRITICAL SUCCESS FACTOR
- BUSINESS PROBLEM
- PROBLEM INVOLVES INFORMATION SYSTEM
- CHANGE ALTERNATIVE

These components are used during review steps in examining products prepared in subsequent stages. They serve as a means whereby management can confirm whether a product is likely to match business desires and support future directions.

Information systems planning can therefore provide a link between business concepts and the subsequent analysis, design and implementation projects and establishes a basis for their proper management.

EXERCISES

A.   *Self-assessment*

7.1   In this chapter, seven topics (business plan, finance, mental models, competition, organization, environment and information technology) are mentioned explicitly as having a bearing on information systems planning.

(a)   Without referring to the text, state the significance of these in the context of information systems planning.

(b)   Describe other possible topics relevant to information systems planning.

7.2   In Sections 7.4 and 7.5, two examples are given of planning processes. The first relates to business problems encountered (and solves them by identifying reasonable options for implementing change within the enterprise); the second relates to the objectives (and establishes the information needs derived from these, and then appropriate information systems).

(a)   Without referring to the text, state the global steps involved in the two approaches.

(b)   Referring to Figure 7.3, describe in what way these two are each other's mirror image and to what extent they coincide.

7.3   Section 7.7 describes the activity of 'business planning' while Section 7.9 describes that of 'information systems planning' proper. The components involved in these are illustrated in Figures 7.4 and 7.5, respectively, and Figure 7.3 shows a consolidation of both.

(a)   Figure 7.3 shows four cross-references reaching across the dividing line between business planning and information systems planning. To what extent do these indicate a need for an interactive planning activity?

(b)   Nine directed relationships cross the same dividing line. To what extent do these indicate a need for an interactive planning activity?

B.   Methodology related

(for those familiar with one or more specific methodologies)

Section 7.11 provides the link from 'information systems planning' to 'business analysis', adding that the way in which this is done is methodology specific.

7.4   Identify the concepts involved in specific methodologies which correspond to those discussed in this section (and Chapter 7, in general).

7.5   Establish the extent to which the methodologies do or do not cover the planning stage described here.

C.   Case studies

7.6   Section 7.1 identifies seven topics of particular relevance to information systems planning and states that components relating to only three of them (business planning, mental models and organization) will be described.

Identify components of the other four topics and show how they can be merged into Figures 7.3, 7.4 and 7.5.

7.7   Appendices B and C describe the business analysis and system design components for a hotel room reservation system at a ski resort. For the sake of the present exercise, the following extra information applies.

The system in Appendices B and C is only one of several systems required throughout the year by a major company providing up-market packaged vacations in many parts of the world.

The company is constantly seeking new business opportunities and negotiating with resort owners and hoteliers to create marketable packages. The company operates its own fleet of jets (contracting additional capacity when needed at peak periods). It arranges local transportation, local tours and entertainment events. The company owns some hotels, two casinos and has a 50% holding in a travel insurance company.

For each of the components identified for the information systems planning stage, identify a feasible set of instances which could be defined during a planning project.

7.8   Appendix D describes three further case studies. For any one of these, define a set of component instances for the components identified for the information systems planning stage.

8

Evolution of an installed information system

8.1 Introduction

This chapter deals with the greater part of the life of an information system – the evolution stage between its initial installation and acceptance and the subsequent stage which leads to its replacement by a new system. During this, its installed life, the system is likely to be changed. The most common aims when instituting change are:

1.   to handle new performance requirements, often because the patterns of usage or the supporting technology have changed;

2.   to accommodate changes in the nature of the business;

3.   to accommodate legislative changes; and

4.   to provide variations of the system, suitable for installation in different locations.

In this chapter, the first three aims will be treated together as leading to evolutionary change. Each leads to changes in requirements and these lead, in turn, to changes in the information systems. This chain of causes and effects can be regarded as fundamental to evolution. The provision of system variations to handle alternative sets of requirements will be treated separately in order to emphasize their administrative implications.

Evolution need not be looked at solely in terms of enhancement through the introduction of changes. Renovation of design products by transferring them to new technologies (including new methodologies) is also treated as part of the evolutionary processes. This may not add functionality in the first instance, but is generally intended to simplify the management and introduction of change thereafter.

The correction of errors, while recognized as a serious problem, is not concerned with change in requirements and will thus not be dealt with as an aspect of evolution. Errors may, however, occasionally stimulate evolution by causing a reassessment of requirements. This item is viewed as an aspect of the iterative nature of the design process.

Today's information systems methodologies treat the topic of evolution very sketchily, if at all. This chapter is therefore a commentary on the subject, based on the experience of the authors and their hopes for the future, rather than an analysis of practice as represented in current methodologies.

Experience shows that enormous resources and effort continue to be expended on information systems after they have been installed. This, the 'maintenance' overhead, may often amount to five or ten times the cost of the original development over the installed life of the system. Too often this is an unrecognized, or greatly underestimated, budget item at the time the information system is proposed.

Implicit in this chapter then is the hope that better methodologies will promote more flexible design, so that the resulting systems will be better able to evolve at lower cost. The ideas in this chapter point to some important features that will need to be supported in these methodologies.

8.2   Evolution and the design process

The life of an information system, as illustrated in Figure 8.1, is one in which planning is followed by design (including construction, installation and phasing out the prior system) then evolution and, finally, replacement by a new system. The need for replacement will not be dwelt on. It results from change in technologies and improvements in perceptions of the nature of information systems and how to develop them. In the future, once the information technology industry has matured, replacement will occur at much lengthier intervals. The careful handling of information system evolution will therefore become all the more important.

For an installed system to evolve, changes must be made to it. If these changes are at all significant then they will affect the description of the system, that is, the design product. Changes to one aspect of the design

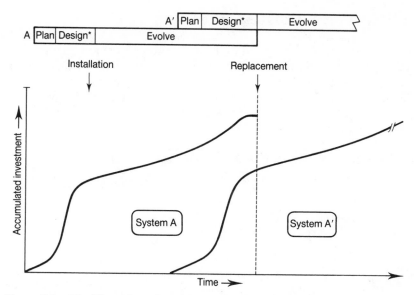

Figure 8.1   The life cycle and replacement of an information system. *Design includes construction, installation and phasing out of prior systems.

product may result in consequential changes elsewhere, even going so far back as to include the information systems plan. To control and manage these changes so that evolution proceeds in an orderly manner, it is necessary to adopt a properly defined design revision process (see Section 1.12). This process provides means whereby change objectives are achieved and it provides control to ensure that the design product is not compromised as a result of the changes.

Design revision and system change are made easier when the design process includes objectives intended to simplify evolution. For example, data independence, as an objective, ensures that a data design is not impacted by alterations to business activities and the subsequent changes to systems.

Similarly, the separation of the logical view from the physical, as with the business model and the design specification, can protect a system from changes to other systems, provided its logical view remains unaffected. Other objectives, such as provision for anticipated change in the design product or provision of clear and comprehensive documentation, will also simplify the task. Tools which provide automated support to the design process may further simplify revision, especially through their ability to assess quickly the full impact of any proposed change.

8.3   The process of design revision

Design revision is often triggered by a system audit or by monitoring the performance or behaviour of a system. Once an opportunity or requirement for change has been identified, changes can, in principle, then be dealt with through a process based on comparable stages to the information systems life cycle. The requirement would therefore pass through the following stages of the life cycle (described in Chapter 3):

- impact assessment (rather than a strategic study),
- information systems (re)planning,
- business analysis,
- system design,
- construction design, and
- construction and workbench test.

Depending on the nature and scale of the change, it may not be necessary to carry out all of the steps within these stages or even all of the stages. Impact assessment will determine what is necessary and what may be bypassed. For example, if the change involves only rearranging fields on a screen layout, there will be no need to perform business analysis.

Today, design revision usually takes place in two very different circumstances.

1.   Where there is a clearly defined design product produced by a methodology which would fit into the framework defined in this text.

2.   Where the system was produced by traditional craft approaches and where there is no clearly defined set of models describing the underlying nature and origin of the system.

Each of these circumstances is examined in detail in Sections 8.4 and 8.5. In practice, systems from each background commonly coexist within mature information systems environments.

The designer faced with a demand for design revision in the second case is placed in a difficult position. There is no adequate means of assessing the implications of proposed changes or of maintaining control over the change process. This problem is worsened where the system has also to remain well integrated with other systems which do have a well defined design product.

An option that is increasingly being adopted is, retrospectively, to develop models making up what appears to have been the design product. The process for doing this is often known as **reverse engineering**. The resultant models then become the baseline for subsequent evolutionary change and, where integrated computer aided systems engineering (CASE) tools are available, this may be initiated by re-creating the system through system generation. This re-creation process is often known as **re-engineering**.

8.4 Design revision with a defined design product

If a change request is raised to alter a system for which there exists a design product developed using a methodology that would fit into the framework defined in this text, then design revision can be controlled by reference to that design product. The principal activities in handling a change request are:

- impact assessment, and
- revision of the design.

Impact assessment involves determining three things – the nature, impact and scale of the proposed change. These allow a decision on whether and how the change should be made. Revision then takes place in the light of what has been agreed.

8.4.1 Impact assessment

In dealing with a proposed change to a system, a usual objective is to minimize the effort required to effect the change. There is no desire to go through all the stages and steps of the design process again, except where the change is a major one. Impact assessment therefore becomes the first step in design revision. It determines the nature of each change and, from this, the level in the design product at which it must be controlled and its implications first considered. Impact assessment also provides a measure of the project effort needed to carry out the change.

Nature of change

The proposed change must be examined and classified to highlight the first component of any stage which it affects. This is needed before all of its implications can be fully described. For example, a program change may affect nothing more than the construction design product, whereas a new business objective may alter the information systems plan, following which the effects may cascade through changes to the business analysis and each level of design. Figure 8.2 illustrates examples from a scheme of the sort needed in classifying information system changes.

Such a scheme must assist in determining which of the kinds of features of the design product and the information system itself are affected by the change. These may range from factors influencing the criteria for prioritization of the system during information systems planning, to the physical characteristics of a proposed replacement terminal type.

A scheme of this kind would include a wide range of types of change, some of which are not described in this text but which have an influence on impact assessment. In Figure 8.2, entries A to E illustrate changes that can have a direct effect on components of the kinds described in this framework. Entries F to H illustrate changes that affect the system technically without directly affecting framework components. Entries I to M illustrate changes that may also have a significant impact but which do so less directly – in most cases, by altering the environment or the context of the system.

Impact of change

Once a proposed change has been classified, the extent of its effects on the products of the life cycle stages can be assessed. Each component which may be impacted is identified, together with the step used to produce it. This shows which stages in the design process must be gone through to introduce the change. The full impact of a proposed change is assessed by first examining the product of the earliest of the stages where a component is directly affected. The structure of the product then allows consequential changes to be identified – changes required because of a dependency between components. The components affected directly and consequentially can then be traced through the products of subsequent stages, in order to determine the full impact of the change. At this point, it becomes possible to see which steps from each stage will have to be carried out and to estimate the cost of doing so. This is important because a usual objective in design revision is to repeat as few steps as possible and minimize the cost of change.

It is apparent from this that the product of any stage can act as the primary vehicle for control over the change process, by highlighting what must and what need not be done. Figure 8.3 contains an example of a possible scheme to show what vehicle might be appropriate at different points.

The impact of a change can be extensive. For example, if a proposed design change is found to require a change to the business analysis models, then all systems dealing with that feature of the business will have to be changed. The evolution of one system may therefore force evolutionary change upon other systems.

Scale of change

The size of a change may be allowed to affect a number of steps in the design process which are revisited when implementing the change. If the change is small, it can be argued that all of its effects are apparent to the implementor. Where this is agreed to, checking and review steps can be eliminated or carried out informally. Change assessment should therefore include some means of determining the size of a change. Figure 8.4 illustrates a scheme that might be used for this purpose.

Changes to components

A. Business activities (that would affect the business analysis models).

B. Entity types (that would affect the business analysis models).

C. Existing user tasks (not affecting the business analysis models but affecting the system design specification or new user tasks to be added).

D. A report or enquiry (when added to the system).

E. Documentation (change to a user guide or operations instructions, for example).

Changes to technical factors

F Database technical characteristics (to improve performance, integrity, security and operability without impacting the construction design product).

G. External forms, when independent of application program logic (screen format changes or report layouts, for example).

H. An application program, not involving any change to the logic (for example, literals or constraints changed)

Changes to contextual factors

I. Housekeeping tasks/programs that support the operation of the system.

J. Systems software parameters (such as new buffer size or new block size) or additional – but identical – hardware (new lines, new terminals or a new processor within the distributed network).

K. System software (such as a new release or a fix).

L. Hardware (such as an upgrade that does not require new systems software).

M. Computing environment (new hardware and systems software).

Figure 8.2   Examples for a change classification scheme.

Initial impact	Control vehicle
1. Replanning	Information systems plan and business models
2. Business analysis	Detailed business analysis models
3. System design	Components of the system design specification
4. Construction design	Components of the construction design
5. Construction and workbench test	Components of the construction design specification
6. Installation	Components of the construction design specification and of the system

Figure 8.3   Vehicles for modification control.

Scale	Characteristics
Minor	No new business activities or entity types involved; only one program's logic is to be altered, or small similar changes are to be made to several programs
Medium	Up to five new programs or tasks, or five major program logic changes, or small similar changes are to be made to many programs; up to five new record types or a small structural change to a database
Major	Anything more complex, which is not considered to be a new business system

Figure 8.4   Example of a change sizing scheme.

8.4.2   Revision of the design

Once the impact of a proposed change is understood and its implications accepted, the change and all consequential changes can be implemented in the design product.

At the start of revision, a proposal is prepared which outlines the preferred means of implementing all aspects of the change. The costs of implementing the proposal are reviewed in the light of the benefits claimed in the request for change. If the proposal is approved, the revision is undertaken. The revision will be to a number of things, principally

- each affected product of the development stages
- all supporting documentation and training
- products for other affected systems,

and it will be implemented in

- the system,
- other affected systems.

At the end of revision everyone affected by the changes must be notified and retrained if necessary. The altered system can then be created and brought into use through the enterprise's usual transition procedures.

8.5 Renovation of existing systems

Many of the changes required in an environment where the information systems are mature, are of the kind that involve modifying a system that was not developed using any of the approaches analysed for the framework in this text.

There may be good business reasons for not mounting a project to replace a system – and its functionality and human interfaces may be largely sound. In such a situation the system needs to be brought up to date and brought into line with other systems so that its continuing evolution may be properly managed. This is **system renovation**. It need not imply changed functionality, but it will make it possible for change to be introduced more easily on subsequent occasions.

Alternative approaches to system renovation are identified as follows:

- restructuring,
- reverse engineering, and
- re-engineering.

Restructuring seeks to improve the overall logical structure of the system without any modification to its functionality.

Reverse engineering seeks to recreate the design specification or analysis model that the system conforms to.

Re-engineering creates a new version of the system by using new technology, often in combination with the results of reverse engineering. It need not seek to alter the system's functionality.

How these approaches relate to the stages of the information systems methodologies framework is shown in Figure 8.5. Also, renovation often acts as a stimulus to wider ranging system enhancement so this is commented on in Section 8.5.4.

8.5.1 Restructuring

Many systems have been built in the absence of good structuring standards. This is true of both program structure and data structure. The process of improving the structuring to a good standard is known as **restructuring**.

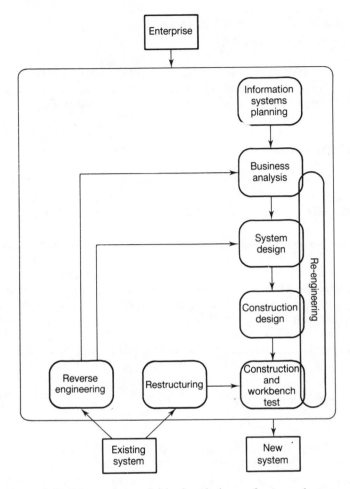

Figure 8.5   Renovation activities in relation to framework stages.

Program restructuring and data restructuring are often carried out as separate activities.

Program restructuring typically involves first an analysis of the working and overall logic of the program. The blocks of logic are then rearranged to conform with good structured programming practice. For example, all logic could be reshaped into combinations of sequence, selection and iteration constructs.

Data restructuring typically involves first an analysis of functional dependencies among items within the current data structure. Based on this, a normalized version of the data structure is created. This may be adopted as the new structure or may be de-normalized in a controlled fashion where known performance optimizations are required.

Once the restructuring is complete the system becomes more readily maintainable, since rendering the program and its data into a clear structure improves the level of comprehensibility and the system's documentation. Doing this often highlights unsatisfactory aspects of the system (which may not have been apparent or else have been only dimly perceived before). It is common, therefore, for restructuring to be followed immediately by enhancement.

Automation is being introduced to this area and tools exist which deal with some of the mechanics of these procedures. 'Intelligent' assessment of the logic of programs is, however, a difficult area in which to provide practical automated support.

8.5.2 Reverse engineering

The most difficult modifications arise when changes to the business have to be accommodated but the business analyst has no analysis models or design specifications to provide guidance in making the modification. To cope with this lack of suitable products, an increasingly common strategy is to employ what will be referred to here as **reverse engineering**.

Reverse engineering requires the analyst to produce models and specifications by extrapolation from existing technical documentation. Once these have been produced they serve as the vehicles for modification control and, like other models and design specifications, may be revised to reflect subsequent accepted modifications.

The process of reverse engineering typically takes place one system at a time when change classification and sizing have been done in response to a request for change. However, it is also possible for all the relevant systems to be processed at once when these systems still have an appreciable, maintainable life.

The process of extrapolation from technical documentation or, indeed, from the system itself must lead to a form of design product which is expressed in the same terms (and by the same means and representations) as the design products for newer systems developed by a methodology fitting the framework defined in this text. This is necessary to provide a common basis for control of modifications and to encourage integration between the systems.

The most common omissions from older systems are the models resulting from business analysis. It is not possible to reconstitute these by examining the systems but it is possible to build a 'system model' to represent what is implemented, using a notation identical to the 'business models'. In this context, the creation of a system model is the reverse engineering process. By way of illustration, one possible approach to the building of such models could be as follows:

1.   Extract a data model (one of the most common omissions is the absence of data models such as those described in Chapter 4) and:

  - Examine the descriptions of major external forms and stores of data; prepare a structured representation of the contents of each (employing normalization principles, for example) using some common notation.

  - Merge these to give a single, synthesized system data model in which each major element can be identified as an entity type and its components as attributes.

  - Identify relationships through the duplication of identifiers.

  - Determine constraints by checking validation procedures in programs, and determine constraint assumptions by searching among comments and test data.

2.   Develop a process model:

  - Examine the programs and prepare a structured representation of their high level procedures, assuming that each may support a business activity.

  - Merge to create a single system model of the business activities supported and their precedence/succedence associations.

  - Identify the data used by the procedures to determine information sets and which activities use the sets.

3.   Determine a behaviour model:

  - Examine the transactions and other program triggers to identify system events.

  - Consolidate the set of events and examine program control structures to determine event precedence/succedence associations and event constraints.

This illustrates the principle of reverse engineering. In practice a more detailed approach would, of course, be required. Moreover, it may not always be necessary to go through all three of these modelling exercises. What is actually done will depend on the extent and quality of existing documentation.

It must be remembered that system models and specifications derived by this kind of approach will only indicate what has been implemented within the systems. They cannot be viewed as business models since the original design process may have omitted or merged components, or may even have got some wrong. Inspection of a system model will not show where this has occurred. However, a system model in conjunction with a business model, developed using a methodology consistent with the framework described in this text, does provide a sound base from which to control subsequent system modification.

8.5.3 Re-engineering

When new or improved methodologies or system development technologies become available there may be a case for transferring a system and its design products to that technology. The process of re-creating the products through carrying out this transfer is known as **re-engineering**. It does not imply any increase in the basic functionality of the system – although the new technology may bring with it enhanced technical facilities.

For example, if a system has been reverse engineered it becomes manageable by using the methodology whose conventions it now adheres to. To make this management as completely controllable as possible the system can be constructed afresh by applying the methodology to move forward from whatever product has resulted from the degree of reverse engineering undertaken. A new version of the system emerges from this procedure. It has exactly the same functionality as the old one but now corresponds to current best practice as exemplified by the methodology.

Reverse engineering is not a prerequisite for re-engineering. Any system developed using a methodology consistent with the framework described in this text can be re-engineered to take advantage of new developments in the methodology or, for example, new CASE system capabilities.

Overall, re-engineering is an important measure in protecting the current investment in systems and in enabling the concepts captured in current systems to be reused in enhanced systems.

8.5.4 Enhancement

Occasionally, when it is apparent from the models that some important business feature is missing or poorly supported, the exercise of renovation may trigger enhancement of a design product in the ways described in Section 8.4.

Enhancement implies a significant improvement in functionality and leads to a version of the system in a higher evolutionary state. This sort of procedure is becoming increasingly common with the availability of automated system generation tools. It increases the ability of existing systems to coexist with newer systems built using the methodology. It also improves the existing systems' ability to be integrated with the new ones, where that is needed.

8.6 Development of variations

It may prove necessary to create alternative forms of a system suitable for installation in different environments. These can be called **system variations**.

It may be argued that variations do not contribute to the proper evolution of a system. However, they undoubtedly add to the problems of managing change, hence the brief discussion which follows. The designer or the constructor may seek to avoid system variations – possibly by employing a technique such as parameterization. This section discusses the circumstances in which variations may arise, how they are developed and the subsequent control problem.

A system variation is a system modified in certain respects to suit a specific (set of) location(s) or organization unit(s). It is based on a system designed for the activities of another location or organization unit within the same business.

8.6.1 Reasons for variations

In general, variations are introduced either to deal with some compelling reason for introducing change or because of some pragmatic decision to accept a less than theoretically ideal end product during the design project.

The compelling reasons are often imposed by outside agencies and are therefore contextual factors in the development scenario (see Chapter 2), while the pragmatic decisions often seek a faster return on the enterprise's investment and are therefore technical factors in the scenario.

Examples of compelling reasons requiring the production of variations are:

- **Legal** Different countries or states may have different legal requirements. Variations may be designed to cope with this.
- **Language** A possible variation is to produce a system which interfaces with the user in a different language.
- **Physical** The physical layout of buildings or locations often leads to the development of unique local procedures. It may be necessary to provide a system variation which acknowledges and supports the need for such procedures.
- **Political** It may be impossible to change working practices in a location for political reasons. For example, where there are strong employee pressure groups a variation may be necessary, despite both long and short term costs.

Examples of pragmatic reasons for producing variations are where:

- It was not possible to examine all the locations in detail during business analysis and, at one location, some difference in the way business is conducted was not discovered.
- The first system design project had a scope which deliberately excluded certain locations. This often happens where the requirement for a variation was identified during analysis but it was then decided to implement the new system elsewhere first, usually in order that the system could be 'seen to be working' sooner.

- A design specification project excluded support of some business activities because they were only required in some locations.

These pragmatically produced variations do have shortcomings, but these are understood by the enterprise and accepted as a trade-off against other benefits.

8.6.2 Stages in variation development

The stages required to create system variations are typically as follows:

1. Review the requirements for a variation.
2. Revise the business analysis.
3. Extend the system design.
4. Perform construction design.
5. Perform construction and workbench testing.
6. Install.

These stages are conducted in essentially the same manner as conventional stages. If the variation is the first version of the system to have been built then there is no difference. If the variation has the more limited aim of creating a modified version of a system already built then the stages are conducted as for a design revision.

8.7 Configuration control

Configuration control, in the context of the framework that is the subject of this text, is that aspect of the broader subject of configuration management that deals with change to products of the information systems methodology. Configuration control *as a whole* is beyond the scope of this text but must be mentioned here to emphasize its importance in the context of both evolution and variations.

Evolution is about change. There is a need during the information systems life cycle to promote change yet at the same time to retain management control over the development process. This control must be capable of recognizing and keeping track of the many, possibly coexisting, versions of models and systems and system variations, both current and previously used. It must also deal with both single and multi-user forms of development and with the relationships between the work activities and work products of individuals involved. There is therefore a need to deal with topics as diverse as:

- managing access rights to design product components,
- managing the dependencies between components, and
- managing the steps of change control.

This general topic is commonly known as **configuration control**.

Configuration control for variations can be extremely complex, requiring sophisticated configuration management techniques. This requirement can be reduced (almost completely) by incorporating all variations within the system. The installed system, therefore, has every alternative feature and nothing more than a selection needs to be made at installation time. However, the resulting system then contains a high level of redundancy. This redundancy adds significantly to the system's complexity to the point where it may even require configuration control to manage its internal structure, thereby defeating the original purpose.

8.8 Conclusion

It is difficult to overstate the importance of the evolution period in the life of an information system. The system must bend with the winds of business change and must respond constantly to novel demands. As systems become more highly integrated and come closer to providing support to all business activities, it becomes more difficult and more expensive to achieve systems improvement by the traditional strategy of starting again and discarding what exists.

A more likely strategy for the future will be to manage the evolution. For this to succeed two things, at least, are necessary. The first is the availability of a clear description of all the systems involved and a definition of their components – in terms of the kinds of components described in this framework. The second is deliberate provision for flexibility in preparing the design product. It is the intention of this chapter to provide a reminder of how essential these are.

EXERCISES

A. *Self-assessment*

8.1   Without referring to the text, summarize the reasons for changing existing information systems. Give examples of *minor*, *medium* and *major* changes in this context.

8.2   Describe the distinction between 'system evolution' and 'system replacement'. Why may system evolution prove difficult?

8.3   Outline the process of design revision for an employee remuneration system when the government imposes a new form of personal taxation.

8.4   What is 'reverse engineering' and why may it be needed?

8.5   'System renovation without increased functionality squanders the enterprise's resources.' Refute this assertion.

8.6   Indicate why and in what circumstances 'system variations' are useful. When would one stop speaking of a variation? Illustrate the answers with examples.

B.   *Methodology related*

(for those familiar with one or more specific methodologies)

8.7   If an existing methodology is specific about post-implementation issues, identify the concepts in the methodology which correspond to those presented in this chapter.

8.8   Select a methodology which does not consider post-implementation issues. What extensions would be needed to the methodology to provide the capability needed?

8.9   Select a methodology which offers advice on configuration control and identify the concepts that need to be added to the framework described in this book to cover the topic adequately.

9

Representation and documentation

9.1 Introduction

During the design process, there are various times when the design product components produced by one of the parties involved have to be communicated to one or more other interested persons or groups. Those concerned, in the role of acceptor, designer, constructor or otherwise (see Section 1.5), usually have different backgrounds and experience in relation to the business area and the representation technique. In the need to communicate, both sides must have some minimum level of knowledge about the techniques for representing the design product component in question.

While product components may be described verbally or expressed as strict formal language (the use of which will be discussed in Section 9.7.5), the

263

easiest and most widely used vehicle for communication is some kind of graphical representation. Examples of such representations were given in Chapter 6, for example, activity graphs, data structure diagrams and data flow diagrams.

As can be seen from the representations referred to, different techniques are used for different perspectives. However, representations of the design products containing two or more perspectives may be integrated into a single form. The framework in this book, for example, uses the table format as a uniform expression (see Chapters 4 and 5).

There are two areas where one should be careful with the use of representation techniques. Firstly, when different representation techniques are employed with different perspectives, it is important to pay proper attention to cross-references. Similarly, different representation techniques may be used in different steps or stages. In general, such differences are undesirable since they will add complexity to the transition from one step to the next.

Well chosen representation techniques can contribute considerably to the quality of the design product and to the effectiveness and efficiency of the design process, not only because of the communication aspects but also by structuring the knowledge about the system. The way in which information systems are conceived depends greatly on the way in which the information system is represented. The choice of representation of a design product influences the way in which the system is viewed.

Another use of the representation is in the recording of the design product for future use during the evolution stage (see Chapter 8).

Because people, in their various roles, have different uses for the design product, they may also have different requirements for a representation technique. They have different requirements concerning the ease of learning and the ease of using the representation technique. The technique must be appropriate for the task they are performing.

These requirements can be met using various means, such as the concept of decomposition, the concept of abstraction, the appropriate form (diagrams, matrices, etc.) and automated techniques.

These topics will be discussed in the subsequent sections of this chapter in the following tutorial order:

- Representation and documentation for different human roles.
- Representation and documentation for different purposes.
- Requirements of the different roles.
- Examples of different component representations.
- Management to achieve effective representation and documentation.
- Alternative representation forms.
- Automated tools.

9.2 Representation and documentation for different human roles

Various people, in different roles, are involved in analysis, design and construction (see also Section 1.5). This means that the design product has to be communicated explicitly among a number of people. Figure 9.1 depicts the different human roles and the communication between them. The human roles are organized in a hierarchy, and communication occurs between the different levels of the hierarchy and between the different branches (as shown by the arrows in Figure 9.1).

Whereas the designers and constructors are, in many respects, a rather homogeneous group with a clear role definition, this is not the case for the user community. Various interest groups are involved from the user side. Ultimately, these are the people who will be 'using' the system (in the literature they are sometimes referred to as the 'end users'). Consultation with the users is important for two reasons:

1. Since these are the people on the envisaged (operational) interface between the information system and the organization, their experience with the previous way of working may help elicit information requirements on which the new design is to be based.

2. As actual users, they will be affected by the ergonomics of the information system: their views are essential for arriving at an information system of high quality.

The second party concerned with establishing detailed information requirements and the subsequent design of an information system is the

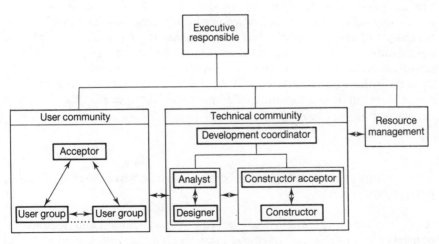

Figure 9.1 Communication among human roles.

ORGANIZATION UNIT whose activities are to be supported. The people (and systems) working in the organization unit are the users and producers of the information and, as such, they are the most important source for the information requirements definition.

The third group to be considered on the user side is the overall management spanning the units for which an information system is to be developed. The management will need to be informed in understandable terms. When – as often happens – the allocation of responsibility is unclear or is delegated to too junior a person, it is all the more important that communication takes place up to the highest level.

Three to four organizational levels may become involved with user aspects of an information system project. Such involvement may arise not only from ongoing development, but also from initiatives from outside the customary units. Senior management, for example, may have perceived the need for a hitherto unrecognized information requirement and will express its wishes in general terms. Likewise, recommendations may come from other units not immediately involved with the information streams, such as a management services section or an information centre.

In some projects, one or more business analysts will act as consultants to the user community and they will report to the user acceptor. In other projects, representatives of the user community will be trained to be business analysts and they will participate, as such, in the design process. Experience has shown, however, that although a mixture of expertise on the user side and/or the technical side has merit, it is advisable to separate the responsibilities of producing and accepting the design. Indeed, one should avoid the situation where the same persons are responsible for accepting what they have produced.

In all cases, it is essential that the requirements and possible solutions can be reviewed extensively by these 'users'. They must therefore be expressible in lay terms, but specified in such a precise way that no misunderstanding will result. Additionally, the ultimate design must be capable of modification at a later stage, in particular when new requirements are identified and the information system needs to evolve. In other words, both the intermediate representation and the final documentation of the information system specifications must be comprehensible to (and debatable by) a variety of non-experts.

9.3 Representation and documentation for different purposes

In this section, different purposes se.ved by representation and documentation techniques such as modelling, mastering complexity, communication and recording the results of steps in the design process are discussed.

9.3.1 Modelling and mastering complexity

The representation of a design product influences the way in which different people perceive the system because of the relationship between the system, the (external) representation and the mental image that people build of the information system (that is, the internal representation). Both the internal and external representations are a model of the system. Figure 9.2 shows the process of communication. Person A builds a mental image corresponding to his or her view of the system and communicates this to person B using an external form. Person B perceives this external form and will then build his or her own mental image. Within this process, the importance of the external representation of a system is clearly demonstrated.

Well chosen representation techniques will induce a clear mental image of the system. By structuring the knowledge of the people involved, external representations can help to master the complexity of the design process and its results. External representation techniques can also facilitate the reasoning about a design product, for example, in making inferences, detecting contradictions or establishing completeness.

Different external representations can be constructed for a single information system using different forms (such as graphs, tables, matrices, natural language prose and formal language). Each of these has its own degree of formality. In any case, a certain kind of formality will be in place, where 'formal' is understood to mean using a restricted set of symbols with a predefined meaning.

When designing complex systems, it is necessary to avoid the situation where different people have to rely on their own interpretation – a situation

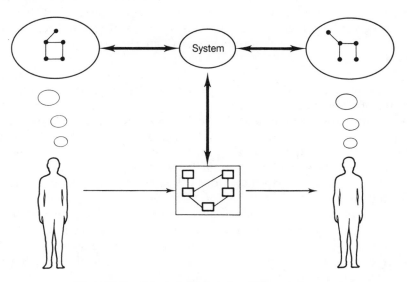

Figure 9.2   Communication for different views.

which inevitably leads to misunderstanding and, eventually, to an error-prone information system. Formality is further important if there is a requirement to reason about the design product, by applying inference rules or integrity rules on the design products. This is true for human reasoning, and it is also true for machine reasoning and the automated transformation of a design product into a working system.

Like human beings, an automated design tool has one internal and several external representations. The internal representation can, for example, be captured in a data dictionary.

Clear thinking and the ability to reason about a design product are essential requirements for all the parties involved. They are essential for recognizing the components and their relationships, for checking the quality characteristics of the design product and for acceptance by different user groups.

9.3.2 Communication

Given the various roles played by different people, it is essential to communicate in order to ensure a common understanding of the desired system. Communication is needed among users, analysts and designers in order to obtain an information system that will satisfy the users' requirements. It is also needed between the designer and the constructor.

In addition to the communication between different parties, there is the communication between various people filling the same role. The various groups on the user side have to communicate in order to obtain agreement on the required system. Analysts and designers have to communicate with each other when producing, modifying or maintaining the design product. Constructors will have their own discussions on completeness and realizability when evaluating a design product on which the construction is to be based.

The nature of the resulting communication will be different in each of the various stages of the information systems life cycle. In principle, two documents should result from the design process. These can be identified as the **acceptor specification** and the **constructor specification**, respectively. The former should represent the basis for a go-ahead on the second, but they cannot possibly be developed independently and precisely in that sequence. Some of the analysis will be intermingled with the design, in the same way that some construction considerations will have to be addressed during the system design stage.

Consequently, there is a need for two interacting forms of representation over an extended period. On the one hand, a specification of the system must be developed in conjunction with the user, but work towards the construction specification can only lag slightly and all involved will have to communicate on that basis.

9.3.3 Recording the results of steps

Keeping records of the results of various steps serves the purpose of communication over a period of time (including communication with one-self). Recording is necessary during the design process since people have only limited memory capacities. In addition, recording makes the design explicit. Documenting which decisions were taken and which were discarded (and why) should be seen as an essential part of the design process.

Various levels of representation and documentation can be distinguished:

- **Capturable** Information is directly written or diagrammed on a permanent medium, for example, using the back of an envelope, a typewriter or a photograph.
- **Updatable** Information is captured and stored using an updatable medium, for example, using a word processor or image digitizer.
- **Verifiable** Information is checked against a set of validation criteria as part of the process of capture, for example, a spelling checker or a diagramming tool.
- **Enhanceable** Information is automatically subject to improvement by applying rules for good practice or rules that describe a field of expertise, for example, an intelligent document editor, an image enhancer or reformatter.

After the system design stage is complete, the recorded design product forms the basis for verification of the construction and will further serve as a basis for maintenance and enhancement.

9.4   Requirements of the different roles

Different human roles make different use of the represented design product. Business analysts and system designers are expert, active and regular users of the representation techniques whereas constructors must be able to read them on a more casual basis. The users of the information system can have more expertise, or less, in the representation techniques. Their use of the representation techniques is basically passive (involving reading only) and it may vary from one-off use to regular use in conjunction with designers.

These different uses pose different requirements for the representation techniques to be used. For beginners (such as some users of the information system), any technique that is employed must be easy to learn and to comprehend. For people who are confronted with the representation only on a casual basis, it should be easy for them to be able to recall the meaning of the formalism used in the representation.

The business analysts and system designers require a certain flexibility in handling the design product and they require the option of controlling the design process.

The requirements of the different roles can be classified as follows:

- appropriateness for each role,
- ease of learning, and
- efficiency in use.

9.4.1   Appropriateness for each role

Appropriateness means that the different purposes listed in Section 9.3 can be achieved in an effective way.

For the designer, this means that the representation technique must have sufficient expressive power. That is to say, the designer must be able to express the things that he or she wants to express because he or she must be able to develop, modify and extend the design product. The user acceptor must be able to evaluate the design product.

The representation technique should hence highlight those aspects which need an evaluation. The constructor must understand what system he or she has to construct and which technical – and other – limitations are imposed. Some constructors will be familiar with only one specific representation technique or will require the design product in a particular form.

A major task for each party is checking the quality of the design product. The user acceptor performs his or her task from a user requirements point of view whereas the constructor does it from a construction point of view. The business analysts and designers have their own rules for assessing the quality of the design product which they have produced. Different representation and documentation techniques will score differently in relation to their ability to assess the quality of a design product. The intrinsic quality characteristics of a design product that must be checked are completeness, correctness and consistency. These characteristics will now be discussed further.

Completeness and level of detail

A design product possesses the characteristic of completeness to the extent that all components which should be present are, indeed, present and each is fully developed. Judgement on completeness should be made by the user acceptor and the constructor. For example, some user acceptors will need detailed EXTERNAL FORM specifications, such as complete screen layouts and printed output report layouts including indentation, while others will be content with a less specific description of the contents. Similarly, the design deliverable to the constructor is complete whenever it is sufficient to construct the correct information system.

An information system methodology must provide representation techniques that allow complete specifications. In other words, the set of representation techniques should be such that one can specify a complete information system. In addition, certain methodologies may provide objective criteria to judge the completeness of a design product but, in many cases, this judgement is a function of the role filled by the persons involved.

Correctness

The design product is correct to the extent that it satisfies true needs within the existing constraints of the development and operational environment. Consequently, correctness also means that one must be able to construct the information system. Some representation techniques will be more suited than others to capturing the true needs of the users and the limitations under which the system must be realized. It is important to note that there is an inevitable element of subjectivity in assessing correctness. A consensus view may be needed.

Consistency

A design product is consistent to the extent that it does not contain contradictions. Formal representation techniques are more suited to detecting contradictions since they allow inferences to be made about the design product.

9.4.2   Ease of learning

Ease of learning is determined by qualities such as structure, conciseness, self-descriptiveness, orthogonality and uniformity of a representation technique.

Ease of learning is also dependent on the prior knowledge of the people who have to learn. Designers and constructors will, in general, have a better background for learning new techniques. However, experience with earlier methodologies may prove to be an impediment when learning new ones.

Ease of learning is essential for the user and user acceptor since they are usually beginners and are casual readers of the design product for evaluation purposes only.

Ease of learning is less important for designers and constructors since use of a representation technique should be part of their professional competence.

9.4.3   Efficiency in use

It is not sufficient for a representation technique to be appropriate for an analysis or design step. It should also be efficient in use. This means that it should be both easy and fast to use. For casual users of the representation technique, such as the user acceptor and – to a certain extent – the constructor, it is important that the meaning of the representation formalism is easy to recall. Since recall is a form of quick relearning, the characteristics described in Section 9.4.2 also play a role.

For the designer, efficiency in use not only means efficiency in the development of the design product, but also efficiency in modifying and maintaining the design product (see Chapter 8). One of the most important tasks for the designer is to keep the design product complete and up-to-date. This is easy in the earlier stages of a project but it becomes more difficult as one progresses. In fact, it is rare for nth version modifications to be recorded properly. There are at least four reasons for this:

1.   A full – but incomplete – design normally gives rise to extensive documentation. Even a minor change will affect the documentation in many places, only some of which will be visibly related to the immediate modification.

2.   Sometimes, the change is only a proposal, which will be attempted temporarily but not necessarily incorporated. Documenting the effects may be regarded as a waste of time during the trials, but this may be forgotten later.

3.   Since the design representation often is not restricted to one medium (such as a formal record, together with explanatory comments), updating at least one of these may be overlooked or postponed until the situation has become chaotic.

4.   Laziness develops on the part of the designer.

Consequently, a designer needs a representation technique that will allow for rapid and consistent modifications.

Finally, the design product is transferred to the constructor and serves as input to the construction stage. The chosen representation technique will influence to what extent the design product can be used, as such, during this stage and how much translation and reinterpretation will be necessary.

9.5   Examples of different component representations

Any component may be represented differently in different methodologies. This section gives an example chosen from each of the perspectives.

9.5.1   Data perspective

As an example within the data perspective, take the 'one to zero, one or more' RELATIONSHIP TYPE discussed in Section 4.5.5. This is depicted in Figure 9.3. Figure 9.4 shows 11 different ways of representing this RELATIONSHIP TYPE,

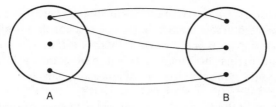

Figure 9.3 One to zero, one or more relationship.

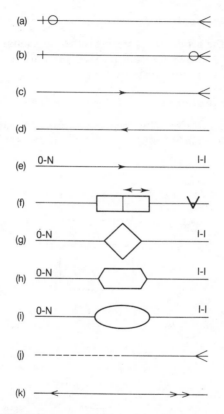

Figure 9.4 Different representations of the 'one to zero, one or more' relationship.

which is a component in various methodologies. These eleven representations have the same meaning. Some of the differences are due to the difference in richness of representation techniques; other differences are purely graphical.

In representation (a) the small circle means optionality, while in representation (b) the small circle means zero cardinality is allowed and the crowsfoot means 'many'. In (c) the arrow means that the existence of ENTITY TYPE A is a prerequisite for the existence of ENTITY TYPE B while in (d) the arrow is interpreted as the mathematical notation for a function.

Representation (e) is similar to (c) but the cardinalities are given explicitly. In (f) the double-headed arrow means that every relationship is identifiable by an entity of ENTITY TYPE B and the symbol ∀ means that every occurrence of B must participate in this particular relationship. Representations (g), (h) and (i) have different symbols for a relationship, each allowing n-ary relationships. Finally, (j) is similar to (a) where the dashed line means optionality and in (k) the double arrow indicates the one or more side of the relationship.

9.5.2 Process perspective

An example within the process perspective is the representation of a BUSINESS ACTIVITY. Figure 9.5 shows six alternative representations which are to be found in various information systems methodologies.

9.5.3 Behaviour perspective

Methodologies also have multiple representations for components of the behaviour perspective, such as BUSINESS EVENT and SYSTEM EVENT depicted

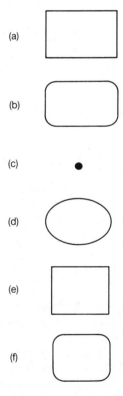

Figure 9.5   Different representations of a BUSINESS ACTIVITY.

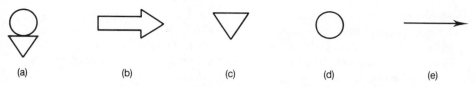

(a)   (b)   (c)   (d)   (e)

Figure 9.6   Different representations of an event.

in Figure 9.6. These representations are for the EVENT TYPE component, which is slightly differently defined in some methodologies.

9.6   Management to achieve effective representation and documentation

The requirements specified in Section 9.4 are met using different means for representation and documentation. Characteristically, a design product is complex and potentially voluminous. It is of partial interest to different groups, each with their own abilities and prior knowledge. These characteristics cannot be avoided but their impact should be managed.

The possible approaches to managing these points are as follows:

9.6.1   Decomposition

This means representing the design product at several levels of detail in order to increase its understandability and to divide the design product into parts relevant to different interest groups.

9.6.2   Abstraction

This means representing parts of the design product by leaving out other parts, for example, using a graphic representation of an entity attribute relationship model on which attributes are not shown.

9.6.3   Choice of suitable forms

Different forms may be used for the representation of the design product. These forms will be discussed in Section 9.7 and include:

- natural language text (structured or prose),
- tables and matrices (cross-reference tables),
- diagrams,
- formal language specifications,
- (elements of) a working system (including a prototype), and
- mixed forms.

One important aspect is that some forms can (at least partially) be derived from others. For example, it is possible to generate a diagram from a table format or to generate a prototype from formal language specifications. The derivation of one form from another is of particular importance in the analysis and design of an information system since several human roles are involved.

9.6.4 Choice of suitable style

Elements of style, such as the format of tables and matrices, indentation of text and graphical layout guidelines, will structure the representation of the design product in a particular way. Depending on the chosen techniques, the representation of the design product will be more concise and more legible.

9.6.5 Ensuring traceability

Traceability of the design deliverables is of the utmost importance. It must be possible to trace components back to earlier stages in order to effect corrections and enhancements in a correct way. This can be achieved by using uniform representation and documentation techniques across stages. For instance, when the same concept is used in different stages, each usage should have the same representation within a given form. For example, the same representation of an ENTITY TYPE should be used in different stages. When different representations are used, the correspondence should ideally be one-to-one, such that translation is minimal and the formalisms can be used interchangeably.

9.6.6 Quality assurance

Using certain representation techniques, it will be more easy to assess the completeness, correctness and consistency of the design product. For example, certain relationships (or the omission thereof) might easily be detected using matrices.

9.6.7 Associated inference techniques

Reasoning about the design product is facilitated if inference rules exist that are closely integrated with the representation techniques. For example, when using predicate logic for representing the design product, the inference rules of predicate logic can be used to draw certain conclusions about the design product.

9.6.8 Explanatory help facilities

Training, explanation and help facilities are essential for learning and using the representation technique. Some representation techniques are more easy to explain and teach than others.

9.6.9   Automation

Automation can have a significant impact on the efficiency and effectiveness of the design process. It can facilitate all of the above approaches by:

- providing automated decomposition and abstraction tools;
- providing automated translation from one to the other;
- enforcing uniform standards for style and graphical symbols;
- providing easy update facilities for representation techniques that are well-suited for quality assurance but hard to update; and
- providing automated inference techniques and automated help facilities.

Automated tools are discussed in more detail in Section 9.8 and in Chapter 10.

9.7   Alternative representation forms

In this section alternative representation forms including diagrams, matrices, tables, natural language, prototypes, simulations, formal languages and mixed forms are discussed.

9.7.1   Diagrams

Acceptor specifications, especially for the user acceptor, typically include diagrams containing various kinds of graphic representation. Experience has shown that users, in particular, tend to deal with concepts more effectively when they can visualize them in graphic form. Because of this, diagrams are easy to understand and help in the correctness and consistency checking. This is why so many of the techniques found in existing information systems methodologies use diagramming techniques.

Examples of typical diagramming techniques currently in use (see Figure 9.7) include:

- data flow diagrams,
- bubble charts,
- data structure diagrams,
- activity graphs,
- binary relationship diagrams, and
- behaviour diagrams.

One problem with the use of diagrams is that they sometimes lead to misinterpretation because people think they understand when they do not.

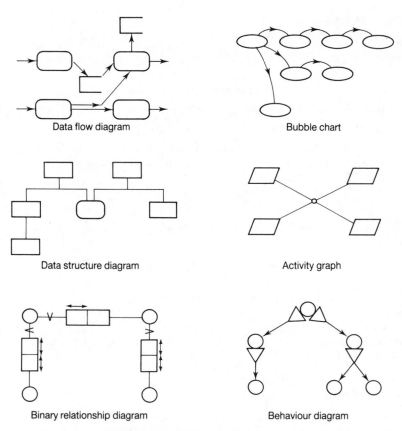

Data flow diagram

Bubble chart

Data structure diagram

Activity graph

Binary relationship diagram

Behaviour diagram

Figure 9.7   Examples of some typical diagramming techniques.

Furthermore, some existing information systems methodologies use diagramming techniques that are too complicated and the resulting pictures are difficult for the average user to assimilate. Some methodologies have attempted to represent as many aspects as possible of a design product in the diagrams. The result has been a set of diagrams which are useful to (and possibly even required by) those responsible for constructing the system but which are not useful to a user acceptor.

A diagramming technique is a way of depicting one or more components and how they are interrelated. The use of such techniques in many existing information system methodologies is so deeply ingrained that, for many methodologies, the diagramming technique and the methodology have become synonymous.

The chief merit in a diagramming technique is in user communication. It should therefore be judged, not on whether it is complete, but rather on whether it communicates effectively.

One can safely assert that the design product for most information systems methodologies would be impossible to display in its totality in the form of diagrams. Hence, the diagramming techniques can only be an aid to communication and should never be regarded as a complete definition of a design product.

9.7.2 Matrices and tables

Matrices and tables are quite structured and concise. The term matrix is used here to refer to a cross-reference table (see for example Section 4.6.3). The table representation form is used extensively in Chapters 4, 5, 6 and 7. Matrices help to establish correct specifications and are excellent for consistency and completeness checking of some specific parts. They can also help by giving an integrated picture. On the other hand, large matrices are not always easily assimilated and they may be applicable to only a part of the design product. It would be very difficult to have complete specifications with matrices only. Matrices are difficult to change in the absence of automated tools. An example of a matrix relating two components is given in Figure 9.8.

9.7.3 Natural language

A traditional form of human communication is natural language. While it is often claimed that 'a picture is worth a thousand words', it must also be asserted that diagrams on their own, as a means of communication with non-technical users, always need to be supplemented with explanatory prose.

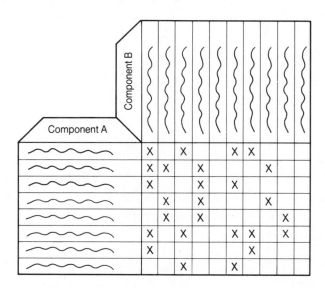

Figure 9.8 Example of a matrix relating two components.

Simple natural language prose is, in general, easily understood by all parties. It allows for complete, correct specifications, it is easy to change (using a word processing system, for example) and can be easily integrated with other forms of specification. On the other hand, natural language prose can be ambiguous and it does not give any support to the detection of incompleteness, incorrectness or inconsistencies. Since the semantics are hard to capture by machine, another translation step is required and natural language can be verbose (and lacking in conciseness).

Natural language can be constrained so that such disadvantages can be overcome. Examples include:

- a subset of English that can be formalized,
- natural language output – generating natural language expressions for the user acceptor on the basis of more formal specifications established by the designer, and
- structured English as used in pseudocode.

Natural language is usually found in combination with other, more formal, representations. For the purposes of documentation and explanation, natural language is indispensable. Figure 9.9 shows an example of a natural language specification and the same specification represented in structured English.

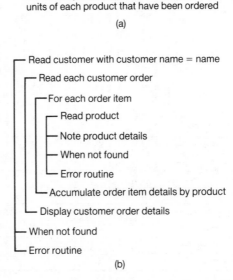

For a named customer, report on orders that
have been placed and on the number of
units of each product that have been ordered

(a)

Read customer with customer name = name
Read each customer order
For each order item
Read product
Note product details
When not found
Error routine
Accumulate order item details by product
Display customer order details
When not found
Error routine

(b)

Figure 9.9   Examples of (a) natural and (b) structured language representations.

9.7.4   Prototypes and simulations

A technique for user communication is rapid prototyping. The term 'proto-typing' typically covers various possibilities, ranging from a 'rough and ready' version of the final system to nothing more than dummy screens containing the kind of picture the user will be shown in the final version.

Different aspects of an information system can be prototyped – such as the user interface, the data model, the behaviour, the program logic or the performance.

Prototypes and simulations are very useful for handling the problem which arises when there is uncertainty about what the designer needs to design. They have the advantage that they are closer to a working system and they assist greatly in getting the visible aspects of a design specification correct.

However, prototypes must be used keeping in mind what one is prototyping. The use of a user interface prototype will not lead to a full evaluation of the correctness, completeness and consistency of elements that show up only indirectly, such as complex computations and integrity rules. The ability to modify the prototype is dependent on the choice of prototyping tool. In a number of cases, analytic techniques will give better results than simulations, especially with respect to the detection of inconsistencies and incompleteness.

When prototypes of complete information systems are used, then system design consists of a very quick pass through a design process into a constructed prototype, which can be evaluated by a user. The ability to use prototyping in a meaningful way depends on the availability of easy to use construction tools. Advanced I-CASE tools (see Chapter 10) allow for efficient and effective generation of complete applications, one of which – after a number of iterations – becomes the installed operational system.

9.7.5   Formal languages

Formal languages, such as First Order Logic, have an excellent expressive power and are well suited to making inferences about design specifications. Conclusions could therefore be drawn about the consistency, completeness and correctness of the design specifications.

A formal language can be hard to learn and difficult to understand and use, depending on the function being used. Figure 9.10 shows examples of two different formal language specifications.

9.7.6   Mixed forms

Most design methodologies use more than one form for the representation of the design product. Graphics play a major role in most of the methodologies. Natural language prose is usually used for documentation and the recording of descriptions of design components.

(a) **when**   QUANTITY in stock for PRODUCT.P **is less than** QUANTITY of reorderpoint of PRODUCT.P **and**
     if   **exists** (GOOD_SUPPLIER that supplies PRODUCT.P)
     then   PRODUCT.P <– reorder.

(b) <u>function</u> inv-cat-of-person-to-invite;
     <u>domain</u>   ip: PERSON-TO-INVITE;
                ic: INVITATION-CATEGORY;
                d: D;
     <u>range</u>   Boolean;
     <u>def</u>   ∀ip∀ic∀d(PERSON-TO-INVITE(ip,d) D(d)
                (∃ y) (PERSON-INVITATION(y) invitee(y) = ip
                invitation-category(y) = ic day(y) < d)
                ––––> inv-cat-of-person-to-invite (ip, ic, d);
     <u>end</u>:

Figure 9.10 Examples of formal language specification.

When using a mixture of different forms, it becomes necessary to monitor the compatibility between the different forms.

With the emergence of automated design tools, different forms (graphics, tables, matrices, prototypes) can be generated from a single storage source, usually referred to as an automated data dictionary, respository or encyclopaedia.

9.8 Automated tools

The issue of representing the design product is complicated by a move in the industry towards computerized support for certain stages in the information systems life cycle.

Automated tools (see Chapter 10) may support one or more steps of one or more methodologies. They may, for example, give support from information systems planning to running applications. Alternatively, a tool may support only a few steps. Also, techniques of more than one methodology may be supported by a given tool, thus allowing mixing and matching. Such tools are usually less powerful since greater power, in terms of analysis and generation capabilities, requires a substantial integration of the various techniques.

As such, automated tools can be of help for the different roles during the design process because of their ability to handle the volume of design specifications and the complexity of the design product. Automation allows for easy expansion, contraction, chaining of graphical objects and for the translation of one form into another, for example, text into graphics or vice versa. These obvious advantages of automated tools should not mean that non-automated tools can be disregarded.

9.9 Conclusions

There is a growing awareness that the user community must be a major source for establishing design specifications. Many methodologies have adopted a new role for the user, shifting the user from a passive victim of the information systems department to a more active participant in the design process. This new role has created new requirements for representation and documentation techniques, quite different from those used for communication among analysts, designers and constructors. It has led to the emergence of rapid prototyping, enhanced diagramming techniques and natural language interfaces.

As a result, representation and documentation is no longer a topic of secondary importance but has become a keystone in the success of any information systems methodology.

EXERCISES

A. *Self-assessment*

9.1 Which human roles have to be considered in connection with the representation and documentation of information system components, in which stages, and for what purposes?

9.2 Name some representation and documentation techniques. How can these contribute to the quality of the design product?

9.3 Discuss in some detail the specific requirements for representation and documentation of different human roles.

9.4 In what way can representation and documentation help manage the complexity and volume of the design product?

9.5 Discuss in some detail the various forms of representation. How do automated tools affect these forms?

B. *Methodology related*

(for those familiar with one or more existing methodologies)

9.6 List the representation techniques of some methodologies. Discuss how the approach taken in these cases supports the requirements for the various human roles, in particular the requirements that cause problems (for example, in connection with communication between persons).

9.7   List and discuss the documentation techniques connected with the various components, as prescribed or suggested by the specific methodologies.

9.8   Discuss how the methodologies in question deal with the complexity and volume of the design product (see Section 9.6).

10

Computer aided systems engineering

10.1 Introduction

The term information systems methodology (see Section 1.1) has been used throughout this text to mean a methodical approach to progressing through the stages of the information systems life cycle, gathering the information necessary to understand requirements for systems, turning that into stage products, then creating systems to match what is specified by those products. It is characteristic of methodical activities which involve significant amounts of information handling that they benefit greatly from computer support. Since the middle of the 1980s that kind of support has been available through software specifically intended to assist all, or aspects of, the development processes provided through information systems methodologies.

Examples of that type of software exist which support all stages of the information systems development cycle. The term 'computer aided systems engineering' (CASE) has come into general use to describe such software systems and is the subject of this chapter. The term 'computer aided software engineering' is also in use but it is limited to tools which support only system design, construction design and construction and workbench test so will not be used in this text.

The chapter starts by considering the nature of CASE systems through a look at some generic features common to the architecture of offerings in the market. It also sets out to examine major concepts from the framework that is the subject of this book and how they can be supported through CASE technology. It then considers some of the consequences to the stages of the information systems life cycle of providing computer assistance in handling them.

It is not the purpose of this chapter to examine individual offerings in the field of computer aided systems engineering or to comment on the nature and future of the CASE market. Neither is it an aim to offer recommendations on appropriate architectures and features in CASE offerings.

10.2   Aspects of CASE

The term 'CASE system' describes a wide variety of commercial offerings and research testbeds. At the most basic level it can refer to a system providing one drawing tool which supports the recording, documentation and representations for a single technique and which may enforce the conventions of that technique. At that level it is likely that the diagrams used as representations will be stored as diagrams, separately from the objects being represented.

At the other end of the spectrum, a CASE system may seek to support the techniques used by a large proportion of the steps in every stage of the information systems life cycle and may seek to integrate these techniques through the use of a single form of storage for each component. At this level, representations such as diagrams will be created when needed by reference to the components currently stored. A consistent and perpetually up-to-date view is therefore provided to each user of such CASE systems. Data generated as a result of performing one step in a design process is stored by the computer and is available at a workstation for the same, or some other, person to perform the next task.

CASE systems may also provide sophisticated support to their users beyond that needed just for individual techniques and steps of a methodology, for example:

- direct manipulation of graphical objects in multiple windows at the same time, for capturing and updating the design product,
- natural language enquiry facilities,
- production of catalogue reports, tables and matrices generated from the stored data,
- generators that propose other parts of the design product based upon parts already defined; for example, report layouts may be proposed by the CASE system on the basis of components with a data perspective, and

- interfaces to various other tools, for example, for project management, performance estimation, presentation graphics or prototype driving.

An outline architecture of the features common to CASE systems suggests a possible appearance of the sort shown in Figure 10.1. The simplest CASE systems provide a (possibly very narrow) vertical slice through the diagram and do not require integration services. The most complex will provide support to all parts.

- The **human/computer interface** enables a person who takes on one of the human roles in information system design (see Section 1.5) to use the computer, to get access to tools appropriate to their current role, and to use the tools in support of that role.
- **Workstation services** provide the operating environment which controls the use of tools and interfaces.
- **Tools** are commonly designed to provide support to techniques (or a technique) used in steps of a particular stage. They can be classified broadly into those that support the predominantly analytic stages (information systems planning and business analysis) and those that support the remaining predominantly prescriptive stages (system design, construction design, construction and workbench test). Occasionally these groupings are referred to by the terms 'upper case' and 'lower case'.
- **Integration services** provide a common interface between the tools and the storage. They enable the tools to share data irrespective of whether they come from one or from several vendors.

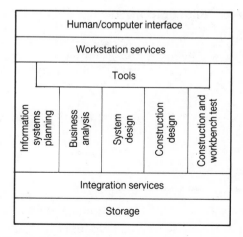

Figure 10.1   Typical CASE system architecture.

- **Storage** contains the information gathered throughout the development process. This may range from the simple recording of text and diagrams, to data that describes instances of framework components discovered during projects and from which representations may be generated. It may also maintain a definition of the methodology processes it can support, the components they allow, and the rules governing their use.

    A variety of terms are used to describe the storage facility; among them are repository, encyclopaedia, database, knowledge base, catalogue, directory and dictionary.

If the tools used in a particular implementation of this architecture come from a single vendor they may be designed to work together in a tightly coupled fashion. In that instance the product may be described as 'integrated CASE' (I-CASE). If the tools come from multiple vendors their coupling will be looser and may require significant human intervention during form conversion steps. In that instance the product may be described as 'component CASE' (C-CASE), where 'component' refers to the fact that each tool supports only a part of the information systems life cycle (that is, it is not used in the framework sense).

10.3   CASE and framework concepts

This section deals with the principal framework concepts introduced in Chapter 1 but handles them in a different order. This is done for tutorial purposes, to introduce the major features of CASE first and then to consider their impact on and relevance to the other concepts.

10.3.1   Techniques and components

The commonest purpose of a CASE system is to automate one or more techniques and by doing so to capture information about components in the methodology being used. To achieve this, the tools may provide functionality to:

- capture specifications of newly identified components (in the framework sense),
- update specifications of existing components,
- view existing components,
- group components as a stage product,
- provide graphic representations of components and stage products,
- convert output from one technique to input for another,

- check that the specifications of components or collections of components are consistent with the rules of the methodology,
- check the completeness of specifications, and
- transfer or map specifications to another life cycle stage.

This functionality implies a high level of support in representing and documenting components and products. That usually comes about by providing automated support to handling the syntax, semantics and graphic representations employed in a technique, and enforcing their consistent use.

In doing these things to automate techniques it is clear that data about components is the data that CASE systems work with. It is also clear that the tools provided in a CASE system may have a marked effect in several step categories and on the ability of their users to manage representations of products. These are discussed more fully in Sections 10.3.3 and 10.3.5.

The fact that a CASE system provides automated support to techniques and can deal with components must not be taken to suggest that it automates a design process or even has the functionality to manage products of stages of the information systems life cycle (see Section 10.4).

10.3.2 Products

The product of any stage is the collection of the components of that stage with all necessary descriptions and with some appropriate means of representation. A CASE system can manage a product for any stage if it provides sufficient tools and storage functionality to capture and retain details of all the components. This implies a degree of integration, at least for that stage, and therefore the use of an I-CASE system rather than a C-CASE one. It also implies an ability to provide appropriate representations to whoever will need to work with the product, for example, when the product is to be used as an acceptor specification.

10.3.3 Step categories

CASE tools do not provide the same level of support to all methodology activities. Some categories of step lend themselves readily to automated support while others demand intelligent human intervention:

- **Abstraction** steps are readily supported through CASE systems since the majority of techniques used in planning and analysis are aimed at this type of activity.

  Typically the tools provide support simply by recording results from the abstraction step and by providing necessary representations of these results. Intelligent or knowledge based systems can prompt or advise during an abstraction step and an I-CASE system can support the user by offering, through models it already has in storage, a context within which further abstractions can be placed.

- **Checking** steps are also ideally suited to automation, especially those concerned with consistency checking. The potential for supporting checking stems from the fact that the CASE system can become the source of all relevant information on components and products produced during the application of a methodology. The range, diversity and complexity of checking that is possible increases with the degree of integration among the CASE system's tools.

  CASE systems therefore also have potential for assisting in the management of projects based on a methodology. At a simple level they can help the project manager by reporting on the completeness of the descriptions of components, by checking that all inputs conform to the syntax and semantics of the methodology and by providing reports and representations of products suitable for inspection at checkpoints or milestones in a project.

  Certain representations lend themselves well to supporting checking. For example, matrices provide a simple, visual form of cross-checking that can be readily scanned and also used for automated exception reporting; more sophisticated representations such as prototypes (see Section 9.7.4), system mock-ups or simulations allow users to check system functionality and behaviour.

- **Form conversion** steps are well suited to automation whenever there are definable rules governing what is to be done. If the rules can be expressed as algorithms then the conversion becomes fully automatic. If, however, judgement is required then an expert system style of approach can be used, with guided human intervention.

  Since form conversion often takes the output from one technique and converts it to be suitable as input to another, this functionality demands a level of integration typical of an I-CASE system.

- **Review** steps are supported largely through the provision of information about products and components and by graphic representations of them. A desirable feature of any CASE system is an ability to provide graphic representations suitable for presentation purposes. This may imply summary level representations or representations using less formal notations and icons than those employed in the underlying techniques.

  A variety of audiences may be targeted in different types of review. It is important that each audience be able to look at the products under review in ways that suit them and, therefore, that may be markedly different from the developers' representations. There is no reason, for example, why entity types such as 'warehouse' and 'person' should not be represented by pictures or pictograms of a warehouse and a person rather than by boxes on a diagram. Icons to suit different types of user may therefore be valuable.

It is sometimes the case that a review step exists for routine quality control purposes to demonstrate that appropriate checks have been undertaken. Such review steps may become completely unnecessary where the checks are fully automated.

- **Decision** steps should in principle not be automated, unless automation makes them unnecessary. However, as with review steps, CASE systems can provide the necessary information in the representation most appropriate to assist the decision taking.

10.3.4 Human roles

An opportunity exists with CASE systems to make them sensitive to the role an individual is filling when working with the system:

- The **executive responsible** may wish the system to provide no more than a management summary of progress on projects.
- The **development coordinator** requires capabilities which support configuration control (see Section 8.7) and the administration of data gathered by development projects.
- The **business analyst, designer** and **constructor** need tools which automate the techniques being employed and which help in developing the products which are to be delivered as the final results of their particular efforts.
- The **user acceptor** and **constructor acceptor** require that the CASE system should produce specifications in a form that allows them to review them easily and to confirm that they meet requirements.
- The **resource manager** requires detailed, project specific information on resource expenditure within steps and stages in projects which are either under way or in planning.
- The **user** requires the CASE system to provide adequate representations of models that emerge at each stage, so that the user's participation in the development process can be effective.

10.3.5 Representations

An important feature of many CASE systems is their ability to provide and manage representations that are appropriate to the context. Ideally this should extend to providing representations that are attuned to any relevant combination of technique, stage, step category, human role and scenario (see Chapter 9).

10.3.6 Perspectives

A perspective is supported when the CASE system provides tools to automate techniques that provide components relevant to the perspective. An emphasis on any one perspective may influence the market positioning of the system. Those which support components of the behaviour perspective are often marketed more in the area of engineering and manufacturing systems; others, which give support to components of the data perspective, are targeted particularly to the administrative systems market. Explicit inclusion of all perspectives is characteristic of a CASE system intended to support a design process for creating interworking systems in a cooperative or open systems environment.

10.3.7   Scenarios

CASE systems' support to multiple scenarios demands that the use of the tools be tailorable to suit particular situations or development environments. Ideally, the tools would be reconfigurable and capable of adjusting their behaviour to suit whatever circumstances were presented. In practice, this means that once a scenario is defined, and a way of working is agreed upon among those involved in a project, the CASE system would need to be able to accept this way of working and present only the required facilities to its users.

10.4   Impact on stages

CASE systems have the potential to change our view of the stages in an information systems methodology by changing steps in a development process and even by hiding complete stages.

The outline architecture typical of CASE systems, which is shown in Figure 10.1, is representative of several in common use. It is, however, misleading in that it can be taken to imply that the tools provided will automate steps of the stages under which the tools are grouped. In practice, the tools often automate techniques rather than steps, so they can be employed wherever there is a step that can use that technique. This means that some tools can be used in more than one stage; for example, entity modelling is often used in both the information systems planning and the business analysis stages. It also means that CASE systems can, in principle, support multiple design processes.

The support given by CASE systems to stages and their steps is, therefore, often more implicit than explicit. CASE systems that seek to automate fully the stages and steps of a design process require some form of I-CASE functionality and need to incorporate some representation of the stages and steps of the design process.

10.4.1   Analytic stages

In the information systems planning and business analysis stages, CASE systems provide tools that give support for the gathering of information, for recording, detailing and documenting the results of investigations, and for modelling the business and specifying components. They provide enterprises with the ability to handle the versions of models and views of models required throughout the development process. They also marshal facts and present information in ways that assist in reviews, aid prioritization and enable the taking of decisions on future progress.

None of these features changes the nature of those stages. Even the addition of automated, expert analytic support may not fundamentally change the stages until that support becomes sufficiently advanced for the tools to 'interview' users while these users work with the tools to produce and synthesize their own models directly.

However, by issuing CASE systems whose storage is already populated with generic industry models, such as a retail banking model or a steel rolling mill model, then significant changes can be brought about. These models act as a 'starter pack', and the purpose of the analytic stages is then to tailor the models, rather than develop them afresh as tends to be the assumed way of working in many methodologies. This approach provides a means of capturing business concepts and making them reusable.

10.4.2   Prescriptive stages

At the system design, construction design and construction and workbench test stages, increasing amounts of automation are possible. The translation of data models into database specifications can be done automatically; logic for stereotyped computer procedures can be generated. In this and similar instances, original steps are altered or disappear. In construction design and construction and workbench test, most steps can be wholly automated by the use of system generators capable of automatically generating all of the program code, database descriptions and control language needed for a complete system, and also capable of link-editing the modules and compiling them ready for test. This level of automation can cover all steps in design, enabling CASE systems to generate usable applications based on the results of analysis. These applications may well be viewed as prototypes, but the steps in design are then devoted simply to tailoring them to match user tastes and tuning them where performance is a critical requirement.

Much of this capability is achieved by providing reusable specifications – reusable in the sense that the designer can request certain forms of functionality and have the CASE system automatically incorporate them in the design product and match them to the data structure as it does so, updating all data names.

10.4.3   Evolution

CASE systems have the potential to assist considerably in managing system evolution in an orderly manner. Where analysis and design products are held in storage, modification can be done easily. If these products are then to be used to drive a system generator, evolution can be completed accurately and quickly.

Tools for reverse engineering may also appear as elements of CASE systems (see Figure 8.5). They can be used to examine existing programs and databases or files and to deduce the likely, intended structure of the original products of the design or even the analytic stages. Details of these original products can then be retained in the storage. There, they can be used either to support future maintenance and progressive evolution of the system from its current state or to allow it to be re-engineered by using the generator to create a wholly new version of the system. In either instance the system is sub-sequently managed within the disciplines of the information systems methodology being used.

An effect of this may be to promote more frequent, but smaller scale, enhancements throughout the life of the system (a more truly evolutionary development). Every enhancement implies some knock-on change to other systems and procedures but these may be handled more easily because the CASE system will be able to offer automated support to this internal migration.

Reverse engineering of programs is more difficult than that of data structures. Restructuring tools may be used first, to render the program into a properly structured format. Subsequent interpretation, however, demands some way of determining which parts of the program provide design logic and which business logic, and then deducing what purpose the business logic serves.

With data structures, the rules of normalization and the mapping rules for data management systems often provide a reasonable basis for inter-pretation. The principal area of difficulty arises when data is embedded in program code. This data may be identified by manual inspection or by reporting on every element of program logic that changes a data variable. Again, the interpretation of the meaning of this data and the determination of its functional dependencies may not be simple, though inferences are possible from the program logic.

10.4.4 Management of stages

Direct support becomes possible if the CASE system can handle information about the stages and steps of a methodology, about types of scenario and about specific scenarios for each project. Under these conditions CASE systems can be used actively in support of project management.

Version management and configuration control provide mechanisms to assist in managing work-in-progress on projects and are valuable in supporting coordination of effort. The coordination may be among members of a project team, between projects belonging to the same stage and between projects of different stages. It may also need to be applied to effort used in creating system variations. For all of these requirements, however, it seems likely that the functionality needed will be possible only through I-CASE systems.

10.5   Conclusions

CASE systems can and do provide substantial levels of automated support to information systems methodologies and to many of the concepts discussed in this framework. There is less support to the behaviour perspective than the others, but as methodologies seek to embrace that perspective this is expected to change. Similarly, support to the management processes around the use of information systems methodologies offers potential to future CASE system developers.

As in other areas of endeavour, the advent of automation causes significant changes in methodologies. The rigour introduced by automation does away with the need for many review and decision steps. Similarly, many form conversion steps can be wholly automated or, in the case of highly integrated tools, may become unnecessary. Increased levels of automation are also achieved by building reusability of concepts into the tools – possibly in the form of industry templates or stereotyped specifications. This allows analysts and designers to get off to a flying start on any project by exploiting the 'canned' expertise available.

Increased use of formal models may also help in achieving increased levels of automation, by further enhancing the rigour achievable and by guaranteeing the correctness of mappings or transformations undertaken.

CASE heralds a move from a craft based to something more like a production line based approach to systems development. CASE systems that support individual techniques provide tools to the craftsman, and those that give support to the design process itself enable a level of production line operation. When embedded in an appropriate organization structure and handled with appropriate management procedures, the more advanced CASE systems offer an exceptionally efficient approach to creating information systems.

EXERCISES

A.   *Self-assessment*

10.1   Without referring to the text, summarize the impact of CASE systems on steps of each of the five step categories. Distinguish between the respective impacts of I-CASE and C-CASE approaches.

10.2   Describe briefly the relevance of an advanced storage facility such as an encyclopaedia or repository to CASE systems and to the use of an information systems methodology.

10.3   The text suggests that CASE systems may influence analytic steps in a methodology rather differently from prescriptive steps. Why is this? What differences do you anticipate?

10.4   'Reverse engineering tools remove the need for themselves.' Discuss this proposition.

10.5   Why is configuration management a critical issue in the use of I-CASE systems?

10.6   Describe how a formal definition of a design process might be developed in a way that could be used by a CASE system to manage its automation of that design process.

Concluding remarks

11.1 Review

This text has presented a framework for the understanding and appreciation of information systems methodologies. The detail of the framework is to be found in Chapters 4, 5 and 7. The detail consists of an enumeration of 127 different components, allowing for some duplication between the information systems planning stage components described in Chapter 7 and the business analysis stage components described in Chapter 4.

It can be seen that the framework has an essentially data oriented perspective. It lists the kinds of things produced by different methodologies. Each such 'kind of thing' is referred to as a **component**. A component is analogous to the concept of an ENTITY TYPE but on the level of the framework rather than on the level of business analysis.

One design process might generate N components (where N is a number less than the total in the framework). Another design process might generate the same N components, but in a different sequence, which is what causes it to be regarded as a different design process. Another aspect of this is that another design process might generate the same N components in the same sequence as the first, but might package the steps differently and include more of the kind of steps, such as review steps, which do not generate components.

The framework is presented in terms of components which have a data oriented perspective and in terms of stages and steps, each of which has a process oriented perspective, as illustrated in Chapter 6. While it is possible to itemize all the components, some selection of which will be generated by any information systems methodology, a comparable itemization of steps could be made only in terms of the components used and created by each step. The number of possible steps in such an itemization would be very high.

Since this attempt to prepare such a framework is the first at this level of detail, there are bound to be omissions. There are, almost certainly, components which have not been recognized. It would not be difficult to find further relationships and cross-references between pairs of existing components. In addition, some new methodology dependent components might be introduced to enable the combination of two or more existing components into a new component on a higher abstraction level.

It might be seen as an unfortunate omission that this framework does not cover the construction design stage, although one of the reasons for omitting this was that construction design is felt to be tool dependent – as pointed out in Section 3.2.4. The tools which are being developed for the construction of computerized information systems are, at time of writing, undergoing a significant evolution.

The traditional tools, as epitomized by standardized procedural programming languages such as FORTRAN, COBOL, BASIC and Ada (in order of age), are being supplemented – and in some installations replaced – by a myriad of new languages, most of which claim to be 'fourth generation'. The same is true of older, widely used, non-procedural languages such as RPG (Report Program Generator) which has been in use in various forms since the 1960s.

A component analysis for the construction design stage, at a detail level comparable to that carried out for information systems planning, business analysis and system design in this book, would probably have revealed as many components as the current exercise has done for all three stages together.

11.2   Components checklist

The components which have been identified in this text are scattered throughout Chapters 4, 5 and 7. The aim of this section is to bring them all together in one place so that the reader has a checklist which can be used during the initial stages of checking how a methodology fits into the framework.

An enumeration of so many components can, on an initial reading, be rather overwhelming. Many readers will wish to go through the exercise of taking their favourite methodology and trying to check which components it

· generates. To do this accurately, it is necessary to start with the methodology dependent components.

RELATIONSHIP CLASS
RELATIONSHIP TYPE
VALUE CONSTRAINT TYPE
POPULATION OVERLAP TYPE
INFORMATION OR MATERIAL
INVOLVEMENT TYPE
FLOW TYPE
BUSINESS EVENT ROLE

Figure 11.1 Methodology dependent components from business analysis.

11.2.1 Methodology dependent components

The concept of a methodology dependent component has been explained in Section 3.8.1 as a component, the instances of which should be prescribed by a methodology designer rather than by a methodology user as is the case for other components. Figure 11.1 lists the eight methodology dependent components in the business analysis stage.

It will be noted that the methodology dependent component INVOLVE-MENT TYPE is presented twice in Chapter 4 on the basis that it might have different options prescribed by the methodology definer for each kind of use.

Figure 11.2 lists the 15 methodology dependent components for the system design stage.

Figure 11.3 lists the three methodology dependent components for the information systems planning stage.

ASSIGNMENT TYPE
DATA TYPE
CONSTRAINT TYPE
DISPLAY OPTION
ON LINE OR BATCH
TASK CATEGORY
HOMING IN OR OUT-OF-THE-BLUE
MENU-DRIVEN OR FAST TRACK
INITIATIONS MEANS
TASK TO TASK INITIATION TYPE
ACCESS PATH NODE TYPE
TASK DATA USAGE TYPE
FORM USAGE CLASS
TRIGGER CATEGORY
CONDITION ROLE

Figure 11.2 Methodology dependent components from system design.

```
DEVELOPMENT STATUS
PRIORITY
PROJECT STATUS
```

Figure 11.3   Methodology dependent components from information systems planning.

The first task for a person wishing to check how a methodology fits into the framework is to go through each of these methodology dependent components, determining whether the component is relevant and, if so, which options for the component are applicable to the methodology under examination. It is important to note that the options shown in Chapters 4, 5 and 7 are illustrative. A methodology might well use options which are not illustrated in this text.

11.2.2   Business analysis components

The next step is to review the other components, namely those which are generated by a user of a methodology rather than a specifier of a methodology. The data oriented components for the business analysis stage are listed in Figure 11.4.

Care should be exercised with components such as ENTITY TYPE NAME and ATTRIBUTE NAME. They are included as separate components to cater for analysis techniques which allow for synonyms to be recorded. If such techniques are not supported, then the only name of each ENTITY TYPE and of each ATTRIBUTE would be recorded with those components.

Care should also be exercised with the RELATIONSHIP and CONSTRAINT components where there is some scope for duplication (as pointed out in Chapter 4).

The process oriented components for the business analysis stage are displayed in Figure 11.5.

```
ENTITY TYPE
ENTITY TYPE NAME
ENTITY TYPE USES NAME
RELATIONSHIP
ENTITY TYPE IN RELATIONSHIP
ATTRIBUTE NAME
ATTRIBUTE
ATTRIBUTE GROUP
ATTRIBUTE IN GROUP
ATTRIBUTE OF RELATIONSHIP
VALUE CONSTRAINT
POPULATION OVERLAP
```

Figure 11.4   Data perspective components from business analysis stage.

BUSINESS ACTIVITY
BUSINESS ACTIVITY NAME
BUSINESS ACTIVITY USES NAME
ACTIVITY PRECEDENCE/SUCCEDENCE
INFORMATION/MATERIAL SET
SET NAME
INFORMATION/MATERIAL SET USES NAME
ACTIVITY USES SET
ACTIVITY PRECONDITION
PRECONDITION ENABLES ACTIVITY
ORGANIZATION UNIT
ACTIVITY RESPONSIBILITY
EXTERNAL UNIT
FLOW
ACTIVITY INVOLVES FLOW
FLOW INVOLVES INFORMATION/MATERIAL SET
FLOW OF SET IN ACTIVITY
FLOW PRECONDITION
PRECONDITION ENABLES FLOW

Figure 11.5   Process perspective components from business analysis stage.

BUSINESS EVENT
BUSINESS EVENT NAME
BUSINESS EVENT USES NAME
EVENT PRECEDENCE/SUCCEDENCE
BUSINESS EVENT CONDITION
CONDITION FOR BUSINESS EVENT
BUSINESS ACTIVITY INVOLVES ENTITY TYPE
BUSINESS ACTIVITY INVOLVES ATTRIBUTE
ACTIVITY TRIGGER
BUSINESS EVENT INVOLVES ENTITY TYPE
BUSINESS EVENT INVOLVES ATTRIBUTE
CONDITION USES ENTITY TYPE
CONDITION USES ATTRIBUTE

Figure 11.6   Behaviour perspective and cross-reference components from business
analysis stage.

Similar cautions are appropriate for components introduced to allow
for the analysis of synonyms such as BUSINESS ACTIVITY NAME and SET
NAME. As already indicated in Chapter 4, the component INFORMA-
TION/MATERIAL SET is intended to cover the widely used term 'data store', as
well as the name of any information which is involved in a FLOW.

Figure 11.6 covers the remainder of the business analysis stage, namely
the behaviour perspective and the cross-reference components between
components. The total number of components which need to be checked for
the business analysis stage is hence 44 (excluding methodology dependent
components).

11.2.3   System design components

Moving to the system design stage, the number of components is somewhat less than for the business analysis stage. The components for the data perspective are listed in Figure 11.7. The list in Figure 11.7 contains a number of cross-reference components, each of which may be used to relate a system design component with a business analysis component. The component CONSTRAINT, indicated with a double asterisk, is also used in the business analysis stage.

Figure 11.8 contains the process perspective components for the system design stage together with the cross-reference components between data and process perspectives.

TABLE
ENTITY TYPE TO TABLE ASSIGNMENT
COLUMN NAME
COLUMN
ATTRIBUTE TO COLUMN ASSIGNMENT
COLUMN GROUP
COLUMN IN GROUP
**CONSTRAINT
RELATIONSHIP TO CONSTRAINT ASSIGNMENT
ROW
EXTERNAL FORM
EXTERNAL FORM ELEMENT
COLUMN ON FORM ELEMENT

Figure 11.7   Data perspective components from system design stage.

TASK
MENU
MENU HIERARCHY
TASK IN MENU
ACCESS CONTROL CLASS
TASK IN ACCESS CONTROL CLASS
TASK TO TASK INITIATION
TASK USES TABLE
TASK USES COLUMN
ALGORITHM
ALGORITHM REFERENCES COLUMN
TASK USES ALGORITHM
TASK USES EXTERNAL FORM

Figure 11.8   Process perspective components and cross-reference components between data and process perspectives for system design.

SYSTEM EVENT
BUSINESS EVENT TRIGGERS SYSTEM EVENT
SYSTEM EVENT PRECEDENCE/SUCCEDENCE
CONDITION
CONDITION REFERENCES COLUMN
CONDITION ROLE FOR SYSTEM EVENT
SYSTEM EVENT TRIGGERS TASK

Figure 11.9 Behaviour perspective components and cross-reference components
with data and process perspectives for system design.

BUSINESS PROBLEM
**ORGANIZATION UNIT
UNIT IN ORGANIZATION
INTEREST GROUP
ORGANIZATION UNIT INVOLVED WITH INTEREST GROUP
OBJECTIVE
PROBLEM FOR OBJECTIVE
GOAL
INFORMATION/MATERIAL SET
CRITICAL SUCCESS FACTOR
**BUSINESS ACTIVITY
OBJECTIVE TARGETS BUSINESS ACTIVITY
**ACTIVITY USES SET
**ENTITY TYPE
**BUSINESS ACTIVITY INVOLVES ENTITY TYPE
INFORMATION FROM ENTITY TYPE
**RELATIONSHIP
**ENTITY TYPE IN RELATIONSHIP
NEED FOR CHANGE
CHANGE ALTERNATIVE

Figure 11.10 Components from information systems planning stage for business
plan, organization and mental model.
(Double asterisk means component also used in business analysis stage.)

Finally for the system design stage, Figure 11.9 contains the behaviour
oriented components from the system design stage, together with the cross-
references between behaviour components and those with one of the other
two perspectives. The total number of components to analyse for the system
design stage is 33 (again excluding methodology dependent components).

11.2.4 Information systems planning components

The components enumerated in Chapter 7 for the information systems
planning stage are not categorized according to the three perspectives – data,
process and behaviour – but in terms of the following two aspects of the
stage:

1.   Business plan, organization and mental model.
2.   Information systems plan and cross-references.

Figure 11.10 lists the components identified as relevant to the first aspect. Figure 11.11 lists the components relevant to the information systems plan including the cross-references to components relevant to the first aspect.

It should be noted that some of these components have already been included as business analysis components and these are again indicated with a double asterisk.

In general, the information systems planning components will consist of far more textual information than those for the other two stages. It should also be noted that the number of information systems methodologies which attempt to cover information systems planning is far fewer than those covering business analysis and system design.

For completeness, it is noted that the number of components from the information systems planning stage which are not already identified in connection with business analysis is 26.

11.2.5 General comments on components

When checking an information systems methodology to see how it fits into the framework described in this text, it may be tempting to use the lists of components presented in Figures 11.4 to 11.11, deleting from these lists any component not generated by the methodology. This approach will work only if the analyst has a good in-depth understanding of the meaning of the component, as presented in Chapters 4, 5 and 7.

INFORMATION SYSTEM
ENTITY TYPE GROUP
BUSINESS AREA
INFORMATION SYSTEMS PLAN
INFORMATION SYSTEMS SUPPORT FOR OBJECTIVE
PLAN PROJECT
PRIORITIZATION CRITERION
PROJECT PRECEDENCE/SUCCEDENCE
INFORMATION SYSTEM IN PLAN PROJECT
ENTITY TYPE GROUP IN PLAN PROJECT
BENEFIT
COST
PROBLEM INVOLVES INFORMATION SYSTEM
PROBLEM INVOLVES ENTITY TYPE GROUP

Figure 11.11   Components from information systems planning stage for
information systems plan and cross-references.

Differences in terminology in the field of information systems methodologies are considerable and have caused major problems during the preparation of the framework. It would be dangerous to assume a meaning for a term, such as 'attribute', 'task' or 'condition', without a full understanding of how it is used in the context of the framework.

A preferred approach to investigating how a methodology fits into the framework would be to use a copy of the structure diagrams given in Chapters 4, 5 and 7 and to annotate each rectangle to indicate whether the component is generated using the methodology and, if so, what name the methodology uses for the component. In the same way, each arrow between two rectangles can also be annotated to indicate whether the methodology handles the implied relationship. This kind of analysis is difficult to achieve with lists of components such as those presented in this chapter.

It is, of course, quite possible for a methodology to generate a component or a relationship between two components which is not identified in the framework. Another possibility is for one component in the methodology under examination to be on a higher abstraction level than those presented in the framework and, as a result, to be represented in the framework by two or more framework components.

A final dimension to the exercise of fitting a methodology into the framework is that of identifying the sequences of steps. Some methodologies are broken down fairly neatly into a sequence of clearly identified steps. Others are presented in a less structured manner.

A way of relating components to the steps in which they are generated is shown for each of the examples presented in Chapter 6. A step number is included in the rectangle indicating the step in which the component is generated.

11.3   Levels of description

The use of **levels of description** in this framework is most apparent when data concepts are considered. Figure 1.6 shows a data structure diagram of the key concepts used in the framework and how these are interrelated. Figure 5.1 then shows a data structure diagram for the data perspective components in the system design stage. Finally, Figure 5.2 shows a data structure diagram for the inventory control example. It is clear that each of these diagrams relates to a different level of description.

The top level used in this text provides the general concepts for the framework. These general concepts help in categorizing specific concepts used in methodologies. The specific concepts exist in turn to categorize the many instances of things specific to individual enterprises or business areas. Ultimately, the enterprise may store data in an operational information system about these relevant 'things', but no examples of such data are presented.

Figure 11.12 illustrates and suggest a name for each of the four levels, including the bottom one. In practice, it is useful to identify levels only when, at the same time, it is necessary to show what the level describes. It is helpful

Level	Illustrative level concept
Framework structure	Component
Framework content	Entity type
Dictionary database structure	
Dictionary database content	Employee
Application database structure	
Application database content	Smith

Figure 11.12   Data levels relevant to this book.

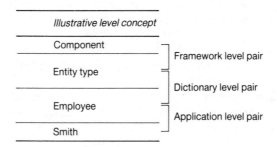

Illustrative level concept	
Component	Framework level pair
Entity type	Dictionary level pair
Employee	Application level pair
Smith	

Figure 11.13   Data level pairs.

to formalize the notion of a description and what is described. In the '*ISO Reference Model of Data Management*' (ISO 10032), this notion is referred to as a **level pair**. Figure 11.13 shows the level pairs applicable to Figure 11.12.

An important feature of level pairs is that they interlock or possibly overlap. This is because descriptive concepts often describe the level of description below their own, at the same time as being an instance in the level pair above. For example, in Figure 11.13 'Entity type' is a dictionary level pair concept describing such concepts as 'Employee', while at the same time 'Entity type' is an instance of a 'Component' with respect to the framework level pair.

The notion of multiple levels of description is pervasive in thinking related to methodologies and in practice. The levels of description used are not always explicit. The aim of drawing attention to this notion here is that consideration of the levels used in a particular methodology can make that methodology easier to understand.

11.4   Comparing methodologies

Some enterprises will wish to standardize on one methodology on the basis that if it is good for one job, it is good for another. Others will find several different ones being assimilated by different departments. Some will wish to find the right tool for the job in the case of each major information system when the time comes for it to be implemented or reimplemented.

Comparing two or more methodologies could start with carrying out the exercise described in the previous section for each methodology under consideration. This will give a useful insight into how the methodologies are similar and where they are different.

Deciding on the most suitable methodology to use in a given situation is a far more difficult task and one that calls for an understanding of the various situations discussed in Chapter 2. A methodology which is appropriate for one situation may be inadequate for another situation.

A major aspect of any methodology is the amount of the information systems life cycle which it covers. If it is felt to be important to carry out information systems planning, then a methodology which covers this stage will be preferable to one which does not. If it is felt, rightly or wrongly, that there is sufficient insight and structured understanding of the business area available to be able to take the risk of going straight into system design, then a methodology offering elaborate business analysis techniques, and not much else, will be rated accordingly.

After some experience with several methodologies, one can think in terms of the underlying concepts and techniques. One can learn to combine the approach to analytic data modelling promoted in one methodology with the approach to data flow analysis in another, cross-referencing the results of the two analyses in a way not supported in either. One can learn to recognize 'overkill' in a methodology, particularly in the business analysis stage. Overkill would call for generating a large number of components such that the problems of intercomponent consistency introduced outweigh any extra insight and understanding gleaned from carrying out the analysis.

A word of warning is in order about the number of components generated by a methodology. One should not necessarily assume that the greater the number of components identified in this text that a methodology supports, the more highly that methodology should be rated.

Figure 11.14 shows a hypothetical graph of how quality might vary according to the number of components. The basis for the hypothesis is that a very low number of components is clearly an indication of an inadequate methodology and that as the number of components increases initially, the adequacy and hence the quality should also improve. As indicated, an ill-chosen mix of too many components can represent 'overkill' and therefore the optimum lies somewhere between the two extremes.

Figure 11.14 suggests that the quality of the methodology improves with the number of components as far as some maximum, after which the quality decreases. This picture should be borne in mind when creating new methodologies. The graph does not take into account the fact that some components may be more important than others. The omission of specific quantitative measures along the axes is deliberate.

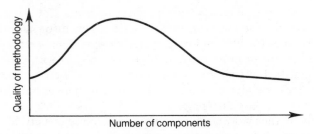

Figure 11.14   Hypothetical graph of methodology quality as a function of number of components.

One of the main objectives of this text is to disseminate a general understanding of methodologies as a class of man-made device. If it enables users to compare one methodology with another, it will have gone some way towards meeting this goal.

11.5   Researchable topics

This book may well be accused of raising more problems than it solves. Hopefully, it will be viewed as stimulating research work in the area of information systems methodologies. In order to give some pointers to work which could usefully be done, the following eight topics are suggested:

1.   Study of techniques.
2.   Techniques for scenarios.
3.   Framework for construction design.
4.   Role of graphic symbols.
5.   Abstract framework.
6.   Evolution of an installed system.
7.   Computerized framework for methodology generation.
8.   Extended framework for research oriented methodologies.

Each of these topics will briefly be discussed in turn, in the form and sequence identified in this text. It is, of course, possible for these topics to be broken down and packaged differently.

11.5.1   Study of techniques

This text has introduced the concept of a technique, such as entity modelling, flow analysis, organizational studies, etc. (see Section 1.8). Several techniques were identified in Chapter 6 in the illustrations of design processes and the steps in each. However, the text has not formalized the concept of a technique further than the implication in Chapter 1 that each step may use one or more techniques (see Figure 1.6).

The first research topic would be to identify the basic techniques covered by the components in this text and to indicate which components are relevant to which techniques. Some components will be relevant to more than one technique. A first extension to this would be to identify the possible variants of the basic techniques, partly in terms of options for methodology dependent components and partly in terms of basic components created.

11.5.2 Techniques for scenarios

This project requires the preceding project to have been completed. In Chapter 2, the concept of a scenario was introduced. Various factors influencing each scenario were identified. It was pointed out that there could be a very large number of possible scenarios if all alternative values of all scenario factors were taken into account.

Possibly one of the most valuable projects which could be undertaken on the basis of this text would be to analyse the value of various techniques for each scenario factor. This kind of analysis could be superficial, for example, by restricting the study to some very specific situations. Alternatively, it could be extensive, by investigating what opportunities exist in the first place and considering the full range of factors.

Conclusions in this area will inevitably be somewhat subjective. The guidance many practitioners will be looking for over the next decade, when they start to understand that a methodology is a compendium of techniques, is which technique to use in a given situation. Research into means of recognizing and specifying these would find immediate applicability. Additionally, it would be very useful to find ways of making some of the existing methodologies less rigorous and of allowing more flexibility to the user.

This research project would cause new methodologies to emerge which would have the capability to guide the practitioner in the selection of the most useful options.

11.5.3 Framework for construction design

This text has established a style for a framework by analysing extant methodologies and identifying the components relevant to three stages, namely information systems planning, business analysis and system design. The role of the next stage, construction design, has been discussed (see Sections 3.2.4 and 5.12). It has been pointed out that construction design is regarded as tool dependent.

There are three complementary parts to this project. One is to take as a starting point a set of methodologies which purport to cover the design of application programs, and to create a framework for the construction design stage similar to those created in this text for the earlier stages.

The second is to take a set of commercially available fourth generation languages which claim to be usable for constructing information systems more rapidly and inexpensively than conventional techniques. On the basis of these, a framework can be created for the construction design stage similar to those in this text for the earlier stages.

The final part of the project is to review the two frameworks created in the first and second parts. The duplication between the two should be carefully noted. On the basis of this review, a combined framework can be prepared which covers both the methodologies and the tools.

11.5.4   Role of graphic symbols

Chapter 9 discusses the different ways in which components could be represented graphically. Eleven ways of displaying a 'one to zero, one or more' relationship were shown in Figure 9.4 and six ways of representing a business activity in Figure 9.5.

This work needs to be taken further and the range of alternatives analysed for each of the major components (excluding methodology dependent components). It would be useful if this analysis could include some evaluation of how widespread the use of a given alternative has become. On the basis of this analysis, it should be possible to propose a set of graphic symbols for each of the components and to show how diagrams associated with each of the separately identified techniques can be prepared.

Another important aspect of this topic is the applicability of various forms of representation to the various human roles. Some graphic representations will be more appropriate for users and others for constructors.

11.5.5   Abstract framework

The discussion in Section 4.13 defended the abstraction level chosen for the components of the business analysis and system design stages. The argument was that the abstraction level was comparable with that found in a majority of extant methodologies which were being used in a commercial environment.

It should be recognized that a higher abstraction level should lead to a more generally applicable framework and the preparation of such a framework is suggested as a research project. How the abstract components relate to those in this text should be analysed, together with an indication of what new representation capability is achieved and its practical value.

Researchers aiming for a higher abstraction level framework should be careful to avoid recreating parts of Figure 1.6, which shows the key concepts used to define the framework.

11.5.6 Evolution of an installed information system

Chapter 8 introduced this topic and indicated the very considerable investment of resources which typically takes place using today's technology after an information system has been installed until a decision is taken to phase out the system and to replace it with a different one.

The chapter indicated ways of handling what is a well recognized problem in a given situation once it has occurred. The problems are caused more by the way in which the analysis, design and construction stages are performed.

The researchable topic is how to minimize the costs of evolving an information system once it has been installed. Solutions will, almost certainly, call in general terms for more investment in the earlier stages of planning, analysis and design, together with faster (and hence less expensive) construction techniques. More specific guidelines are needed.

Are certain techniques (and hence certain components) critical in the early stages? How does one design for extensibility, and which components are critical in this context? On the hypothesis that it is not enough merely to identify the critical components but, in addition, to specify them in a certain way, what guidelines are applicable in this context?

11.5.7 Computerized framework for methodology generation

Part of the framework presented in this text is essentially a data model containing a significant number of entity types (each referred to as a component). As indicated earlier in this chapter, it is possible to design a methodology by selecting a related set of components and defining a sequence of steps in which the instances of the components are to be created.

. This research project calls for the availability of suitable hardware and software resources. The aim is to create a computerized methodology generator, such that a methodology designer can sit at a terminal and review the available components and how they are interrelated, and then select a set of components which he or she can use as a basis for specifying a methodology suitable to his or her needs. In addition to the components, a sequence of steps in different categories for each stage covered would need to be identified. The inclusion of components and techniques not described in the current text but possibly developed during research projects covering other topics is to be expected.

If the system created by the researcher allowed a methodology user (as opposed to a methodology designer) to take over and use this methodology in a given business area, then this would be a major achievement.

11.5.8 Extended framework for research methodologies

The framework presented in this text has been designed to cover the kinds of methodology which are in commercial use in various parts of the world.

However, it is noted that there is considerable research activity on information systems methodologies and it is more than likely that the present framework would need extension to cover them effectively.

This research project calls for a set of research oriented information systems methodologies to be analysed and an attempt made to fit each into the framework described earlier in this chapter. This attempt should identify new techniques, components and associated steps that are needed and point the way for appropriate extensions.

The research project for creating a higher abstraction level framework should also be taken into consideration here since the higher abstraction level components could handle some of the concepts introduced in the new research oriented methodologies.

11.6   Opening questions revisited

In the introduction to Chapter 1, a number of questions were asked. In this concluding chapter, it is appropriate to revisit the four major ones and to see what new insight has been gained.

1.   Are there really so many substantially different ways to design a computerized information system?

There are certainly many different ways to design an information system, as can be seen from the large number of components identified and the theoretically enormous number of different combinations of components and step sequences in which components can be generated. This book has not attempted to evaluate the usefulness of the components, although it has become clear that the number of basic techniques available is not that high.

The present state-of-the-art is that each methodology supports some techniques and possibly also some level of integration among the techniques.

2.   If not, how are these ways similar? If so, how are they different?

The ways are similar in that they use a basic set of techniques based on an enumerable set of components. The ways are often different in that they use different variants of the techniques. The variants can be observed in the various options selected for methodology dependent components.

3.   Should we be using one kind of methodology for one kind of information system and a different methodology for another?

This text has not attempted to categorize 'kinds of information system' except in the very broadest sense in the discussion of scenarios in Chapter 2. Any explicit answer to this question at the present state of understanding would be, at best, subjective. However, it is hoped that this book provides a means of addressing this question – and ultimately achieving some convergence on the answers – by suggesting what one should look for in an information systems methodology.

4.   If so, which methodology should we use for which kinds of system?

This question remains to be addressed in more detail. For the practitioner, the answer will necessarily be based on pragmatism. For the researcher, the project described in Section 11.5.2, and possibly others, remain to be studied.

11.7   Hopes and aspirations

This book has attempted to consolidate and merge the various views on information systems methodologies into a unified framework. The book is about how to view methodologies. It is hoped that this framework will be the first step along the long path of technology convergence in this area. The book does not teach people how to design computerized information systems. There are many available texts which attempt to do this and the views on how the job should be done are so varied that it would be impossible to synthesize a unified view.

It is hoped that this book will help many people – teachers, students, practitioners and researchers – to gain a new perspective on the subject of information systems methodologies. It is hoped that this will be broader than that of the single methodology. As indicated in the introduction, such a perspective is a prerequisite for tackling this book.

Appendix A
Some existing methodologies and relevant frameworks

A.1 Introduction

An information systems methodology is an intellectual tool supporting some of the stages described in this book. This is a broad definition encompassing many existing methodologies which are not all described in this appendix. In the selection, the following criteria have been applied.

A first selection is based on the application domain of the methodologies. This appendix does not include the many methodologies which, according to their authors, essentially aim at different application areas, the main one being control systems.

A second selection limits the choice to those methodologies which are in wide-spread use, or are representative of a particularly interesting approach. For the latter reason, various innovative methodologies are included, although the framework presented in this book is aimed rather at methodologies in use in practitioner environments. These innovative methodologies are not necessarily encompassed at component level, but can still be located in stages and characterized in terms of perspectives.

Finally, the methodologies described can usually be readily accessed in the literature or, for some commercial methodologies, by contacting the supplier (who is always mentioned).

For each methodology, the following information is provided (when available):

- name (acronym and meaning),
- institution from which the methodology originated,
- references (up to four, at least one in English),
- availability (commercially marketed, research status),
- description (around 50 words).

This should provide the reader with an overall impression of the methodology as well as pointers to further sources of information.

The descriptions are based on the available publications and use the terminology of this book. This may sometimes lead to divergences with the opinions of the developers of the various methodologies.

This list does not include techniques that would be hard to describe separately from the methodologies using them. Neither does it attempt to itemize the case tools supporting several of the methodologies.

A.2   Methodologies

ACM/PCM: Active and Passive Component Modelling

Computer Corporation of America (CCA), USA.
Brodie, M.L. and Silva, E., 'Active and passive component modelling: ACM/PCM'. In: Olle *et al.* (1982), pp. 41–92.
Availability: research status.

This methodology, which covers business analysis and system design, includes a data and a process perspective. The former is based on the identification of objects organized by means of abstraction relations (is-a, part-of, member-of) and complemented by constraints in a language inspired by formal logic. The process part is expressed in terms of operations on the data model, possibly subject to preconditions and postconditions.

Activity Modeling/Behavior Modeling

Norwegian Institute of Technology, Norway.
Kung, C.H. and Sølvberg, A., 'Activity modeling and behavior modeling'. In: Olle *et al.* (1986), pp. 145–171.
Availability: research status.

This methodology addresses the stages of business analysis and system design. Activity modelling, the first part of the methodology, is mainly process oriented. It uses data flow diagrams, extended to distinguish data and material flows. The flows are described in a data perspective component using entity-relationship modelling. Behaviour modelling, the second part of the methodology, details each activity in terms of state transitions, using Petri nets with preconditions and postconditions.

AXIAL

IBM, France.
Pellaumail (1986).
Pellaumail (1987).
Availability: commercially marketed by IBM, France.

AXIAL covers the four stages of the framework, with emphasis on information systems planning. It also includes managerial aspects, such as planning and resource allocation. It recommends various diagrammatic techniques belonging to the data and process perspectives.

CIAM: Conceptual Information Analysis Methodology

SYSLAB, Sweden.
Bubenko (1980).
Gustafsson, M.R., Karlsson, T. and Bubenko, J.A., Jr., 'A declarative approach to conceptual information modeling'. In: Olle *et al.* (1982), pp. 93–142.
Availability: research status.

CIAM covers the stages of information systems planning, business analysis and system design. The early stages aim at developing a theory of the application in a mixed data and behaviour perspective, by using the concepts of entity, event, attribute function and relationship function. Entities and their properties are time dependent. Constraints are expressed in a language inspired by first-order predicate calculus, with explicit time values. System design uses a behaviour and process perspective, where transactions are triggered by events.

DADES: DAta oriented DESign

University of Barcelona, Spain.
Olivé, A., 'DADES: a methodology for specification and design of information systems'. In: Olle *et al.* (1982), pp. 285–334.
Availability: research status.

DADES deals mainly with the stages of business analysis and system design. It favours a data perspective and uses a relational model (although it claims not to depend on this choice) of the business complemented by the definition of input and output data. It includes constraints in the form of derivation rules and assertion times which specify when information becomes available. It also provides techniques for checking the validity of the model.

DAFNE: Data And Functions NEtworking

ITALSIEL SpA, Finsiel Group, Italy.
Lojacono (1984).
Caldiera and Quitadamo (1982).
Availability: owned and commercially marketed by the Finsiel Group.

DAFNE incorporates SADT (under exclusive European rights granted by SofTech) and supports the four stages described in this framework together with the implementation stages. It offers a modular approach with simultaneous specification and documentation and it bases the structuring of the software architecture on data. It includes techniques such as Warnier charts, decision tables and entity-relationship-attribute modelling, in addition to those of SADT. DAFNE encourages coordinated decentralization of activities and can also be used for organizational analysis.

D2S2: Design of Data Sharing Systems

CACI, UK.
Macdonald, I.G. and Palmer, I.R., 'System development in a shared data environment'. In: Olle *et al.* (1982), pp. 235-284.
Rock-Evans (1981).
Availability: commercially marketed by CACI Europe B.V., Amsterdam.

A data oriented approach nominally dealing with the four stages of the framework but in practice primarily concerned with business analysis and (to a lesser extent) information systems planning. It employs entity-relationship modelling and functional decomposition as its principal techniques and examines interactions between data and activities by using entity life cycles and process logic analysis. D2S2 can be seen as a precursor of the Information Engineering Methodology.

ERAE: Entity, Relationship, Attribute, Event

Philips Research Laboratory, Belgium.
Dubois *et al.* (1986).
Dubois, E., Hagelstein, J., Lahou, E., Ponsaert, F., Rifaut, A. and Williams, F., 'The ERAE model: a case study'. In: Olle *et al.* (1986), pp. 87-105.
Availability: research status.

ERAE covers the stages of business analysis and system design. It favours a mixed data and behaviour perspective by combining the concepts of entity, relationship and event. A graphical part of the language is used to identify the concepts relevant to the application and a textual part states constraints involving these concepts. In the latest version of the language, the constraints are expressed in temporal logic. ERAE also includes methodological guidance in the form of heuristics for acquiring and validating the information.

HOS: Higher Order Software

Higher Order Software Inc., USA.
Hamilton and Zeldin (1976).
Availability: commercially marketed by Higher Order Software Inc. in the USA and by Sema (France) in Europe.

HOS supports system design and construction design. It favours a process perspective by viewing the information system as a hierarchy of functions, the lowest being defined on abstract data types. Subfunctions can only be combined by means of control structures constrained to obey some axioms. Both the control structures and the data types may be built in or user-defined.

IDA: Interactive Design Approach

University of Namur, Belgium.
Bodart, F., Hennebert, A.M., Leheureux, J.M., Masson, O. and Pigneur, Y., in Teichroew and Davis (1985), pp. 203-216.

Bodart and Pigneur (1983).
Availability: commercially marketed by METSI, France.

IDA, a methodology including DSL and DSA as components, is an extension of PSL/PSA intended to capture more information about the dynamics of the information system. This is achieved by adding to PSL a number of new entities, such as 'event' and 'process', and some new relationships, such as 'triggers'.

IEM: Information Engineering Methodology

James Martin Associates, UK.
Martin (1989).
Martin (1984).
Macdonald (1984).
Macdonald, I.G., 'Information engineering'. In: Olle *et al.* (1986), pp. 173–224.
Availability: commercially marketed by James Martin Associates.

An approach which covers the four stages of this framework. It stresses the development of integrated systems, combines data and process oriented features at each stage and uses business objectives based information systems planning. The approach packages and integrates a large number of techniques and proposes flexible deployment of techniques in different development scenarios.

IML-inscribed High Level Petri Nets

GMD, Germany.
Richter, G. and Durchholz, R., 'IML-inscribed high-level Petri nets'. In: Olle *et al.* (1982), pp. 335–368.
Richter, G. (1981).
Availability: research status.

This work emphasizes the use of concurrency in the process perspective during system design, in order to postpone localization decisions. The technique used is a variant of Petri nets.

INFOLOG: INFOrmation LOGic

University of Lisbon, Portugal.
Fiadeiro, J. and Sernadas, A. (1986).
Availability: research status.

INFOLOG covers the stages of business analysis, system design and construction design. Each stage is treated in a data, behaviour and process perspective. The proposed techniques include a data model inspired by the entity-relationship approach with abstraction mechanisms, a variant of temporal logic for historical descriptions, a behavioural perspective using events, a subdivision of the computer system into subsystems described as processes exchanging messages and updating their records.

ISAC: Information Systems Work and Analysis of Changes

Institut V, Sweden.
Lundeberg *et al.* (1981).
Lundeberg, M., 'The ISAC approach to the specification of information systems and its application to the organization of an IFIP working conference'. In: Olle *et al.* (1982), pp. 173-234.
Availability: commercially marketed by Institut V, Stockholm.

A process oriented methodology concerned principally with information systems planning, business analysis and system design. Information systems planning is driven by an analysis of changes required within the business; business analysis separates activities and data but shows how they are related; system design draws heavily on the Jackson structured programming technique.

JSD: Jackson System Development

Michael Jackson Systems Ltd., UK.
Jackson (1983).
McNeile, A.T., 'Jackson system development'. In: Olle *et al.* (1986), pp. 225-246.
Availability: commercially marketed by Michael Jackson Systems Ltd.

This process oriented methodology models the business application as a network of communicating processes, adds new processes during system design to provide the desired outputs and transforms the whole during construction design into a working system. JSD includes the earlier JSP language which is used to describe process behaviour.

LSDM: LBMS System Development Method

LBMS, UK.
Hall (1983).
Availability: commercially marketed by Learmonth and Burchett Management Systems Ltd., UK.

A data oriented approach geared to system-at-time development. Business analysis employs normalization and entity life cycle analysis starting from the current system. System design focuses on prescriptive mapping techniques for a variety of DBMS and on data flow diagramming. Closely related to SSADM.

MERISE

Sema-Metra, France and Gamma International, France.
Rochfeld and Tardieu (1983).
Tardieu *et al.* (1984).
Tardieu *et al.* (1988).
Rochfeld and Moréjon (1989).
Availability: commercially marketed by several software houses in France.

This approach supports the four stages of information system development and uses the three perspectives. It combines an entity-relationship approach for data and a Petri net based approach for processes.

Method/1

Andersen Consulting (Arthur Andersen & Co. Int'l), USA.
See description in Maddison *et al.* (1983).
Availability: commercially marketed by Andersen Consulting.

A full life cycle project management approach (including planning, analysis, system design and construction design, but also the evolution stage). Starting with planning, three design processes are supported (referred to as new development, package software development and iterative development). Method/1 allows incorporation of various techniques.

NIAM: Nijssen's Information Analysis Method

Control Data, Belgium.
Verheijen, G.M.A. and van Bekkum, J., 'NIAM: an information analysis method'. In: Olle *et al.* (1982), pp. 537-590.
Availability: commercially marketed by Control Data under the names NIAM and IA.

A data and process oriented approach covering business analysis, system design and construction design. The process perspective is reflected in information flow diagrams and the data perspective uses information structure diagrams, based on the binary model. The latter include a great variety of constraints, such as cardinality of relationships, uniqueness, etc. A textual formal language is used to specify how functions are performed.

PROMOD

GEI, Germany,
PROMOD User's Manual, GEI (1987).
Hruschka (1987).
Availability: commercially marketed by GEI, Germany.

This methodology combines the use of structured analysis (part of SASS) for business analysis, of modular design for system design and of pseudocoding and structured programming for construction design.

PSL/PSA: Problem Statement Language/Problem Statement Analyser

University of Michigan, USA.
Teichroew and Hershey (1977).
Availability: commercially marketed by Meta Systems Inc., USA.

This data oriented methodology supports the system design phase. It uses an entity-relationship model to describe various aspects of the information system, such as input/output flow, system structure, data structure and system dynamics. See IDA for an extension of PSL/PSA.

REMORA

University of Paris-1, France.
Rolland, C. and Richard, C., 'The REMORA methodology for information systems design and management'. In: Olle *et al.* (1982), pp. 369-426.
Rolland *et al.* (1986).
Rolland *et al.* (1987).
Lingat *et al.* (1988).
Availability: research status.

Remora supports the stages of business analysis and system design. The basic concepts of Remora are those of object, operation and event. Remora is based on the relational model and integrates the three perspectives, with some emphasis on the behavioural perspective. Both graphical and textual notations are provided. Execution of the formal specification, made using the PROQUEL language, allows the information system prototyping.

RML: Requirements Modelling Language

University of Toronto, Canada.
Greenspan *et al.* (1986).
Availability: research status.

RML is meant for business analysis and possibly system design. It is inspired by knowledge representation techniques, such as frames and predicate logic. A mixed data and process perspective is favoured by the basic concepts of entity, activity and assertion. Entities and their properties are time dependent and assertions may explicitly refer to time intervals.

SADT: Structured Analysis and Design Technique

SofTech Inc., USA.
Ross and Schoman (1977).
Availability: commercially marketed by SofTech Inc. in the USA and by IGL (France) in Europe.

This data and process oriented methodology is mainly applicable during business analysis. It is based on the development of two kinds of diagrams – datagrams and actigrams. The former represent data sets connected by arrows representing the actions using or producing them. The latter are akin to data flow diagrams. Both kinds of diagrams are organized in a hierarchy.

SASS: Structured Analysis and System Specification

Yourdon/De Marco, USA.
De Marco (1979).
Availability: commercially marketed by Atlantic Systems Guild, USA.

SASS is related to the Yourdon approach which it influenced and broke away from. It concentrates on business analysis and system design. It emphasizes strongly the use of data flow diagrams in these stages. Later stages are handled briefly and information systems planning not at all. SASS is essentially process oriented.

SDM: System Development Methodology

Pandata BV, The Netherlands.
Hice *et al.* (1978).
Turner *et al.* (1987).
Availability: commercially marketed by Pandata BV., The Netherlands.

SDM is a methodology which provides first of all a management framework for planning and organization of automation activities. Information and business systems planning are incorporated as phase 0, along the lines of the Information Engineering Methodology.

SF: Set-Function approach

University of Pittsburgh, USA.
Berztiss, A., 'The set-function approach to conceptual modelling'. In: Olle *et al.* (1986), pp. 107–144.
Availability: research status.

SF covers the stages of business analysis and system design. This methodology uses a technique taken from conventional software engineering, namely the algebraic specification of abstract data types. The methodology mixes a data and behavioural perspective. The statics of the information system are modelled by means of data types and functions operating on them. The dynamics are handled in a behavioural perspective, with events specified by preconditions and postconditions involving the data types.

Software through Pictures

University of California in San Francisco, USA.
Wasserman, A., 'The user software engineering methodology: an overview'. In: Olle *et al.* (1982), pp. 591–628.
Wasserman (1985).
Wasserman *et al.* (1986).
Availability: commercially marketed by IDE, USA.

This methodology is geared to the development of interactive information systems. It covers business analysis, system design and construction design. It uses an integrated set of techniques including data flow diagrams, hierarchical data structures, entity-relationship modelling, structured design and transition diagrams. The main originality of the approach lies in the last of these techniques, which allows the rapid prototyping of user interfaces.

SSADM: Structured Systems Analysis and Design Method

Central Computer and Telecommunications Agency, Norwich, UK.
SSADM4 Reference Manual. Published jointly by Butterworth Press and National Computer Centre, Manchester.
Coutts (1987).
Downs *et al.* (1988).
Goodland (1988).
Availability: UK Central Government standard.

SSADM is a government sponsored methodology, the use of which has been promoted in all UK central government projects since 1983. The method was originally based on LSDM. The fourth version, SSADM4, released in mid-1990, covers the business analysis and system design stages. It embodies the use of several techniques including data flow diagramming, entity-relationship modelling, entity life history analysis and data normalization.

STRADIS: STructured Analysis, Design and Implementation of Information Systems

Yourdon Inc., USA.
Gane and Sarson (1979).
Availability: commercially marketed by McDonnell Douglas Information Systems, USA.

Data flow diagramming based approach which emerged from the Yourdon school.

SYSDOC

Central Institute for Industrial Research, Oslo, Norway.
Aschim, F. and Mostue, B.M., 'IFIP WG 8.1 case solved using SYSDOC and Systemator'. In: Olle *et al.* (1982), pp. 15-40.
Availability: commercially marketed by Sysdeco AS, Oslo, Norway.

SYSDOC covers business analysis, system design and construction design, as well as construction and maintenance. It is supported by a computerized tool called Systemator. The methodology uses an entity-relationship model for its data perspective and a very high level programming language for its process perspective. It also emphasizes the definition of user interfaces (layouts, dialogues, etc.) and the description of manual procedures.

Yourdon

Yourdon Inc., USA.
Yourdon and Constantine (1979).
Yourdon (1982).
Page-Jones (1980).
Ward and Mellor (1985).
Availability: commercially marketed by Yourdon Inc., USA.

Prior to 1984 the approach was process oriented, took the current system as its starting point for analysis and focused on system design through data flow diagramming and on construction design through functional decomposition.

Since 1984 it has changed substantially. Business analysis is behaviour oriented, defining the environment in terms of events and behaviour through data flows in response to events, but incorporates entity-relationship modelling. System design focuses on data flow and state transitions for processes. It does not deal with information systems planning.

A.3   Methodology references

Blank, J. and Krijger, M.J. 1982. *Evaluation of Methods and Techniques for the Analysis, Design and Implementation of Information Systems*. The Hague: Academic Service.

Bodart, F. and Pigneur, Y. 1983. *Conception Assistée des Applications Informatiques. Vol. 1: Etude d'Opportunité et Analyse Conceptuelle*. Paris: Masson.

Bubenko, J.A., Jr. 1980. 'Information modelling in the context of system development.' In: *Proceedings of the IFIP Congress, 1980*. Amsterdam: North-Holland.

Caldiera, G. and Quitadamo, P. 1982. 'Conceptual representation of data and logical IMS design'. In: *Entity Relationship Approach to Information Modelling and Analysis*, edited by P.P. Chen. Louisiana: ER Institute.

Couger, J.D. 1973. 'Evolution of business system analysis techniques'. *Computing Surveys*, **September**, 167–198. Also in:

Couger, J.D. and Knapp, R.W. (eds). 1974. *System Analysis Techniques*. Chichester, UK: John Wiley.

Coutts, G. 1987. *SSADM – Structured Systems Analysis and Design Methodology*. London: Paradigm Publishing Ltd.

De Marco, T. 1979. *Structured Analysis and System Specification*. Englewood Cliffs, New Jersey: Prentice-Hall Inc.

Downs, E., Clare, P. and Coe, I. 1988. *Structure Systems Analysis and Design Method: Application and Context*. London: Prentice-Hall International (UK) Ltd.

Dubois, E., Hagelstein, J., Lahou, E., Ponsaert, F. and Rifaut, A. 1986. 'A knowledge representation language for requirements engineering.' *Proceedings of the IEEE*, **74(10)**, 1431–1444.

Fiadeiro, J. and Sernadas, A. 1986. 'The INFOLOG linear tense propositional logic of events and transactions'. *Information Systems*, **11(1)**.

Gane, C. and Sarson, T. 1979. *Structured Systems Analysis: Tools and Techniques.* Englewood Cliffs, New Jersey: Prentice-Hall Inc.

Goodland, M.C. 1988. 'Structured Systems Analysis and Design Method – A UK Government Standard.' In: *Proceedings of the IFIP TC8 Conference on Governmental and Municipal Information Systems, Budapest, Hungary, September 1987.* Amsterdam: North-Holland.

Greenspan, S.J., Borgida, A. and Mylopoulos, J. (1986). 'A requirements modelling language and its logic.' *Information Systems,* **11(1),** 9–23.

Hall, J. 1983. 'The LBMS System Development Method.' In: *Data Analysis Update,* edited by G.J. Baker. UK: British Computer Society Database Specialist Group.

Hamilton, M. and Zeldin, S. 1976. 'Higher Order Software – a methodology for defining software.' *IEEE Transactions on Software Engineering,* **2(1).**

Hice, G.F., Turner, W.S. and Cashwell, L.F. 1978. *System Development Methodology.* Amsterdam: North-Holland.

Hruschka, P. 1987. 'ProMod at the age of 5'. In: *Proceedings of the 1st European Software Engineering Conference, Strasbourg, France, 1987.* Berlin: Springer-Verlag.

Hunke, H. (ed.) 1981. *Software Engineering Environments. Proceedings of the Symposium held in Lahnstein, Germany, 1980.* Amsterdam: North-Holland.

Jackson, M.A. 1983. *System Development.* Englewood Cliffs, New Jersey: Prentice-Hall Inc.

Lingat, J.Y., Collignon, P. and Rolland, C. 1988. 'Rapid application prototyping: the PROQUEL language'. In: *Proceedings of the 14th International Conference on Very Large Databases, Los Angeles, USA, 1988.* Palo Alto, USA: Morgan Kauffman Publishers Inc.

Lojacono, G.M. 1984. *DAFNE – Data and Functions Networking.* Rome: Publ. Italsiel.

Lundeberg, M., Goldkuhl, G. and Nilsson, A. 1981. *Information Systems Development: A Systematic Approach.* Englewood Cliffs, New Jersey: Prentice-Hall Inc.

Macdonald, I.G. 1984. 'Information Engineering – a methodology to match fourth generation tools.' In: *Application Development Tools,* edited by E.E. Tozer. Maidenhead, UK: Pergamon Infotech Ltd.

Maddison, R.N. *et al.* 1983. *Information System Methodologies.* Chichester, UK: Wiley Heyden Ltd, John Wiley and Sons.

Martin, J. 1984. *An Information Manifesto.* Englewood Cliffs, New Jersey: Prentice-Hall Inc.

Martin, J. 1989. *Information Engineering* (3 vols). Englewood Cliffs, New Jersey: Prentice-Hall Inc.

Olle, T.W., Sol, H.G. and Verrijn-Stuart, A.A. (eds). 1982. *Information Systems Design Methodologies: a Comparative Review. Proceedings of the IFIP WG 8.1 Working Conference, Noordwijkerhout, The Netherlands.* Amsterdam: North-Holland.

Olle, T.W., Sol, H.G. and Tully, C.J. (eds). 1983. *Information Systems Design Methodologies: a Feature Analysis. Proceedings of the IFIP WG 8.1 Working Conference, York, UK.* Amsterdam: North-Holland.

Olle, T.W., Sol, H. G. and Verrijn-Stuart, A.A. (eds). 1986. *Information Systems Design Methodologies: Improving the Practice. Proceedings of the IFIP WG*

8.1 Working Conference, Noordwijkerhout, The Netherlands. Amsterdam: North-Holland.

Page-Jones, M. 1980. *The Practical Guide to Structured Systems Design.* New York: Yourdon Press.

Pellaumail, P. 1986. *La Méthode AXIAL. Vol. 1: Conception d'un Système d'Information.* France: Les Editions d'Organisation.

Pellaumail, P. 1987. *Le Méthode AXIAL. Vol. 2: Planification du Système d'Information et Supports Logiciels.* France: Les Editions d'Organisation.

Richter, G. 1981. 'IML-inscribed Nets for modelling text processing and database management systems.' In: *Proceedings of the 7th International Conference on Very Large Databases,* pp. 363–375.

Rochfeld, A. and Moréjon, J. 1989. *Le Méthode MERISE. Vol. 3: Gamme Opératoire.* France: Les Editions d'Organisation.

Rochfeld, A. and Tardieu, H. 1983. *MERISE: An Information System Design and Development Methodology. Information and Management 6.* Amsterdam: North-Holland.

Rock-Evans, R. 1981. *Data Analysis.* Surrey, UK: IPC Electronic Press.

Rolland, C., Foucaut, O. and Benci, G. 1986. *Conception de Systèmes d'Information.* Paris: Eyrolles.

Rolland, C., Benci, G. and Foucaut, O. 1987. *Conception de Systèmes d'Information: la Méthode REMORA.* Paris: Eyrolles.

Ross, D.T. and Schoman, K.E. 1977. 'Structured analysis for requirements definition.' *IEEE Transactions on Software Engineering,* 3(1).

Schneider, H.J. (ed.). 1979. *Formal Models and Practical Tools for Information Systems Design. Proceedings of the IFIP WG 8.1 Working Conference, Oxford, UK.* Amsterdam: North-Holland.

Tardieu, H., Rochfeld, A. and Colletti, R. 1984. *La Méthode MERISE: Principes et Outils.* France: Les Editions d'Organisation.

Tardieu, H., Rochfeld, A., Colletti, R., Panet, G. and Vahée, G. 1985. *La Méthode MERISE. Vol. 2: Démarches et Pratiques.* France: Les Editions d'Organisation.

Teichroew, D. and Davis, G. (eds.). 1985. *System Description Methodologies. Proceedings of the IFIP TC2 Conference, Kecskmet, Hungary, 1983.* Amsterdam: North-Holland.

Teichroew, D. and Hershey, E.A. 1977. 'PSL/PSA: a computer-aided technique for structured documentation and analysis of information processing systems.' *IEEE Transactions on Software Engineering,* 3(1).

Turner, W.S., Langerhorst, R.P., Eilers, H.B., Hice, G.F. and Uittenbroeck, A.A. 1987. *System Development Methodology.* Rijswijk, The Netherlands: Uitgeverij PANDATA.

Ward, P.T. and Mellor, S.J. 1985. *Structured Development for Real Time Systems* (3 volumes). New York: Yourdon Press.

Wasserman, A. 1985. 'Extending state transition diagrams for the specification of human-computer interactions.' *IEEE Transactions on Software Engineering,* 11(8), 699–713.

Wasserman, A. *et al.* 1986. 'Developing interactive information systems with the user software engineering method.' *IEEE Transactions on Software Engineering,* 12(2), 326–345.

Yourdon, E. and Constantine, L. 1979. *Fundamentals of a Discipline of Computer*

Program and System Design. Englewood Cliffs, New Jersey: Prentice-Hall Inc. (First published by Yourdon Press, New York, in 1975.)

Yourdon, E. 1982. *Managing the System Life Cycle*. New York: Yourdon Press.

A.4   Relevant frameworks

There have been various other attempts to specify frameworks which encompass the topic of information systems methodologies. As a result of their broader scope, there is a tendency to go into rather less depth.

The present framework covers three stages in the life cycle in considerable detail, analysing the components which are generated by existing methodologies. As well as categorizing components by a life cycle stage, each component is further categorized as having a perspective which is either data, process, behaviour or some cross-reference between two of the others. It discusses in general terms (that is, terms not specific to any methodology) the concepts of scenario and the alternative forms of representation and documentation.

The other frameworks referenced here will be summarized at a level of detail sufficient to permit an initial comparison with the framework described in this book.

Since frameworks, unlike methodologies, are not normally given a name, they are more easily identified by their authors.

Essink

Essink, L.J.B. 1986. 'A modelling approach to information systems development'. In: *Information Systems Design Methodologies: Improving the Practice. Proceedings of the IFIP WG 8.1 Working Conference, Noordwijkerhout, The Netherlands*. Amsterdam: North-Holland.

Essink's framework is intended for use by methodology designers. It has two dimensions, one of which is referred to as the 'level of abstraction' and the other as 'aspects'. Each aspect is relevant on each level of abstraction.

The four levels of abstraction are each identified as models and are identified as follows:

- object system,
- conceptual information system,
- data system, and
- implementation.

The object system model corresponds closely to the results of the business analysis stage. The conceptual information system model appears to provide a prescriptive model derived from the results of the business analysis stage. The data system model then corresponds to the results of the system design stage. It is the 'result of logical implementation decisions'. Finally, the implementation model can be equated to the result of performing a construction design stage.

The eight aspects which play a role at each level of abstraction are categorized into two groups. The first six are derived from systems theory and identified as follows:

- goal structure,
- environmental interaction,
- functional structure,
- relationships between entity types,
- process structures, and
- system dynamics.

The remaining two, which are called achitectural aspects, are as follows:

- hardware and distribution aspects, and
- organizational and social constraints.

Essink's framework calls for goals to be defined at each stage (or level of abstraction). The goal structure in the framework described in this book is handled to some extent by components of information systems planning (see Section 7.7.8). However, the goals identified in the component analysis for information systems planning would not necessarily apply to, or provide goals for, later stages in the life cycle.

The environmental interaction in Essink's framework is aimed, for each of the four abstraction levels, at identifying boundaries and the interaction across such boundaries. In most methodologies studied, and hence in the current framework, this is an implicit exercise rather than an explicit one. It is determined in terms of business analysis components such as business activity, entity type, organization unit, external unit and interest group.

The functional structure, subsequently referred to in Essink's framework as the 'internal functional structure', appears to relate to the process perspective in the broadest sense (see Section 3.4.2). It is concerned with different problems at each level of abstraction.

The 'entity structure' (relationship between entity types in the above list) relates to the data perspective in its broadest sense (see Section 3.4.1). In Essink's framework, as in the present framework, the entity structure (data perspective) includes the various kinds of static and dynamic constraints.

The process structure appears to relate to the TASK component (see Section 5.6.6) in the process perspective of the system design stage. In Essink's framework, this concept has meaning in earlier stages.

The system dynamics model relates to the process structure. It embraces some of the data/process cross-reference components identified in this framework and hence does not equate simply to the behaviour perspective.

Olivé

Olivé, A. 1983. 'Analysis of conceptual and logical models in information systems design methodologies'. In: *Information Systems Design Methodologies: a Feature Analysis. Proceedings of the IFIP WG 8.1 Working Conference, York, UK.* Amsterdam: North-Holland.

The main dimension for this framework is called the 'level of abstraction'. Five such levels are identified: external, conceptual, logical, architectural and physical. For each of these levels of abstraction a different set of properties is identified. For example, for the conceptual level of abstraction, the following aspects are identified:

- data model,
- how events are modelled,
- how constraints are handled,
- form of derivation rules, and
- input/output aspects.

The framework is created as a basis for comparing 11 methodologies, most of which are listed in Section A.2 of this appendix.

A second dimension for this framework is the 'type of information system'. The two examples given are database systems and decision support systems. The framework points out that different methodologies could be suitable for different types of systems. This second dimension equates to one of the scenario factors mentioned in Chapter 2 of the present framework.

The main dimension, namely 'level of abstraction' is hard to equate to any concept used in the framework described in this book. Life cycle stage is the closest. Whether in fact one becomes more specific (hence less abstract) as one goes through the life cycle stages is open to debate. One could also argue that many of the components in the successive stages are different rather than more or less abstract.

RISE: Reference Model of Information Systems Engineering

ISO/IEC JTC1 SC7 N706. *Information Systems Engineering Reference Model Overview.* (When formally approved, this will be published by ISO as a technical report. The detailed reference model will appear subsequently as an ISO standard.)

ISO/IEC JTC1 SC7/WG5 is producing a reference model of information systems engineering called RISE. The aim of the reference model is to provide a framework in which standards for information systems engineering can be developed.

Information systems engineering is defined as being concerned with six topics. The following list includes a reference to the associated term used in this book and to the section in this book in which the topic is discussed:

- nature of systems that are engineered (type of system, Section 2.4.3),
- activities undertaken (life cycle stages,and steps, Sections 3.2 and 3.5),
- people who carry out engineering activities (human roles, Section 1.5),
- means and tools by which people carry out activities (CASE, Chapter 10),
- means by which people communicate (representation and documentation, Chapter 9), and
- system within which engineering takes place and its boundary (not addressed).

The sixth topic refers to what is often called an 'environment', one example of which might be a CASE environment.

A RISE product is defined as an item produced as a result of an activity which then forms the input to another activity. A product is viewed as a model (compare Section 3.1), and each model is regarded as describing one of the following:

- the information system's environment,
- the information system's external interfaces, and
- the information system's internal interfaces.

A model of an information system's environment can be equated to an analytic model of a business area and hence the results of business analysis. A model of an information system's external interfaces equates to the results of a system design stage. Finally, a model of an information system's internal interfaces should be included in the results of a construction design stage.

Using the term 'implementation' in the sense of 'construction', the RISE identifies three levels of abstraction as follows:

- implementation independent,
- implementation dependent but target technology independent, and
- target technology dependent.

All the stages in the life cycle of the present framework up to and including system design are construction independent. The term 'target technology' is interpreted in RISE as follows. A model is target technology independent if it is abstracted 'over all implementation platforms in a class of similar implementation platforms'. This leaves open the question of which of the following are 'similar implementation platforms':

1. any database management system,
2. any relational database management system,
3. any SQL based product, and
4. a specific SQL based product on any hardware platform.

The definition of the system design stage (see Section 3.2.3) would relate to alternative 1 in the sense that the output from a system design stage would assume the use of some kind of DBMS, but which one to use is a matter for construction design.

A target technology dependent model in RISE relates to the output from a construction design stage.

The 'development process' in RISE is broken down into three parts – namely analysis, design and construction. From the definition of 'design' as producing implementation dependent but technology independent models, it appears that the term 'design' includes both system design and construction design.

RISE also includes aspects such as procurement and use which are not covered in the framework described in this text.

Zachman

Zachman, J.A. 1987. 'A framework for information systems architecture'. *IBM Systems Journal*, **26(3)**, pp. 276-292.

This framework is called a 'framework for information systems architecture'. However, it addresses the problem of creating an information system rather than what it should look like in its constructed state.

The framework is two dimensional. One dimension equates to the perspectives and the other to the life cycle stages. The perspectives are called 'types of description' and the three identified are data, process and network. The dimension of the framework called 'architectural representation produced over the process of building a complex engineering product' equates roughly to the information system life cycle stages. The six 'stages' are identified in terms of what is produced, and for whom the view produced is useful.

The following table lists Zachman's six stages, for whom the view is useful and, in the third column, the equivalent life cycle stage in the current framework.

Stage	Use	Equivalent life cycle stage
(1) Scope description	Ballpark view	Information systems planning
(2) Model of the business	Owner's view	Business analysis
(3) Model of the information system	Designer's view	System design
(4) Technology model	Builder's view	Construction design
(5) Detailed description	Out-of-context view	
(6) Actual system		Operation

To give an indication of what Zachman implies by two of these six 'stages' (at least for the data perspective), the technology model is illustrated by a DL/1 data structure diagram. The detailed description is illustrated by a set of DL/1 data definition statements.

Zachman's framework is based on a study of fields of endeavour external to the information systems community.

Appendix B
Worked example of business analysis components

B.1 Introduction

This example concerns a reservation system for hotel rooms in ski resorts.

An individual or a travel agency may request a reservation. Each request is characterized by the name, address and telephone number of the person who makes the request, the resort requested, the hotel category, the number of rooms and the period that the person requests.

A request can be accepted if there is suitable space available in a hotel of the requested category, in the right resort and for the right period. If these conditions are not satisfied, the request can be wait-listed for a certain period if the person so desires and taken into account by the system as soon as possible.

When a request has been accepted, the system is required to send an acknowledgement to the customer confirming the reservation, namely the name, address and telephone number of the hotel, the period of reservation, the number of rooms reserved and the price per day.

The tariff for the rooms depends on the type of season. The definition of each season is standardized for all hotels and all resorts.

The main aim of the information system is to manage requests and reservations. It must also be possible to take into account any modification resulting either from new requirements (such as cancellation of a reservation) or from a change in the available resources (such as the opening or closing of a hotel).

Finally, the system must manage the customers, that is to say, the persons who have an existing reservation or have had a reservation during the two previous years. This includes details of each person's stay in any hotel, the associated check-in, check-out, miscellaneous charges and final invoice.

B.2 Data perspective

Components of the worked example are presented in the same order as in Section 4.5.

B.2.1 ENTITY TYPES

The ENTITY TYPES of interest can be broken down into four groups as follows:

1.   reservation system resources,
2.   requests,
3.   reservation part, and
4.   invoicing aspects.

Each of these groups is analysed in turn. To be consistent with Chapter 3, the names of components are shown in upper case and the names of entity types specific to this example are shown using initial capitals.

Reservation system resources

The reservation system relates to Rooms in Hotels which are located in Resorts. Each Hotel is of a specific Hotel-Type and each Room in a Hotel of a specific Room-Type. Each Room has several Room-Availability periods, irrespective of any Reservation which may be made. The Room-Tariff is dependent on the Room-Type, Hotel and the Season. The data structure diagram is shown in Figure B.1.

Requests

The data structure diagram is shown in Figure B.2. A Request is made by a Person on a given Date for a specific Resort, specific Room-Type, a particular Hotel-Type, and a given period (between two Dates).

Reservation handling

A Reservation is made for a Hotel by a Customer (who is a Person), on a given Date, for a given period. It corresponds to one particular Request and has a set of Reserved-Rooms.
    A Reservation has different states in time. It becomes a Reservation-In with a Post-Check-In-Assigned-Room, when the Guest (who is a Person) checks-in at the Hotel, and a Reservation-Out when the Guest checks-out. On any Date, a Cancelled-Reservation can be recorded. The data structure diagram is shown in Figure B.3.

Invoicing

During his or her stay at the Hotel, a Guest will incur charges to his or her Room. The Bill must be paid by the Guest on departure. Each Charge-Item is of given Charge-Item-Type and is incurred by whoever is staying in a given Room on a given Date. An amount will be added to the Bill-Line of whichever Guest has a Post-Check-In-Assignment-Room to that Room on that Date.
    The data structure diagram is shown in Figure B.4. The list of ENTITY TYPES with the code number as they appear in Figures B.1 to B.4 is shown in Figure B.5.

B.2.2 ENTITY TYPE NAME

The list of names in Figure B.6 could be generated by users to refer to the various ENTITY TYPES (see Figure B.5).

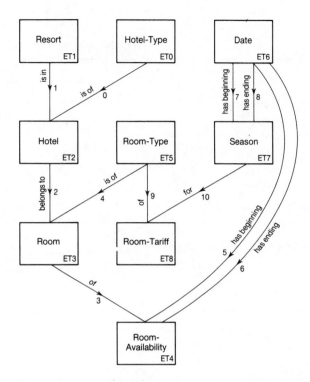

Figure B.1 Reservation system resources. Data perspective – ENTITY TYPES and
RELATIONSHIP TYPES.

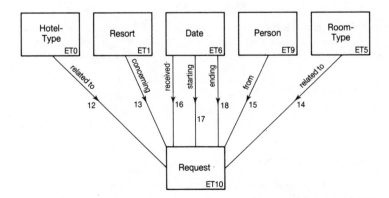

Figure B.2 Requests. Data perspective – ENTITY TYPES and RELATIONSHIP TYPES.

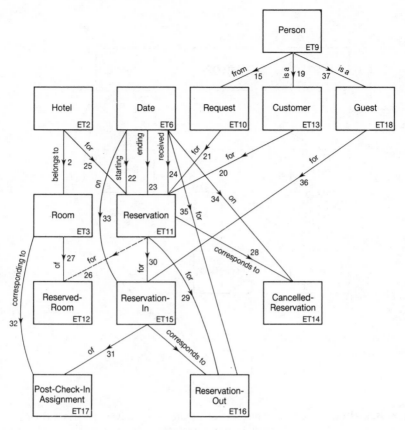

Figure B.3   Reservation handling. Data perspective – ENTITY TYPES and
RELATIONSHIP TYPES.

B.2.3   ENTITY TYPE USES NAME

Five of the 23 ENTITY TYPES identified in Figure B.5 use several of the ENTITY TYPE NAMES listed for the preceding component. Figure B.7 gives synonyms of some ENTITY TYPE NAMES currently used by people in the real system.

B.2.4   RELATIONSHIP CLASS

The only RELATIONSHIP CLASS used in this example is 'binary', as described in Section 4.5.4.

B.2.5   RELATIONSHIP TYPE

Figure B.8 shows the four types of relationship used in this example. It should be noted that in Figures B.1 to B.4, no distinction is made among the four different RELATIONSHIP TYPES used in this example.

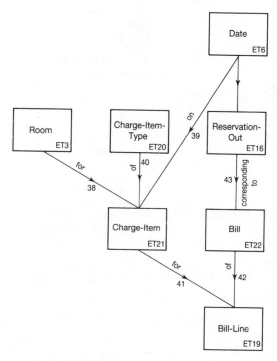

Figure B.4 Invoicing. Data perspective – ENTITY TYPES and RELATIONSHIP TYPES.

B.2.6 RELATIONSHIP

Each RELATIONSHIP belongs to a RELATIONSHIP TYPE and is given a number for possible future reference. The RELATIONSHIPS depicted in Figures B.1 to B.4 are shown in Figure B.9 with their code numbers, descriptions and the RELATIONSHIP CLASS to which each belongs.

B.2.7 ENTITY TYPE IN RELATIONSHIP

Each RELATIONSHIP involves two ENTITY TYPES. However, each RELATIONSHIP is asymmetric and it is therefore useful to distinguish between the two ENTITY TYPES. This is done by identifying one as independent (1) and the other as dependent (3). Figure B.10 shows the RELATIONSHIPS depicted in Figure B.1 (with codes 0 to 10).

B.2.8 ATTRIBUTE NAME

Figure B.11 gives the list of ATTRIBUTE NAMES resulting from an analysis of the 23 ENTITY TYPES listed in Figure B.5.

Entity Type Code	Entity Type Name
ET0	Hotel-Type
ET1	Resort
ET2	Hotel
ET3	Room
ET4	Room-Availability
ET5	Room-Type
ET6	Date
ET7	Season
ET8	Room-Tariff
ET9	Person
ET10	Request
ET11	Reservation
ET12	Reserved-Room
ET13	Customer
ET14	Cancelled-Reservation
ET15	Reservation-In
ET16	Reservation-Out
ET17	Post-Check-In-Assignment
ET18	Guest
ET19	Bill-Line
ET20	Charge-Item-Type
ET21	Charge-Item
ET22	Bill

Figure B.5   List of ENTITY TYPES.

Hotel-Type	Reservation-In
Resort	Reservation-Out
Hotel	Post-Check-In-Assignment
Room	Guest
Room-Availability	Bill-Line
Room-Type	Charge-Item-Type
Date	Charge-Item
Season	Bill
Room-Tariff	Hotel-Class
Person	Room-Category
Request	Check-In
Reservation	Room-Category
Demand	Check-In
Reserved-Room	Check-Out
Customer	Cancelled-Reservation

Figure B.6   List of ENTITY TYPE NAMES.

B.2.9   ATTRIBUTE

Each ATTRIBUTE NAME of the list in Figure B.11 must be an ATTRIBUTE of an ENTITY TYPE. Figure B.12 shows the assignment of ATTRIBUTE NAMES to the 23 ENTITY TYPES.

Entity Type Name	Entity Type Synonym Name
Hotel-Type	Hotel-Class
Room-Type	Room-Category
Request	Demand
Reservation-In	Check-In
Reservation-Out	Check-Out

Figure B.7   List of ENTITY TYPE synonyms.

Relationship Type Code	Relationship Type Description
C1	One to 'zero, one or more'
C2	One to 'one or more'
C3	One to 'zero or one'
C4	is-a

Figure B.8   List of RELATIONSHIP TYPES.

B.2.10   ATTRIBUTE GROUP

ATTRIBUTE GROUPS are needed to be able to specify CONSTRAINTS imposed on the values of the ATTRIBUTES. Figure B.13 shows the ATTRIBUTE GROUPS with a Group Code for each and the ENTITY TYPES in which the ATTRIBUTE GROUPS are needed to express CONSTRAINTS.

B.2.11   ATTRIBUTE IN GROUP

An ATTRIBUTE of an ENTITY TYPE may belong to more than one ATTRIBUTE GROUP. Figure B.14 is a cross-reference table which shows which ATTRIBUTE belongs to which ATTRIBUTE GROUP.

B.2.12   ATTRIBUTE OF RELATIONSHIP

The RELATIONSHIPS identified for this example belong to RELATIONSHIP TYPES which do not have ATTRIBUTES.

B.2.13   VALUE CONSTRAINT TYPE

The permitted VALUE CONSTRAINT TYPES are prescribed for each approach to data analysis. In this example, the three kinds of VALUE CONSTRAINT TYPE presented in Section 4.5.13 are used.

B.2.14   VALUE CONSTRAINT

In this example, one uniqueness VALUE CONSTRAINT is defined for each ENTITY TYPE. Figure B.15 shows the 22 VALUE CONSTRAINTS. Each such VALUE CONSTRAINT is

Relationship Number	Relationship Type	Description
0	C1	Hotel is of a certain type
1	C1	Hotel is in one resort
2	C2	Room belongs to one hotel
3	C2	Availability period of a room
4	C1	Room is of a certain type
5	C1	Start date of availability period
6	C1	End date of availability period
7	C3	ɔtart date of season
8	C3	End date of season
9	C1	Tariff for a type of season
10	C1	Tariff for a given season
11	C2	Tariff for a given hotel
12	C1	Request related to one hotel-type
13	C1	Request concerning one resort
14	C1	Request related to a room-type
15	C2	Person initiating a request
16	C1	Date of request
17	C1	Start date of a request
18	C1	End date of a request
19	C4	Customer 'is a' person
20	C2	Customer of a reservation
21	C3	Reservation of a request
22	C1	Start date for a reservation
23	C1	End date for a reservation
24	C1	Date reservation made
25	C1	Hotel of a reservation
26	C2	Reserved rooms for a reservation
27	C1	Room of reserved rooms
28	C3	Cancelled reservation corresponding to a reservation
29	C3	Reservation check-out
30	C3	Reservation check-in
31	C2	Rooms allocated on check-in
32	C1	Room corresponds to check-in assignment
33	C1	Date of check-in
34	C1	Date of cancellation
35	C1	Date of a check-out
36	C2	Guest of a check-in reservation
37	C4	Guest 'is a' person
38	C1	Room of a charge item
39	C1	Date of a charge item
40	C1	Charge for a charge item type
41	C3	Charge item for an invoice line
42	C2	Invoice line of a bill
43	C3	Bill corresponding to a check-out

Figure B.9   RELATIONSHIPS.

Relationship Number	Entity Type Name	Dependency
0	Hotel-Type	I
0	Hotel	D
1	Resort	I
1	Hotel	D
2	Hotel	I
2	Room	D
3	Room	I
3	Room-Availability	D
4	Room-Type	I
4	Room	D
5	Date	I
5	Room-Availability	D
6	Date	I
6	Room-Availability	D
7	Date	I
7	Season	D
8	Date	I
8	Season	I
9	Room-Type	I
9	Room-Tariff	D
10	Season	I
10	Room-Tariff	D

Figure B.10 ENTITY TYPES IN RELATIONSHIPS.

hot-type	req-nb-room
hot-type-desc	req-state
resort-no	req-date
resort-name	res-no
hotel-no	canc-no
hotel-ad	res-date
hotel-phone	canc-date
hotel-name	res-beg-date
room-no	res-end-date
room-type	cust-code
av-beg-date	res-date
av-end-date	arrival-date
room-type-desc	guest-id
start-date	departure-date
end-date	bill-no
season-type	total-amount
price	invoice-line
person-name	line-amount
person-id	cit-code
address	cit-desc
phone	charge-date
req-no	amount
req-beg-date	req-end-date

Figure B.11 ATTRIBUTE NAMES.

Column Name	Entity Type Code ET																						
	0	1	2	3	4	5	6	7	8	9	10	11	12	13	14	15	16	17	18	19	20	21	22
hot-type	x	x								x													
hot-type-desc	x																						
resort-no		x																					
resort-name	x									x													
hotel-no			x	x	x		x				x				x								
hotel-add			x																				
hotel-phone			x																				
hotel-name			x													x							
room-no				x	x						x					x							
room-type				x		x		x	x														
av-beg-date					x																		
av-end-date					x																		
room-type-desc						x																	
start-date								x															
end-date								x															
season-type								x	x														
price								x															
person-name									x														
person-id									x	x			x					x					
address									x														
phone									x														
req-no										x	x												
req-beg-date										x													
req-end-date										x													
req-nb-room										x													
req-state										x													
req-date										x													
res-no											x	x	x	x	x	x	x						
res-date										x													
res-beg-date										x													
res-end-date										x													
canc-no														x									
canc-date														x									
cust-code										x		x											
arrival-date														x									
guest-id														x			x	x	x				
departure-date															x			x	x				
bill-no																		x					
total-amount																		x					
invoice-line																		x					
line-amount																		x					
cit-code																					x	x	
cit-desc																					x		
charge-date																		x					
amount																		x					

Figure B.12   ATTRIBUTE OF ENTITY TYPE.

Group Code	Attribute Group	Entity Type Name
G1	hotel-no room-no	Room
G2	hotel-no room-no av-beg-date	Room-Availability
G3	hotel-no room-type season-type	Room-Tariff
G4	cit-code room-no charge-date hotel-no	Charge-Item
G5	bill-no invoice-line	Bill-Line
G6	res-no room-no	Reserved-Room
G7	res-no arrival-date	Reservation-In
G8	res-no arrival-date room-no	Post-Check-In Assignment

Figure B.13   ATTRIBUTE GROUPS.

Attribute Name	Group Code							
	G1	G2	G3	G4	G5	G6	G7	G8
hotel-no	x	x	x	x				
room-no	x	x		x		x		x
av-beg-date		x						
room-type			x					
season-type			x					
cit-code				x				
charge-date				x				
bill-no					x			
invoice-no					x			
res-no						x	x	x
arrival-date							x	x

Figure B.14   ATTRIBUTE IN GROUP.

Entity Type Name	Attribute Name
Resort	resort-no
Hotel	hotel-no
Room	hotel-no
	room-no
Room-Availability	room-no
	hotel-no
	av-beg-date
Room-Type	room-type
Hotel-Type	hot-type
Season	start-date
Room-Tariff	room-type
	hotel-no
	season-type
Charge-Item-Type	cit-code
Charge-Item	cit-code
	room-no
	⁄narge-date
	hotel-no
Bill	bill-no
Bill-Line	bill-no
	invoice-line
Request	req-no
Reservation	res-no
Reserved-Room	res-no
	room-no
Person	pers-id
Customer	cust-code
Guest	guest-id
Cancelled-Reservation	canc-no
Reservation-In	res-no
	arrival-date
Reservation-Out	res-no
	departure-date
Post-Check-In-Assignment	res-no
	arrival-date
	room-no

Figure B.15   Uniqueness CONSTRAINTS.

expressed either for a single ATTRIBUTE or for one of the ATTRIBUTE GROUPS listed in Figure B.13.

41 of the 44 RELATIONSHIPS listed in Figure B.9 represent a referential CONSTRAINT. This is because the technique used in this example is based on binary RELATIONSHIPS.

The table in Figure B.16 indicates the ENTITY TYPE and the constrained ATTRIBUTES for each of the 41 RELATIONSHIPS. The RELATIONSHIPS with numbers 19 and 37 are 'is-a' RELATIONSHIPS which do not belong to this table. The CONSTRAINT is on the values of one or more ATTRIBUTES in one of the ENTITY TYPES involved in the RELATIONSHIPS.

Relationship Number	Description	Entity Type Name	Attribute Name
0	Hotel is of a certain type	Hotel-Type	hot-type
1	Hotel is in one resort	Resort	resort-no
2	Room belongs to one hotel	Hotel	hotel-no
3	Availability period of a room	Room	hotel-no + room-no
4	Room is of a certain room type	Room-Type	room-type
5	Start date of availability period	Date	av-beg-date
6	End date of availability period	Date	av-end-date
7	Start date of season	Date	start-date
8	End date of a season	Date	end-date
9	Tariff for type of room	Room-type	room-type
10	Tariff for given season	Season	season-type
11	Tariff for given hotel	Hotel	hotel-no
12	Request related to hotel-type	Hotel-Type	hot-type
13	Request concerning one resort	Resort	resort-name
14	Request related to room-type	Room-Type	room-type
15	Person initiating request	Person	pers-id
16	Date of request	Date	req-date
17	Start date of request	Date	req-beg-date
18	End date of request	Date	req-end-date
20	Customer of a reservation	Customer	cust-code
21	Reservation of a request	Request	req-no
22	Start date of a reservation	Date	res-beg-date
23	End date of a reservation	Date	res-end-date
24	Date reservation received	Date	res-date
25	Hotel of reservation	Hotel	hotel-no
26	Reserved rooms for reservation	Reservation	res-no
27	Room of reserved-rooms	Room	hotel-no + room-no
28	Cancelled reservation	Reservation	res-no

Figure B.16   Referential CONSTRAINTS.

Relationship Number	Description	Entity Type Name	Attribute Name
29	Reservation check-out	Reservation	res-no
30	Reservation check-in	Reservation	res-no
31	Room of check-in	Reservation-In	res-no + arrival-date
32	Room corresponding to check-in assignment	Room	hotel-no + room-no
33	Date of check-in	Date	arrival-date
34	Date of cancellation	Date	canc-date
35	Date of a check-out	Date	departure-date
36	Guest of a check-in reservation	Guest	guest-id
38	Room of charge item	Room	hotel-no + room-no
39	Date of charge item	Date	charge-date
40	Charge for charge item type	Charge-Item-Type	cit-code
41	Charge item for invoice line	Charge-Item	cit-code + hotel-no + room-no + charge-date
42	Invoice line of bill	Bill	bill-no
43	Bill corresponding to check-out	Reservation-Out	res-no + departure date

Figure B.16   *Cont'd*

Examples of check CONSTRAINTS are as follows:

1.   The end-date of a season must be greater than the start-date for the same season.

2.   The canc-date of a Cancelled-Reservation must be greater than or equal to the reg-date of the corresponding request.

B.2.15   POPULATION OVERLAP TYPE

The permitted POPULATION OVERLAP TYPES are prescribed for each approach to data analysis. In this example, the three alternatives listed in Section 4.5.15 are considered.

B.2.16   POPULATION OVERLAP

Figure B.17 contains the POPULATION OVERLAP component which is, in effect, a CONSTRAINT consistent with the two 'is-a' RELATIONSHIPS.

Population Overlap Type	First Entity Type	Number	Percentage also in second Entity Type	Second Entity Type	Number	Percentage also in first Entity Type
C	Guest	12 750	100	Person	15 000	85
C	Customer	13 500	100	Person	15 000	90

Figure B.17   POPULATION OVERLAP.

B.3 Process perspective

Components of the worked example are presented in the same order as in Section 4.7.

B.3.1 BUSINESS ACTIVITY

The breakdown previously analysed to categorize ENTITY TYPES was as follows:

- reservation system resources,
- requests,
- reservation handling, and
- invoicing.

Each item corresponds to a class of BUSINESS ACTIVITY as follows:

- resource management,
- request management,
- reservation management, and
- invoice management.

These are now studied from the process perspective. Figure B.18 shows the BUSINESS ACTIVITIES of the four classes. The numbering system of the BUSINESS ACTIVITIES is the same as that used in Section 4.8.1.

B.3.2 BUSINESS ACTIVITY NAME

Examples of BUSINESS ACTIVITY NAME are shown in Figure B.18 under the column headed 'Description'.

B.3.3 BUSINESS ACTIVITY USES NAME

A BUSINESS ACTIVITY can have one or more BUSINESS ACTIVITY NAMES. Figure B.19 shows a table which merges the two components, BUSINESS ACTIVITY and BUSINESS ACTIVITY USES NAME, presenting some synonyms of the BUSINESS ACTIVITY NAMES used in Figure B.18.

B.3.4 ACTIVITY PRECEDENCE/SUCCEDENCE

See Figure B.20.

B.3.5 INFORMATION OR MATERIAL

This component is methodology dependent and would be the same for all examples.

Set Type Code	Description
I	Information set
M	Material set

Activity Number	Description
1	Resource management
1.1	Hotel creation/closing
1.2	Room creation/closing
1.3	Resort creation
2	Request management
2.1	Request creation
2.2	Person creation
2.3	Request acceptance
2.3.1	Reservation choice
2.3.2	Availability updating
2.4	Customer identification
2.5	Request postponement
2.6	Managing postponed request
2.6.1	Acceptance of postponed requests
2.6.1.1	Reservation choice
2.6.1.2	Availability updating
2.6.2	Deletion of postponed requests
3	Reservation management
3.1	Cancellation of reservation
3.1.1	Availability updating
3.2	Reservation check-in
3.3	Guest identification
3.4	Reservation check-out
4	Invoicing
4.1	Guest charging
4.2	Guest billing

Figure B.18   BUSINESS ACTIVITY breakdown.

Activity Number	Activity Name	Activity Synonym Name
1	Resource management	Hotel-resort management
2	Request management	Demand management
2.4	Customer identification	Customer-id Customer-definition
3.2	Reservation check-in	Check-in
3.4	Reservation check-out	Check-out

Figure B.19   BUSINESS ACTIVITY USES NAME.

Preceding Activity		Succeeding Activity	
2	Request management	3	Reservation management
2	Request management	4	Invoicing
3	Reservation management	4	Invoicing
2.2	Person creation	2.1	Request creation
2.4	Customer identification	2.3	Request acceptance
2.5	Request postponement	2.6	Managing postponed requests
3.3	Guest identification	3.2	Reservation check-in
3.2	Reservation check-in	3.4	Reservation check-out
4.1	Guest charging	4.2	Guest billing

Figure B.20   BUSINESS ACTIVITY PRECEDENCE/SUCCEDENCE.

B.3.6   INFORMATION/MATERIAL SET

Figure B.21 gives a list of INFORMATION/MATERIAL SETS that are involved in BUSINESS ACTIVITIES.

Set Type Code	Set Number	Description
I	1	List of hotel changes
I	2	List of available rooms
I	3	List of room changes
M	4	List of hotels
M	5	List of rooms
I	6	New resorts
M	7	Resorts
I	8	New requests
I	9	List of requests
M	10	New persons
M	11	List of persons
I	12	List of reservations
M	13	List of customers
I	14	List of postponed requests
I	15	Postponed requests deleted
I	16	List of cancelled reservations
I	17	Cancellation requests
I	18	New check-in
I	19	Check-in list
M	20	List of guests
I	21	New check-out
I	22	Check-out list
M	23	Services
M	24	Guests
I	25	Charges
I	26	Invoices

Figure B.21   INFORMATION/MATERIAL SET.

B.3.7   SET NAME

The following names are examples which may be used to identify either information or material sets:

- list of hotels
- list of rooms
- new requests
- list of customers
- hotels
- rooms
- incoming requests
- customers
- postponed requests
- list of postponed requests

B.3.8   INFORMATION/MATERIAL SET USES NAME

The same INFORMATION/MATERIAL SET may be identified by different names. Figure B.22 merges a presentation of the two components, SET NAME and INFORMATION/MATERIAL SET USES NAME, giving some synonyms for the SET NAMES introduced in Figure B.21.

Set Number		Set Synonym Name
4	(List of hotels)	Hotels
5	(List of rooms)	Rooms
8	(New requests)	Incoming requests
13	(List of customers)	Customers
14	(List of postponed requests)	Postponed requests

Figure B.22   INFORMATION/MATERIAL SET synonyms.

B.3.9   INVOLVEMENT TYPE

This component is methodology dependent. The two INVOLVEMENT TYPE codes used are the following:

R   Information/material set *input* to ACTIVITY USES SET
U   Information/material set *output* to ACTIVITY UPDATES SET

B.3.10   ACTIVITY USES SET

Figure B.23 shows which INFORMATION/MATERIAL SETS are created or used by BUSINESS ACTIVITIES.

Activity Number	Involvement	Set Number
1.1	R	1
1.1	U	2
1.2	R	3
1.2	U	2
1.1	U	4
1.2	U	5
1.3	R	6
1.3	U	7
2.1	R	8
2.1	U	9
2.2	R	10
2.2	U	11
2.3	U	9
2.3	R	12
2.3	R	2
2.4	U	12
2.4	R	13
2.5	U	9
2.5	R	14
2.6	U	14
2.6	U	12
2.6	R	2
2.6	U	15
3.1	U	17
3.1	R	16
3.2	U	18
3.2	R	19
3.3	U	24
3.3	R	20
3.4	U	21
3.4	R	22
4.1	R	23
4.1	U	25
4.2	R	25
4.2	R	21
4.2	U	26

Figure B.23   BUSINESS ACTIVITY USES SET.

B.3.11   ACTIVITY PRECONDITION

An ACTIVITY PRECONDITION is a condition which has to be satisfied in the business area for one or more BUSINESS ACTIVITIES to be able to take place. Figure B.24 gives some examples of PRECONDITIONS which may need to hold before some of the BUSINESS ACTIVITIES listed in Figure B.18 can take place. Figure B.25 is a cross-reference between PRECONDITIONS and BUSINESS ACTIVITIES.

Precondition Number	Precondition Description
1	New hotel installed
2	New resort created
3	New room opened
4	Hotel closed
5	Room closed

Figure B.24   ACTIVITY PRECONDITIONS.

B.3.12   PRECONDITION ENABLES ACTIVITY

Precondition Number	Activity Number
1	11 (Hotel created/closed)
4	11 (Hotel created/closed)
3	12 (Room created/closed)
5	12 (Room created/closed)
2	13 (Resort created)

Figure B.25   PRECONDITION ENABLES ACTIVITY.

B.3.13   ORGANIZATION UNIT

Each of the BUSINESS ACTIVITIES listed in Figure B.18 is under the responsibility of an ORGANIZATION UNIT. Figure B.26 lists the ORGANIZATION UNITS of the reservation system and Figure B.27 is a cross-reference between the two components, BUSINESS ACTIVITY and ORGANIZATION UNIT, which indicates which ORGANIZATION UNITS are responsible for performing each BUSINESS ACTIVITY and vice versa.

Organization Unit Code	Organization Unit Name
A	Accounting
S	Guest Services
R	Reservation and request
I/O	Check-in and check-out

Figure B.26   ORGANIZATION UNITS.

B.3.14   ACTIVITY RESPONSIBILITY

Organization Unit Code	Activity Number	Activity Name
R	1	Resource management
R	2	Request management
R	3.1	Cancellation of reservation
I/O	3.2	Reservation check-in
I/O	3.3	Guest identification
I/O	3.4	Reservation check-out
S	4.1	Guest charging
A	4.2	Guest billing

Figure B.27   ACTIVITY RESPONSIBILITY.

B.3.15   EXTERNAL UNIT

External Unit	Description
G	Guest
P	Person
H	Hotel

Figure B.28   EXTERNAL UNIT.

B.3.16   FLOW TYPE

This component is methodology dependent.

Flow Type Code	Description
EI	External to internal
IE	Internal to external
II	Internal

B.3.17   FLOW

Movements of information either between EXTERNAL UNIT and ORGANIZATION UNIT or between two ORGANIZATION UNITS are identified as FLOWS. Figure B.29 shows FLOWS between units in the reservation system.

Flow Type Code	Flow Number	Description	Organization Unit Source	Organization Unit Recipient	External Unit
EI	1	Resource modification		Reservation	Hotel
EI	2	Requests		Reservation	Person
EI	3	Guests		I/O	Guest
IE	3	Guests	I/O		Guest
II	4	Decisions on postponed requests	Reservation	Reservation	
II	5	Charges	Service	Accounting	
IE	6	Invoices	Accounting		Guest

Figure B.29   FLOWS.

B.3.18   ACTIVITY INVOLVES FLOW

Figure B.30 shows a cross-reference table which indicates which FLOWS are involved in which BUSINESS ACTIVITIES.

Activity Number	Flow Number
1	1
2.1, 2.2, 2.3, 2.4, 2.5	2
3.1	2
2.6	4
3.2, 3.3, 3.4	3
4.1	5
4.2	6

Figure B.30   BUSINESS ACTIVITY INVOLVES FLOW.

B.3.19   FLOW INVOLVES INFORMATION/MATERIAL SET

This component indicates which INFORMATIN/MATERIAL SETS are involved in which FLOW and vice versa, as depicted in Figure B.31.

Set Number	Flow Number
1	1
3	1
6	1
8	2
17	2
10	2
18	3
24	3
21	3
14	4
15	4
16	4
25	5
26	6

Figure B.31   FLOW INVOLVES INFORMATION/MATERIAL SET.

B.3.20   FLOW OF SET IN ACTIVITY

Flow Type Code	Flow Number	Activity Number	Set Type Code	Set Number
EI	1	1.1	I	1
EI	1	1.2	I	3
EI	1	1.3	I	6
EI	2	2.1, 2.3, 2.5	I	8
EI	2	2.2, 2.4	I	10

Figure B.32   FLOW OF SET IN ACTIVITY.

Flow Type Code	Flow Number	Activity Number	Set Type Code	Set Number
EI	2	3.1	I	17
EI	3	3.3	M	24
EI	3	3.2	M	18
EI	3	3.4	M	21
II	4	2.6.1	I	14
II	4	2.6.2	I	15
II	5	4.1	I	25
IE	6	4.2	I	26

Figure B.32   *Cont'd.*

B.3.21   FLOW PRECONDITION

Precondition Number	Precondition Description
1	New room opened
2	Room closed

It should be noted that these examples of FLOW PRECONDITIONS are based on those used to illustrate ACTIVITY PRECONDITIONS in Section B.3.11. Some techniques may have these two components combined into one component.

B.3.22   PRECONDITION ENABLES FLOW

Precondition Number	Flow Type Code	Flow Number
1	EI	1
2	EI	2

The first example shows that the precondition for a flow of information from a hotel to the reservation centre is that either a new room is opened or else a room is closed.

B.4   Behaviour perspective

Components of the worked example are presented in the same order as in Section 4.9.

B.4.1   BUSINESS EVENT

The main component in the behaviour perspective of the business analysis stage is BUSINESS EVENT. These events are perceived in the application environment as being pertinent to the business. An event is something which happens at a given point in time and may be a trigger for the organization.

Event Number	Description
1	Request arrival
2	Cancellation request
3	Check-in
4	Check-out
5	Guest serviced
6	New day starts
7	Resource modification

Figure B.33   BUSINESS EVENT.

Event Number 6 in Figure B.33 is a calendar-dependent event which allows for a systematic examination of postponed requests.

B.4.2   BUSINESS EVENT NAME

Figure B.34 shows a table of synonyms of BUSINESS EVENT NAMES introduced in Figure B.33.

Event Number	Synonym Name
2 (Cancellation request)	Demand for reservation cancellation
6 (New day starts)	Diary

Figure B.34   BUSINESS EVENT NAME synonyms.

B.4.3   BUSINESS EVENT USES NAME

BUSINESS EVENTS may have different names, as shown in Figure B.34.

B.4.4   EVENT PRECEDENCE/SUCCEDENCE

Succeeding Event	Preceding Event
2	1
3	1
4	3
5	3

Figure B.35   BUSINESS EVENT PRECEDENCE/SUCCEDENCE.

B.4.5   BUSINESS EVENT ROLE

This is a methodology dependent component.

Event Role Code	Event Role Description
B (before)	Precondition
A (after)	Postcondition

B.4.6   BUSINESS EVENT CONDITION

A BUSINESS EVENT CONDITION is a condition that must hold for a BUSINESS EVENT to take place. Figure B.36 lists CONDITIONS to be associated with the BUSINESS EVENTS for the reservation system.

Condition Number	Condition Description
1	New request arrives
2	Cancellation of an existing reservation requested
3	Existing reservation
4	New guest checks-in
5	Customer who checks-in was out of the hotel
6	Guest in
7	Guest asks for a service
8	Service provided to a guest
9	New date
10	System resources are in a given state
11	System resources have changed state
12	Guest departs

Figure B.36   BUSINESS EVENT CONDITION.

B.4.7   CONDITION FOR BUSINESS EVENT

Figure B.37 shows the CONDITIONS which must hold before (precondition) and after (postcondition) a BUSINESS EVENT for each of the seven BUSINESS EVENTS introduced in Figure B.33.

Event Number	Precondition Number	Postcondition Number
1	—	1
2	3	2
3	5	4
4	6	12
5	7	8
6	—	9
7	10	11

Figure B.37   Pre- and postCONDITIONS FOR BUSINESS EVENTS.

Entity Type Name	1.1	1.2	1.3	2.1	2.2	2.3	2.4	2.5	2.6	3.1	3.2	3.3	3.4	4.1	4.2
Hotel-Type	U					R	R	R							
Resort			U			R	R	R							R
Hotel		U				R	R	R							R
Room						R	R	R							R
Room-Availability	U	U				U		R	U	U					
Room-Type															
Calendar															
Season															
Room-Tariff					U										
Person				U	U										
Request						R	R		R		R				
Reservation						R	R	U	U	U	R				
Reserved-Room						U			R	U					
Customer							U		R						
Cancelled-Reservation										R					
Reservation-In											U				
Reservation-Out													U		
Post-Check-In-Assignment											U				R
Guest														U	
Bill-Line												U			
Charge-Item-Type															R
Charge-Item														U	R
Bill														U	U

Activity Number

Figure B.38   BUSINESS ACTIVITY INVOLVES ENTITY TYPE.

B.5 Business analysis — cross-references between perspectives

Components of the worked example are presented in the same order as in Section 4.11.

B.5.1 INVOLVEMENT TYPE

This is a methodology dependent component and, for the purposes of this worked example, the following codes are used:

Involvement Code	Involvement Description
R	Reads information about
U	Updates information about

B.5.2 BUSINESS ACTIVITY INVOLVES ENTITY TYPE

INFORMATION SETS defined in the process perspective and ENTITY TYPES relevant to the data perspective describe the same kind of reality. They are alternative views of the information types involved in an enterprise. It may be useful to define the cross-reference table between BUSINESS ACTIVITIES and ENTITY TYPES, as shown in Figure B.38.

In the data perspective, ENTITY TYPES are defined as representations of real world entities. In the process perspective, INFORMATION SETS are regarded as existing only during the performance of BUSINESS ACTIVITIES.

B.5.3 BUSINESS ACTIVITY INVOLVES ATTRIBUTE

To illustrate this component, only one BUSINESS ACTIVITY, namely,

1.1   (Hotel creation/closing)

is used. This BUSINESS ACTIVITY involves two ENTITY TYPES, namely ET2 (Hotel) and ET4 (Room-Availability), as shown in Figure B.39.

Entity Type Code	Attribute Name	Activity Number	Involvement Code
ET2	hot-type	1.1	U
ET2	hotel-no	1.1	U
ET2	hotel-ad	1.1	U
ET2	hotel-phone	1.1	U
ET2	hotel-name	1.1	U
ET4	hotel-no	1.1	U
ET4	room-no	1.1	U
ET4	av-beg-date	1.1	U
ET4	av-end-date	1.1	U

Figure B.39   BUSINESS ACTIVITY INVOLVES ATTRIBUTE.

B.5.4   ACTIVITY TRIGGER

A BUSINESS EVENT may trigger one or more BUSINESS ACTIVITIES and, in this way, influences the behaviour of an enterprise.

Figure B.40 indicates which BUSINESS EVENT triggers which BUSINESS ACTIVITY. In the behaviour perspective, each BUSINESS ACTIVITY is identified as being a consequence of one or more BUSINESS EVENTS.

Each BUSINESS ACTIVITY is first associated with a triggering BUSINESS EVENT. The decomposition of BUSINESS ACTIVITIES then results in a graph (event-activity) which reflects the pertinent real world state transitions.

Event Number	Event Description	Activity Number	Activity Description
1	Request arrival	2.3	Request acceptance
		2.4	Customer identification
		2.5	Request postponement
2	Cancellation request	3.1	Cancellation of reservation
3	Check-in	3.2	Reservation check-in
		3.3	Guest identification
4	Check-out	3.4	Reservation check-out
		4.2	Guest billing
5	Guest serviced	4.1	Guest charging
6	New day starts	2.6.1	Acceptance of postponed requests
		2.6.2	Deletion of postponed requests
7	Resource modification	1	Resource management

Figure B.40   ACTIVITY TRIGGER.

B.5.5   BUSINESS EVENT INVOLVES ENTITY TYPE

Each BUSINESS EVENT corresponds to a type of system state change, represented as a type of state change of ENTITY TYPES. The involvement of ENTITY TYPES in BUSINESS EVENTS is presented in Figure B.41.

B.5.6   BUSINESS EVENT INVOLVES ATTRIBUTE

To illustrate this component, only BUSINESS EVENT 2 (Cancellation request) is considered. It can be seen in Figure B.42 that this involves two ENTITY TYPES, namely ET14 (Cancelled-Reservation) and ET11 (Reservation).

B.5.7   CONDITION USES ENTITY TYPE

Each BUSINESS EVENT is characterized by CONDITIONS that must hold for an occurrence of the BUSINESS EVENT to take place. PRECONDITIONS and POSTCONDITIONS are

Entity Type Name	Event Number						
	1	*2*	*3*	*4*	*5*	*6*	*7*
Request	U						
Cancelled-Reservation		U					
Reservation		R	R				
Reservation-In			U	R	R		
Reservation-Out				U			
Charge-Item					U		
Calendar						U	
Hotel							U
Room							U
Resort							U

Figure B.41 BUSINESS EVENT INVOLVES ENTITY TYPE.

Entity	*Attribute Name*	*Event Number*	*Involvement Code*
ET14	res-no	2	U
ET14	canc-no	2	U
ET14	canc-date	2	U
ET11	res-no	2	R

Figure B.42 BUSINESS EVENT INVOLVES ATTRIBUTE.

Entity Type Name	Condition Number											
	1	*2*	*3*	*4*	*5*	*6*	*7*	*8*	*9*	*10*	*11*	*12*
Request	x											
Hotel-Type	x											
Room-Type	x											
Resort	x									x	x	
Hotel										x	x	
Room										x	x	
Cancelled-Reservation		x										
Reservation			x		x							
Reservation-In				x	x	x	x					
Reservation-Out						x	x					x
Guest						x	x	x				
Charge-Item-Type								x				
Charge-Item								x				
Calendar									x			
Customer					x							

Figure B.43 CONDITION USES ENTITY TYPE.

shown in Figure B.36 and their associations with EVENTS is shown in Figure B.37. The evaluation of CONDITIONS uses information belonging to ENTITY TYPES. Figure B.43 shows which ENTITY TYPES are used by each CONDITION.

B.5.8 CONDITION USES ATTRIBUTE

To illustrate this component, only CONDITION 1 (New request arrives) is used. It can be seen in Figure B.44 that four ENTITY TYPES are used to check the CONDITION, namely:

- ET10 (Request),
- ET0 (Hotel-Type),
- ET5 (Room-Type), and
- ET1 (Resort).

The CONDITION checks that the requested Hotel-Type, Room-Type and Resort are correct for the request received.

Entity Type Code	Attribute Name	Condition Number
ET10	hot-type	1
ET10	resort-name	1
ET10	room-type	1
ET0	hot-type	1
ET5	room-type	1
ET1	resort-name	1

Figure B.44   CONDITION USES ATTRIBUTE.

Appendix C
Worked example of system design components

C.1 Data perspective

Components of the worked example are presented in the same order as in Section 5.4.

C.1.1 TABLE

Figure C.1 gives a list of 19 TABLES. Each is given a code for future reference.

Table Number	Description
T1	Hotel-Type
T2	Resort
T3	Hotel
T4	Room
T5	Room-Availability
T6	Room-Type
T7	Season
T8	Room-Tariff
T9	Person
T10	Request
T11	Reservation
T12	Reserved-room
T13	Reservation-In
T14	Reservation-Out
T15	Post-Check-In-Assigned-Rooms
T16	Bill
T17	Bill-Line
T18	Charge-Item-Type
T19	Charge-Item

Figure C.1 List of TABLES.

C.1.2   ASSIGNMENT TYPE

This is a methodology dependent component. The two ASSIGNMENT TYPE codes used are as shown in Figure C.2.

1	One ENTITY TYPE to one TABLE
2	Two or more ENTITY TYPES to two or more TABLES

Figure C.2   ASSIGNMENT TYPE.

C.1.3   ENTITY TYPE TO TABLE ASSIGNMENT

Figure C.3 shows a cross-reference table between the TABLES listed in Figure C.1 and the ENTITY TYPES which result from the business analysis stage. It should be noted that four of the ENTITY TYPES from the business analysis stage, namely Customer (ET13), Guest (ET18), Date (ET6) and Cancelled-Reservation (ET14), have not been included as TABLES.

Entity Type Code	1	2	3	4	5	6	7	8	9	10	11	12	13	14	15	16	17	18	19
ET0	1																		
ET1		1																	
ET2			1																
ET3				1															
ET4					1														
ET5						1													
ET6																			
ET7							1												
ET8								1											
ET9									2										
ET10										1									
ET11											1								
ET12												1							
ET13									2										
ET14																			
ET15													1						
ET16														1					
ET17															1				
ET18									2										
ET19																1			
ET20																	1		
ET21																		1	
ET22																	1		

Figure C.3   ENTITY TYPE TO TABLE ASSIGNMENT.

C.1.4 DATA TYPE

This is a methodology dependent component. The three DATA TYPES used in this worked example are as follows:

C   Character
D   Date
N   Numeric

C.1.5 COLUMN NAME

The list of COLUMN NAMES in Figure C.4 consists of ATTRIBUTE NAMES from Section B.2.8.

hot-type	req-beg-date
hot-type-desc	req-end-date
resort-no	req-nb-room
resort-name	req-state
hotel-no	req-date
hotel-ad	res-no
hotel-phone	res-date
hotel-name	res-beg-date
room-no	res-end-date
room-type	cust-code
av-beg-date	arrival-date
av-end-date	guest-id
room-type-desc	departure-date
start-date	bill-no
end-date	total-amount
season-type	invoice-line
price	line-amount
name	cit-code
person-id	cit-des
address	charge-date
phone	amount
req-no	

Figure C.4   List of COLUMN NAMES.

C.1.6 COLUMN

The assignment of COLUMNS NAMES to TABLES is presented in Figure C.5.

C.1.7 ATTRIBUTE TO COLUMN ASSIGNMENT

The ATTRIBUTES represented by an 'X' in the cross-reference table in Figure B.12 may be cross-referenced to the COLUMNS shown in the cross-reference table in Figure C.5.

| Column Name | \<-- | | | | | | | | Table Number | | | | | | | | | --> | |
	1	2	3	4	5	6	7	8	9	10	11	12	13	14	15	16	17	18	19
hot-type	X	X								X									
hot-type-desc	X																		
resort-no			X	X															
resort-name	X									X									
hotel-no			X	X	X		X				X								
hotel-ad				X															
hotel-phone				X															
hotel-name				X															
room-no				X	X							X			X				
room-type				X		X	X			X									
av-beg-date					X														
av-end-date					X														
room-type-desc						X													
state-date							X												
end-date							X												
season-type							X	X											
price								X											
name									X										
person-id									X	X									
address									X										
phone									X										
req-no										X	X								
req-beg-date										X									
req-end-date										X									
req-nb-room										X									
req-state										X									
req-date										X									
res-no											X	X	X	X	X	X			
res-date											X								
res-beg-date											X								
res-end-date											X								
cust-code											X								
arrival-date												X		X					
guest-id												X					X		X
departure-date													X		X				
bill-no														X					
total-amount														X					
invoice-line																X			
line-amount																X			
cit-code																	X	X	X
cit-des																		X	
charge-date																	X		X
amount																			X

Figure C.5 COLUMNS.

There are four fewer TABLES than ENTITY TYPES (see Section C.1.3). For example, the ATTRIBUTES associated with the ENTITY TYPES Customer and Guest are absorbed in the COLUMNS for the TABLE Person.

C.1.8 COLUMN GROUP

The need for COLUMN GROUPS is based on the requirement to be able to specify the CONSTRAINTS which are to be imposed on the values in the COLUMNS. Figure C.6 gives COLUMN GROUPS which are used for the CONSTRAINTS presented in Figures C.8 and C.9.

Group Code	Column Name
G1	hotel-no room-no
G2	hotel-no room-no av-beg-date
G3	hotel-no season-type room-type
G4	start-date end-date
G5	room-no res-no
G6	res-no arrival-date
G7	res-no departure-date
G8	bill-no invoice-line
G9	cit-code change-date guest-id

Figure C.6 COLUMN GROUPS.

C.1.9 COLUMN IN GROUP

A COLUMN in a TABLE may belong to more than one COLUMN GROUP. Figure C.7 contains the cross-reference table showing which COLUMN belongs to which COLUMN GROUP.

Column Name	Group Code								
	G1	G2	G3	G4	G5	G6	G7	G8	G9
hotel-no	x	x	x						
room-no	x	x			x				
av-beg-date		x							
room-type				x					
season-type				x					
start-date					x				
end-date					x				
res-no						x	x	x	
arrival-date							x		
departure-date								x	
bill-no									x
invoice-line									x
cit-code										x
charge-date										x
guest-id										x

Figure C.7   COLUMN IN GROUP.

C.1.10   CONSTRAINT TYPE

This is a methodology dependent component. There are four CONSTRAINT TYPES identified in Section 5.4.10. Figure C.8 illustrates uniqueness CONSTRAINTS and Figure C.9 illustrates referential CONSTRAINTS.

C.1.11   CONSTRAINT

There should be at least one uniqueness CONSTRAINT defined for each of the 19 TABLES. Each such CONSTRAINT is expressed either on a single COLUMN or on a COLUMN GROUP of that TABLE. The uniqueness CONSTRAINTS are listed in Figure C.8.

Figure C.9 lists the referential CONSTRAINTS for the worked example. Some CONSTRAINTS are based on single COLUMNS and some are based on COLUMN GROUPS. For example, the CONSTRAINT on TABLE 8 (Room-Tariff) implies that the value in the COLUMN season-type must correspond to one of the values of the COLUMN with the same name in the TABLE 7 (Season).

C.1.12   RELATIONSHIP TO CONSTRAINT ASSIGNMENT

Figure C.10 shows which of the 44 RELATIONSHIPS defined in Figure B.9 are related to the CONSTRAINTS presented in Figure C.9.

C.1.13   ROW

Of the 19 TABLES listed in Section C.1.1, none would require the content of any of the ROWS to be prescribed by the designer.

Table Name	Column Name
Hotel-Type	hot-type
Resort	resort-no
Hotel	hotel-no
Room	hotel-no
	room-no
Room-Availability	hotel-no
	room-no
	av-beg-date
Room-Type	room-type
Season	start-date
	end-date
Room-Tariff	hotel-no
	season-type
	room-type
Person	person-id
Request	req-no
Reservation	res-no
Reserved-Room	room-no
	res-no
Reservation-In	res-no
	arrival-date
Reservation-Out	res-no
	departure-date
Post-Check-In-Assignment	room-no
	res-no
Bill	bill-no
Bill-Line	bill-no
	invoice-line
Charge-Item Type	cit-code
Charge-Item	cit-code
	charge-date
	guest-id

Figure C.8 Uniqueness CONSTRAINT.

Table Name	Column Name	Referred Table	Column or Column Group
Season	season-type	Room-Tariff	
Hotel-Type	hot-type	Hotel	
		Request	
Resort	resort-name	Request	
Resort	resort-no	Hotel	
Hotel	hotel-no	Room	
		Room-Tariff	
		Reservation	
Room	hotel-no	Room-Availability	
	room-no	Reserved-Room	
		Post-Check-In	
		Assigned Rooms	
Room-Type	room-type	Room	
		Request	
		Room-Tariff	
Person	person-id	Request	guest-id
		Reservation-In	cust-code
		Reservation	guest-id
		Charge-Item	
Request	req-no	Reservation	
Reservation	res-no	Reserved-Room	
		Reservation-In	
		Reservation-Out	
Reservation-In	arrival-date	Post-Check-In	
	res-no	Assigned-Rooms	
Charge-Item-Type	cit-code	Charge-Item	
Reservation-Out	res-no	Bill	
	departure-date		
Charge-Item	cit-code	Bill-Line	
	charge-date		
	guest-id		
Bill	bill-no	Bill-Line	

Figure C.9   Referential CONSTRAINTS.

Table Name	Column Name	Referred Table	Column or Column Group	Relationship Number
Season	season-type	Room-Tariff		10
Hotel-Type	hot-type	Hotel		0
		Request		12
Resort	resort-name	Request		13
	resort-no	Hotel		1
Hotel	hotel-no	Room		2
		Room-Tariff		11
		Reservation		25
Room	hotel-no	Room-Availability		3
	room-no	Reserved-Room		27
		Post-Check-In-Assigned-Rooms		32
Room-Type	room-type	Room		4
		Request		14
		Room-Tariff		9
Person	person-id	Request		15
		Reservation-In	guest-id	36
		Reservation	cust-code	20
		Charge-Item	guest-id	38
Request	req-no	Reservation		21
Reservation	res-no	Reserved-Room		25
		Reservation-In		30
		Reservation-Out		29
Reservation-In	arrival-date res-no	Post-Check-In-Assigned Rooms		31
Charge-Item-Type	cit-code	Charge-Item		40
Reservation-Out	res-no departure-date	Bill		43
Charge-Item	cit-code charge-date guest-id	Bill-Line		41
Bill	bill-no	Bill-Line		42

Figure C.10 RELATIONSHIP TO CONSTRAINT ASSIGNMENT.

C.1.14   EXTERNAL FORM

One example of an EXTERNAL FORM for reservation control is a list of reservations for a given hotel during a given period. This would consist of information extracted from the following TABLES:

- Reservation
- Reserved-Room
- Hotel
- Room

This EXTERNAL FORM would be designed as a screen display format in order to be displayed on a screen on demand.

C.1.15   EXTERNAL FORM ELEMENT

The following is a set of possible elements on a 'list of reservations':

1. header,
2. row heading,
3. column heading, and
4. item line.

The last three would be repeated for each day of the period to be considered.

C.1.16   DISPLAY OPTION

The alternative DISPLAY OPTIONS are independent of any specific example. Examples related to screen displays are as follows:

1. normal,
2. reverse video, and
3. flashing.

C.1.17   COLUMN ON FORM ELEMENT

Figure C.11 indicates which of the COLUMNS listed in Section C.1.6 are used in an EXTERNAL FORM, and in which of the four ways the COLUMN is used. The EXTERNAL FORM contains the hotel name and hotel address in the heading data about room type and person in the body of the form.

C.2   Process perspective

Components of the worked example are presented in the same order as in Section 5.6.

Column Name	External form element			
	1	*2*	*3*	*4*
hotel-name	x			
hotel-address	x			
hotel-phone	x			
room-no				
room-type			x	x
date	x			
reservation-no				
person-id			x	x
address			x	x

Figure C.11   COLUMN ON FORM ELEMENT.

C.2.1   ON LINE OR BATCH

This is a methodology dependent component. The codes used in the worked example are as follows:

    L   On line
    B   Batch

C.2.2   TASK CATEGORY

This component is methodology dependent. The categorization of TASKS used in this example is as follows:

    R   Retrieval
    U   Update

C.2.3   HOMING IN OR OUT-OF-THE-BLUE

This component is methodology dependent and has the following values:

    H   Homing in
    O   Out-of-the-blue
    N   Neither

C.2.4   MENU-DRIVEN OR FAST TRACK

This is a methodology dependent component. The following codes are used in the example:

    M Menu-driven
    F   Fast track
    B   Both menu-driven and fast track

C.2.5 INITIATION MEANS

This component is prescribed as follows:

P   Person at terminal
C   Calendar clock
V   Value related condition
R   Real time interrupt

C.2.6 TASK

Figure C.12 shows the TASKS derived by decomposition of the BUSINESS ACTIVITIES listed in Figure B.18. Each TASK is categorized according to the five methodology dependent components listed in the preceding five sections.

Each of the TASKS listed in the column headed 'Task' is numbered based on the number of the BUSINESS ACTIVITY from which it is derived.

C.2.7 MENU

The limited list of TASKS introduced in Figure C.12 is sufficient to illustrate three MENUS, as shown in Figure C.13.

The two second level MENUS (MENU FOR RESOURCE CHANGE and MENU FOR DAY TO DAY OPERATIONS) correspond to the decomposition of each of these two lines on the top level MENU.

C.2.8 MENU HIERARCHY

Calling Menu	Called Menu
Top	1
Top	2

C.2.9 TASK IN MENU

Figure C.14 shows the cross-reference between TASK and MENU. TASKS are those listed in Figure C.12 and lines of MENU are those on the second of the three menus in Figure C.13 (MENU FOR RESOURCE CHANGE).

The choice of TASKS and associated MENUS is somewhat arbitrary. To make this choice less arbitrary, the designer may prescribe behaviour oriented components. In this way, he or she is able to make a better definition of TASKS by taking into account the SYSTEM EVENTS which trigger each TASK. On this basis, the designer can decide on what are the lines of the MENU by considering the TASKS which are associated with BUSINESS EVENTS.

C.2.10 ACCESS CONTROL CLASS

The list of kinds of individuals on page 376 shows who would be allowed to initiate TASKS in each of the classes:

Activity Number	Activity Description	Task	Task Description	Task Categorization Code
1	Resource management			
1.1	Hotel creation/closing			
		1.1.1	Create new hotel	L A H M P
		1.1.2	Delete hotel	L D H M P
		1.1.3	Modify hotel	L M H M P
1.2	Room creation/closing			
		1.2.1	Create new room	L A H M P
		1.2.2	Delete room	L D H M P
1.3	Resort creation			
		1.3.1	Create new resort	L A B M P
		1.4	Modify season	L M B M P
		1.5	Create season	L M B M P
		1.6	Create tariff	L A H M P
		1.7	Modify tariff	L M H M P
		1.8	Update room availability	L M H M P
		1.9	Create hotel-type	L A B M P
		1.10	Create room-type	L A B M P
		1.11	Delete hotel-type	L D B M P
		1.12	Delete room-type	L D B M P
2	Request management			
2.1	Request creation			
		2.1.1	Create request	L A H M P
		2.1.2	Delete request	L D H M P
2.2	Person creation			
		2.2.1	Create person	L A B M P
		2.2.2	Delete person	L D B M P
2.3	Request acceptance			
2.3.1	Reservation allocation	2.3.1	Allocate reservation	L A H M P
2.3.2	Availability updating	2.3.2	Update availability	L M H M P
2.4	Customer identification			
		2.4.1	Check customer known	L R B M P
2.5	Request postponement			
		2.5.1	Modify request	L M H M
2.6	Managing postponed request			

Figure C.12   TASKS corresponding to decomposition of the BUSINESS ACTIVITY.

Activity Number	Activity Description	Task	Task Description	Task Categorization Code
2.6.1	Acceptance of postponed requests	2.6.1	Allocate postponed request	L M H M P
2.6.1.1	Reservation allocation			
2.6.1.2	Availability updating			
2.6.2	Deletion of postponed requests	2.6.2	Delete postponed request	L D H M P
3	Reservation management			
3.1	Cancellation of reservation			
3.1.1	Availability updating	3.1.1	Update availability	L A H M P
3.2	Reservation check-in			
		3.2.1	Record guest check-in	L A H M P
3.3	Guest identification			
		3.3.1	Check guest identity	L R H M P
3.4	Reservation check-out			
		3.4.1	Record guest check-out	L A H M P
4	Invoicing			
4.1	Guest charging			
		4.1.1	Add charge item	L A H M P
4.2	Guest billing			
		4.2.1	Generate invoice	L R H M P

Figure C.12 *Cont'd*

A   Data administrator
B   Hotel manager
C   Resort information centre

C.2.11   TASK IN ACCESS CONTROL CLASS

This is a cross-reference component which indicates the assignment of TASKS to ACCESS CONTROL CLASSES, as shown in Figure C.15.

C.2.12   TASK TO TASK INITIATION TYPE

The codes on page 378 are used for the following component:

TOP LEVEL MENU

1   Resource change
2   Day to day operations

MENU FOR RESOURCE CHANGE

1. Create hotel
2. Close hotel
3. Create room
4. Create resort
5. Close room
6. Season updating
7. Tariff updating
8. Hotel modification

9.   Season creation
10. Tariff creation
11. Room-availability-updating
12. Hotel-type creation
13. Room-type creation
14. Hotel-type deletion
15. Room-type deletion

MENU FOR DAY TO DAY OPERATIONS

1   Request analysis
2   Management of postponed requests
3   Check-in
4   Check-out
5   Cancellation
6   Invoicing

Figure C.13   MENUS.

Task Code		Menu 1	
1.1.1	(Creation of new hotel)	1	(Create hotel)
1.1.2	(Delete hotel)	2	(Close hotel)
1.1.3	(Hotel modification)	8	(Hotel modification)
1.2.1	(Creation of new room)	3	(Create room)
1.2.2	(Delete room)	5	(Close room)
1.3.1	(Creation of new resort)	4	(Create resort)
1.4	(Season modification)	6	(Season updating)
1.5	(Season creation)	9	(Season creation)
1.6	(Tariff creation)	10	(Tariff creation)
1.7	(Tariff modification)	7	(Tariff updating)
1.8	(Room-availability-updating)	11	(Room-availability-updating)
1.9	(Hotel-type creation)	12	(Hotel-type creation)
1.10	(Room-type creation)	13	(Room-type creation)
1.11	(Hotel-type deletion)	14	(Hotel-type deletion)
1.12	(Room-type deletion)	15	(Room-type deletion)

Figure C.14   TASK IN MENU.

Task Code	Access Control Class		
	A	B	C
1.1.1	x		x
1.1.2	x		x
1.1.3		x	
1.2.1		x	
1.2.2		x	
1.3.1	x		x
1.4	x		
1.5	x		
1.6		x	
1.7		x	
1.8	x		
1.9	x		
1.10	x		
1.11	x		
1.12	x		

Figure C.15   TASK IN ACCESS CONTROL CLASS.

A   TASK A automatically initiates TASK B on completion

C   TASK A conditionally initiates TASK B

S   Successful completion of TASK A is necessary to enable initiation of TASK B

C.2.13   TASK TO TASK INITIATION

Figure C.16 illustrates this component for TASKS 1.1 to 1.12 introduced in Figure C.12.

C.3   Cross-reference between data and process perspectives

Of the seven components in this group presented in Section 5.8, three are methodology dependent. The other four are specific to this worked example.

C.3.1   ACCESS PATH NODE TYPE

This component is methodology dependent:

S   Starting point
T   Target

C.3.2   TASK DATA USAGE TYPE

This component is methodology dependent:

Initiating Task		*Initiated Task*		*Initiation type*
1.1.1	(Creation of new hotel)	1.2.1	(Creation of new room)	S
		1.9	(Hotel-type creation)	C
1.1.2	(Delete hotel)	1.2.2	(Delete room)	A
		1.11	(Hotel-type deletion)	C
1.1.3	(Hotel modification)	1.9	(Hotel-type creation)	C
		1.11	(Hotel-type deletion)	C
1.2.1	(Creation of new room)	1.10	(Room-type creation)	C
		1.8	(Room-availability-updating)	A
		1.6	(Tariff creation)	C
1.2.2	(Delete room)	1.8	(Room-availability-updating)	A
		1.12	(Room-type deletion)	C
		1.7	(Tariff modification)	C
1.3.1	(Creation of new resort)	1.1.1	(Creation of new hotel)	S

Figure C.16 TASK TO TASK INITIATION.

A   Add
R   Retrieve
M   Modify
D   Delete

C.3.3 TASK USES TABLE

As an illustration of this component, Figure C.17 indicates the TASK DATA USAGE TYPE and ACCESS PATH NODE TYPE for each intersection point at which a TASK uses a TABLE. TASKS are based on those presented in Figure C.12 and TABLES are the same as those listed in Figure C.1.

Figure C.18 is an alternative representation of Figure C.17 for the first eight TABLES of Figure C.1 only. Figure C.18 does not show the ACCESS PATH NODE TYPE, but it provides an easier overview of the TASKS perform on each TABLE.

C.3.4 TASK USES COLUMN

Figure C.19 indicates, for each of 16 TASKS identified in Figure C.12, which COLUMNS in each TABLE are used when that TASK is performed and the TASK DATA USAGE TYPE for each case.

Task	1 Hotel-Type	2 Resort	3 Hotel	4 Room	5 Room-Availability	6 Room-Type	7 Season	8 Room-Tariff	9 Person	10 Request	11 Reservation	12 Reserved-Room	13 Reservation-In	14 Reservation-Out	15 Post-Check-In-Assignment	16 Bill	17 Bill-Line	18 Charge-Item-Type	19 Charge-Item
1.1.1		RS	AT																
1.1.2		RS	DT																
1.1.3		RS	MT																
1.2.1		RS	RP	AT															
1.2.2		RS	RP	DT															
1.3.1		AS																	
1.4							MS												
1.5							AS												
1.6						RS	RS	AT											
1.7						RS	RS	MT											
1.8		RS	RP		MT		RS												
1.9	AS																		
1.10						AS													
1.11	DS																		
1.12						DS													
2.1.1					AT				RS	AT									
2.1.2					AT				RS	MT									
2.2.1									AS										
2.2.2									DS										
2.3.1		RS	RP	RP															
2.3.2		RS	RP	RP															
2.4.1									RS										
2.5.1									RS	MT		AT							
2.6.1									RS	RP	AT								
2.6.2									RS	DT									
3.1.1		RS	RP	RP	MT						RS								
3.2.1									RS		RP		AT		AT				
3.3.1									RS					AT					
3.4.1									RS		RP	RP	RP						
4.1.1													RP		RP	RP	RP	RS	AT
4.2.1		RS	RP	RP							RS	RS	RP		RP	RT	RT	RS	RT

Figure C.17   TASK USES TABLE.

Table Number	Task Code	Task Data Usage Type			
		Add	Delete	Modify	Retrieve
1	1.9	x			
	2.1		x		
2	1.3.1	x			
3	1.1.1	x			
	1.1.2		x		
	1.1.3			x	x
4	1.2.1	x			
	1.2.2		x		
5	1.8			x	x
6	2.0	x			
	2.2		x		
7	1.4			x	x
	1.5	x			
8	1.6	x			
	1.7			x	x

Figure C.18   TASK USES TABLE. This alternative version of Figure C.17 does not show the ACCESS PATH NODE TYPE.

C.3.5   ALGORITHM

The action that is to be performed when a TASK is initiated can be non-trivial and the cross-reference component TASK USES COLUMN may not give enough precision about the action performed.

An algorithm is illustrated in Figure C.20, with more detail for TASK 1.8 (Room-availability-updating).

C.3.6   ALGORITHM REFERENCES COLUMN

Figure C.20 indicates that the ALGORITHM references several of the COLUMNS which are listed in Figure C.5. It references all four COLUMNS in TABLE T5 – Room-availability.

C.3.7   TASK USES ALGORITHM

TASK 1.8 uses the ALGORITHM shown in Figure C.20. Other TASKS may use other ALGORITHMS.

C.3.8   FORM USAGE CLASS

This component is methodology dependent:

Table no	Table Name Column Name	Task Number														
		1.1.1	1.1.2	1.1.3	1.2.1	1.2.2	1.3.1	1.4	1.5	1.6	1.7	1.8	1.9	1.10	1.11	1.12
1	Hotel-Type													A	D	
	hot-type													A	D	
	hot-type-desc													A	D	
2	Resort							A								
	resort-no							A								
	resort-name							A								
3	Hotel															
	hot-type	A	D	M												
	resort-no	A	D													
	hotel-no	A	D	R												
	hotel-phone	A	D	M												
	hotel-name	A	D	M												
	hotel-ad	A	D	M												
4	Room															
	hotel-no				A	D										
	room-no				A	D										
	room-type				A	D										

5   Room-Availability
      hotel-no   R
      room-no   R
      av-beg-date   M   A   D
      av-end-date   M   A   D

6   Room-Type
      room-type
      room-type-desc

7   Season
      start-date   M   A
      end-date   M   A
      season-type   M   A

8   Room-Tariff
      season-type   A
      price   A   M
      room-type   A   R
      hotel-no   A   R

Figure C.19   TASK USES COLUMN.

Task 1.8: Room-availability-updating

Natural language description

This task modifies a set of rows of TABLE T5 (Room-Availability). If the updating is done after the creation of a new room (Task 1.2.1), it must insert a new row in TABLE T5, corresponding to the new room.

   If the updating follows deletion of a room (Task 1.2.2), then all the rows describing periods of availability of the room must be deleted.

'SQL like' description

In: V = (hotel-no, room-no, type-mode) %input parameters%
Body: IF   V.type-mode = 'Creation'
      THEN INSERT (V.hotel-no, V.room-no, CURRENT-DATE, 1)
            INTO room-availability;
      IF   V.type-mode = 'Deletion'
      THEN DELETE room-availability
            WHERE V.hotel-no = hotel-no
            AND   V.room-no = room-no;

Figure C.20   ALGORITHM.

1.   Input to task;

2.   Output from task, and

3.   Input and output.

C.3.9   TASK USES EXTERNAL FORM

One example of this component is the form describing one hotel as an output of TASK 1.1.1.

C.4   Components of system design — behaviour perspective

Components of the worked example are presented in the same order as in Section 5.10.

C.4.1   SYSTEM EVENT

A SYSTEM EVENT is a kind of event which is prescribed by the designer to take place in the computerized system under design. For example, it could be such that a new row is added to the TABLE Request.

   When a SYSTEM EVENT occurs, it may be necessary to initiate one or more TASKS. Figure C.21 lists the SYSTEM EVENTS of the worked example.

System Event Number	Description
1	Request arrival
2	Cancellation arrival
3	Check-in
4	Check-out
5	Guest serviced
6	Availability increasing
7	Hotel creation
8	Resort creation
9	Room creation
10	Hotel closing
11	Room closing

Figure C.21   SYSTEM EVENTS.

C.4.2   TRIGGER CATEGORY

This is a methodology dependent component:

    A   Automatic
    M   Manual intervention

C.4.3   BUSINESS EVENT TRIGGERS SYSTEM EVENT

The relationship between SYSTEM EVENTS and BUSINESS EVENTS identified in the business analysis stage is presented in Figure C.22 with the corresponding TRIGGER CATEGORY.

Business Event		System Event		Trigger Category
1	(Request arrival)	1	(Request arrival)	M
2	(Cancellation request)	2	(Cancellation arrival)	M
3	(Check-in)	3	(Check-in)	M
4	(Check-out)	4	(Check-out)	M
5	(Guest serviced)	5	(Guest serviced)	M
6	(New day starts)	6	(Availability increasing)	A
7	(Resource modification)	7	(Hotel creation)	M
7		8	(Resort creation)	M
7		9	(Room creation)	M
7		10	(Hotel closing)	M
7		11	(Room closing)	M

Figure C.22   BUSINESS EVENT TRIGGERS SYSTEM EVENT.

The BUSINESS EVENT 'Resource modification' is decomposed into five SYSTEM EVENTS, namely:

- Hotel creation
- Resort creation
- Room creation
- Hotel closing
- Room closing

C.4.4   SYSTEM EVENT PRECEDENCE/SUCCEDENCE

Succeeding System Event	*Preceding System Event*
2 (Cancellation arrival)	1 (Request arrival)
3 (Check-in)	1 (Request arrival)
4 (Check-out)	3 (Check-in)
5 (Guest serviced)	3 (Check-in)
6 (Availability increasing)	2 (Cancellation arrival)
6 –	9 (Room creation)
6 –	7 (Hotel creation)
6 –	8 (Resort creation)
7 (Hotel creation)	8 (Resort creation)
9 (Room creation)	7 (Hotel creation)
10 (Hotel closing)	7 (Hotel creation)
11 (Room closing)	9 (Room creation)

Figure C.23   SYSTEM EVENT PRECEDENCE/SUCCEDENCE.

Further figures give more details with respect to SYSTEM EVENT 1 (Request arrival) only.

C.4.5   CONDITION

This component is used to identify any CONDITIONS which are necessary for a given SYSTEM EVENT to take place. Figure C.24 shows two conditions associated with SYSTEM EVENT 1 (Request arrival).

Condition Number	*Condition Description*
1	A new row must be inserted in the TABLE T10 (Request)
2	A new row has been inserted in the TABLE T10 (Request)

Figure C.24   SYSTEM EVENT 1 CONDITIONS.

C.4.6   CONDITION REFERENCES COLUMN

Figure C.25 illustrates how a condition is defined in terms of COLUMNS in various TABLES.

Condition Number	Table Name	Column Name
2	Request	resort-name
2	Request	room-type
2	Request	reg-no
2	Request	person-id
2	Request	reg-end-date
2	Request	reg-nb-room
2	Request	reg-state
2	Request	reg-date
2	Hotel-type	hot-type
2	Resort	resort-name
2	Room-type	room-type

Figure C.25   CONDITION REFERENCES COLUMN.

C.4.7   CONDITION ROLE

This is a methodology dependent component. There are two possible roles which a CONDITION can play with respect to a SYSTEM EVENT:

B   Precondition
A   Postcondition

C.4.8   CONDITION ROLE FOR SYSTEM EVENT

This is a cross-reference component which indicates which CONDITION is involved with which ROLE within each SYSTEM EVENT. For example, for SYSTEM EVENT 1 (Request arrival) the ROLES of CONDITIONS 1 and 2 are shown in Figure C.26. An occurrence of SYSTEM EVENT 1 occurs when a new row of the TABLE T10 (Request) satisfies the integrity constraint and has been inserted in the database.

System Event	Condition Number	Condition Role
1 (Request arrival)	1	B
1 (Request arrival)	2	A

Figure C.26   CONDITION ROLE FOR SYSTEM EVENT 1.

C.4.9   SYSTEM EVENT TRIGGERS TASK

A given SYSTEM EVENT will typically trigger one or more TASKS. Figure C.27 illustrates this component using SYSTEM EVENT 1. The triggering of a TASK by a SYSTEM EVENT can be conditional. CONDITIONS c1 and c2 introduced in Figure C.27 are described using free-form text in Figure C.28, and in terms of COLUMNS OF TABLES in Figure C.29.

System Event	Task Number	Task Description	Triggering Condition Code
1	1	Identification of person	—
	2	Allocate reservation	C1
	3	Choice of reserved-rooms	C1
	4	Identification of customer	C1 ˆ C2
	5	Room-availability updating	C1
	6	Request acceptance	C1
	7	Request postponement	C1

Figure C.27   SYSTEM EVENT TRIGGERS TASK.

Entries in the Task Number column and in the Task Description column do not correspond to the entries in Figure C.12.

Triggering Condition Code	Condition Description
C1	One hotel in the requested resort having the requested category with at least the number of requested rooms available during the requested period for the right room-type.
C2	The person who makes the request is not yet a customer.

Figure C.28   Textual description of triggering conditions.

Triggering Condition Code	Table Name	Node Type Code Data Usage Type	Column Name
C1	Request	RS	
	Resort	RT	resort-name
	Hotel	RT	hotel-type
	Room	RT	room-type
			hotel-no
	Room-Availability	RT	hotel-no
			room-no
			av-beg-date
			av-end-date
C2	Request	RS	
	Person	RT	person-id
	Reservation	RT	cust-code

Figure C.29   Description of triggering conditions in terms of COLUMNS of TABLES.

The TASKS used to illustrate the components in this behaviour perspective are not identical to the TASKS shown in the process oriented perspective. TASKS in the behaviour perspective are treated as processes which express actions on TABLES resulting from SYSTEM EVENTS when they occur.

Figure C.30 is a cross-reference table between TASKS and TABLES.

Tasks Number	Request	Person	Reservation	Reserved-Room	Room-Availability
1	AS	AT			
2	AS		AT		
3	AS			AT	
4	AS		MT		
5	AS				MT
6	AS				
	MT				
7	AS				
	MT				

Figure C.30 Cross-reference between TASKS and TABLES.

Appendix D
Case studies

This appendix contains a description of three case studies which are to be used in the exercises at the end of Chapters 4, 5 and 7.

The three case studies are similar to the worked example presented in Appendices B and C, in that each applies to a reservation system. The nature of the reservation system, however, is quite different in each of the four cases.

The three case studies in this appendix apply to the following business areas:

1.   theatre seat reservation,

2.   airline seat reservation, and

3.   car hire reservation.

An important aspect of each case study is that a time continuum is covered in each case. This places emphasis on the behavioural perspective.

The case studies are each non-trivial, although the theatre is somewhat easier than the other two. They are very suitable for handling by groups of three or four students with prior experience of one or more specific methodologies and less challenging examples.

D.1 Theatre seat reservation system

A single theatre wishes to computerize its seat reservation and invoicing system.

The theatre puts on a varied repertoire of plays, operas, operettas and concerts, each of which is called a type of piece. The programme of performances for a season is planned several months in advance and the theatre is prepared to accept seat reservations only for the period for which the programme has been established. More than one performance may be planned for some dates.

The theatre is divided into various areas and the price of the seats is fixed within an area but varies from area to area. The price tariff is established in advance for a given season and the prices depend on the area of the theatre, the type of piece, the type of day (working day or weekend) and the part of day during which the performance is to be held. Another factor influencing the price of the seats is the fact that certain kinds of person (such as military personnel in uniform) are given a reduced rate.

A reservation may be made for one or more seats by a reserver (who is not necessarily the person who will use the seat). The reservation may be made directly with the theatre by telephone, giving a credit card number. Other customers reserve in writing by sending a cheque. A reservation may be for a group of several people who may wish to attend different performances or for the same performance at different prices.

A customer may also make a reservation in person at the box office, paying by cash, cheque or credit card. Each such customer is issued tickets at the time of reservation. Another form of reservation is through a travel agent or theatre ticket office.

A reservation may cover several more seats, possibly at different prices, for the same performance. If the person concerned wishes to reserve for different performances, then it is regarded as a group reservation.

Seats for a performance are allocated to a reservation and it is necessary to keep track of whether tickets for the seats have been issued to the customer. The tickets may be sent by post or arrangements may be made to collect the tickets prior to the performance.

In the case of reservations involving third parties, such as credit card companies and ticket offices, the theatre has to prepare and submit a periodic invoice. Such an invoice may cover more than one reservation.

D.2   Airline seat reservation system

A single airline wishes to computerize its seat reservation and invoicing system.

The airline has authority to fly several routes between several airports. Some routes are single sector routes between two airports while others are multisector routes involving intermediate landings at other airports along the route. A sector is defined as being between two airports. The same sector can belong to one or more routes.

The airline offers one or more flights along each route and publishes a timetable for a planning period showing the flights between pairs of airports and the days of the week on which each flight will be scheduled. The timetable shows that, for certain flights, a different route may be taken on different days of the week. The timetable also shows which type of aircraft is planned for use on each flight. Scheduled departure and arrival times at each airport along the route of each flight are also given.

The tariff to be charged by the airline is established in advance for a given planning period. There are both route tariffs and sector tariffs. The tariff for a given route depends on the tariff class (such as first, economy or standby) as does the tariff for a given sector. There are special tariffs for some types of passenger, such as airline personnel, children and pensioners.

Some passengers make their own reservations directly with the airline and others use a travel agent or have their company handle the reservation. A group of passengers, such as those on a company outing, may be travelling together and their reservations would need to be treated as a single block for invoicing and payment purposes. The means of payment is normally noted at the time the reservation is made.

The reservation for one passenger covers one or more connecting legs of the journey that he or she wishes to make, along connecting sectors of routes flown by the airline. The passenger may be charged either on the basis of a route tariff or on the basis of a series of sector tariffs. A passenger may hold a ticket for several legs of a journey which entitles him or her to travel along a sector without a confirmed reservation for a specific departure of a flight along that sector.

A passenger may arrive at an airport wishing to make a journey without having made a reservation or purchased a ticket. In such cases, the airline would go through the normal reservation and ticketing process. If a passenger is flying on a standby fare, then the ticket would indicate this. A passenger may also be waitlisted for a given departure in a tariff class other than standby.

The allocation of a seat on a departure to a passenger with a reservation may be made either at the time the reservation is made, on the day of departure or on check-in at the airport. Alternatively, there is sometimes no prior seat allocation.

A passenger or group of passengers travelling together may pay by credit card, cheque or even using bank notes. Alternatively, prior arrangements may have been made for an invoice to be sent to a company for payment.

An itemized invoice has to be sent periodically to each credit card company whose cards the airline has agreed to accept. In the case of a block reservation, all reservations covered may be handled by credit card only if all are handled by the same credit card.

D.3   Car hire reservation system

A car hire company wishes to computerize its car reservation system and its invoicing system. The company operates from one single location.

All vehicles are taken from that location and returned to that location. Although the company is, at present, concerned only with private cars, it may wish to branch out into other forms of vehicle rental at a later date and would like to be able to use the same reservation system.

The company has several different models of car in its hire fleet, from different manufacturers. The models are grouped into a small number of price classes. At any time, the company should have several cars of each model listed in its advertising.

The company has a number of different rental plans available to customers. These include a daily time and kilometre rate, a daily rate which includes unlimited kilometres, corresponding weekly rates and a special weekend rate to attract non-business customers.

The tariff charged by the car hire company is established in advance for a given planning period. The tariff for a given model depends on the price class, the type of customer and the charging plan chosen. Business customers get a special discount on the normal rates but not on the special weekend rate.

The company finds it important to have information available on the options which may be fitted on certain models of car, such as automatic or manual gear change, two or four doors, and saloon (sedan) or hatchback. The information on what is actually fitted to the cars in the hire fleet must correspond to the information on options provided by the supplier of the cars. There is no charge for such options but a customer will often request an option when reserving a car and the company wishes to try to meet this request.

In addition to the fitted options, there are optional non-fitted extras, such as roof-rack, trailer, snow-chains and child seats, which customers may request and for which the company does make a special charge. Certain kinds of optional insurance are also handled as an extra charge. The tariff for such chargeable extras is established in advance for the same planning period as for the car rental.

A customer may make his or her own reservations directly with the company or may use a travel agent. Alternatively, the customer's company may handle the reservation. The reservation may specify certain fitted options as well as certain chargeable extras. The means of payment is normally noted at the time the reservation is made.

Sometimes a reserver wishes to make a block booking for several cars and to have the invoices for all rentals on the reservation handled together. As soon as a car is checked out to a customer, an invoice is opened. A single invoice may cover one or more rentals.

The company is willing to accept reservations for a given advance period. It knows when new cars will be available and wishes to be able to rent them out as soon as possible after they are delivered. A car is allocated to a reservation according to its known availability.

A car may or may not be available for hire on a given day. Hire cars need frequent preventive maintenance and, in addition, any damage to a car has to be repaired as soon as possible. The company wants the reservation system to keep track of car availability on each day by recording, in the system, the various kinds of event that can happen to a car between the date on which it is acquired and the date on which it is disposed of.

The company wants the system to be reasonably foolproof. The things that can happen to a car can only occur in a prescribed sequence. A car cannot be returned by a customer before it has been taken out, for example.

Normally a customer will settle the invoice when the car is returned but, in some cases, the invoice must be sent to a company (such as the customer's employer). When the customer pays by credit card, the amount involved has to be billed to the credit card company, together with other rentals using the same kind of credit card.

Index

In this index, terms which refer to formally defined components and to acronyms are given in upper case and other terms in lower case. In some instances, the same term appears in both upper and lower case. The main reference to each component appears in bold.